T0301393

Field Guide for Research in Community Settings

Field Guide for Research in Community Settings

Tools, Methods, Challenges and Strategies

Edited by

M. Rezaul Islam

Institute of Social Welfare and Research, University of Dhaka, Bangladesh

Niaz Ahmed Khan

Department of Development Studies, University of Dhaka, Bangladesh

Siti Hajar Abu Bakar Ah

Department of Social Administration and Justice, University of Malaya, Malaysia

Haris Abd Wahab

Department of Social Administration and Justice, University of Malaya, Malaysia

Mashitah Binti Hamidi

Department of Social Administration and Justice, University of Malaya, Malaysia

ELGAR FIELD GUIDES

Cheltenham, UK • Northampton, MA, USA

Published by
Edward Elgar Publishing Limited
The Lypiatts
15 Lansdown Road
Cheltenham
Glos GL50 2JA
UK

Edward Elgar Publishing, Inc.
William Pratt House
9 Dewey Court
Northampton
Massachusetts 01060
USA

A catalogue record for this book
is available from the British Library

Library of Congress Control Number: 2021933702

This book is available electronically in the **Elgar**online
Business subject collection
http://dx.doi.org/10.4337/9781800376328

ISBN 978 1 80037 631 1 (cased)
ISBN 978 1 80037 632 8 (eBook)

Printed and bound by CPI Group (UK) Ltd, Croydon, CR0 4YY

Contents

Figures

Tables

Contributors

Hamedi M. Adnan, PhD, is Professor at the Department of Media and Communication Studies at University of Malaya, Malaysia. He has published 40 research articles on media agenda, social media, advertisement, social capital, and media publishing. He served as a Director of University Malaya Press for six years (2001–2006), Head of Department of Media Studies (2009–2010 and 2011–2016), and Deputy Dean, Faculty of Art and Social Sciences, University Malaya (2010–2011). He is the President of Malaysian Editors Association since 2011.

Siti Hajar Abu Bakar Ah, PhD, is Professor at the Department of Social Administration and Justice and Deputy Dean at the Faculty of Arts and Social Sciences, University of Malaya, Malaysia. Her core area of expertise is social policy. Over the last 20 years, she has been involved in developing and promoting the teaching, learning and research opportunities in the field of social policy and social work. She teaches social policy, social welfare system, social planning, social evaluation and monitoring, research methodology and social theories. Her research interests focus on social care programmes for at-risk children in Malaysia, children's well-being and social development for vulnerable social groups.

Raja Noriza Binti Raja Ariffin, PhD, is Associate Professor at the Department of Administrative Studies and Politics, University of Malaya, Malaysia. Currently, she is Deputy Director of International Institute of Public Policy & Management (INPUMA), University of Malaya, Malaysia.

Rajendra Baikady, PhD, is a social work educator and researcher. He is currently a URC Post Doctoral Fellow at the Department of Social Work, University of Johannesburg, South Africa. He is the winner of Golda Meir Post-Doctoral Fellowship at Hebrew University of Jerusalem, Israel (2019–2020) and Confucius Studies Understanding China Fellowship (Post-Doctoral Research) at Shandong University People's Republic of China (2018–2019). His most recent books (co-edited) are *Social Welfare Policies and Programmes in South Asia* (Routledge), *Building Sustainable Communities: Civil Society Response in South Asia* (Palgrave Macmillan), *Social Welfare in India and China: A Comparison* (Palgrave Macmillan) and *Palgrave Handbook of Global Social Work Education* (Palgrave Macmillan).

Presently he is at Paul Baerwald School of Social Work and Social Welfare, Hebrew University of Jerusalem Israel.

Adekunle Daoud Balogun, PhD, is currently a PhD Fellow at the Faculty of Law and International Relations, Universiti Sultan Zainal Abidin, Terengganu Malaysia. He served as a part-time lecturer at the Department of Social Administration and Justice, University of Malaya, Malaysia. His research interests include social work, public policy, international relations, public administration, international political economy, foreign policy of the major powers, and international organizations.

Ramy Bulan, PhD, is Associate Professor and the Founding Director of the Centre for Legal Pluralism and Indigenous Law at the Faculty of Law, University of Malaya, Malaysia. She was the Deputy Dean of the Faculty (2006–2009) and also headed the University Malaya's Centre for Malaysian Indigenous Studies until 2017. Dr Bulan's book *An Introduction to the Malaysian Legal System* (Oxford Bakti) is a standard text for undergraduate students. She teaches international human rights with an emphasis on indigenous peoples, and also comparative native title. She writes and speaks extensively on issues relating to indigenous peoples at local and international forums.

Shofiqur Rahman Chowdhury, PhD, is Professor at the Department of Social Work, Shahjalal University of Science & Technology, Bangladesh. His interests include community development, faith-based NGOs and community empowerment. He has a wide range of involvement in community activities in Bangladesh.

Nasa'i Muhammad Gwadabe, PhD, is Lecturer of International Relations at Yusuf Maitama Sule University, Kano, Nigeria. His area of interest includes foreign policy and diplomacy, humanitarianism and international organizations, and the politics of the Middle East.

Mashitah Binti Hamidi, PhD, is Senior Lecturer at the Department of Social Administration and Justice, University of Malaya, Malaysia. She obtained her PhD in Sociology from La Trobe University, Australia. Her research interests include social work for marginalized groups focusing on labour and gendered migration, stateless people and refugees.

Mohammad Hamiduzzaman, PhD, is Research Fellow in the College of Medicine & Public Health at Flinders University, and has undertaken extensive research in personalized dementia care, health determinants, beliefs and behaviours and virtual healthcare.

Rosila Bee Mohd Hussain, PhD, is Senior Lecturer at the Department of

Anthropology and Sociology, University of Malaya, Malaysia. She has expertise in cross-cultural study, identity, social inequality, youth culture and contemporary social issues.

Md. Rafiqul Islam, PhD, is Professor at the Department of Peace and Conflict Studies, University of Dhaka, Bangladesh. Dr Islam completed his Bachelor degree in Political Science, and Master's and MPhil in Peace and Conflict Studies from the University of Dhaka, Bangladesh. He has also completed his MA degree in Environmental Security and Peace from the University for Peace, Costa Rica. He received his PhD from Flinders University, Australia. His primary research interests include peace, conflict, democracy and development. Dr Islam's PhD thesis has been selected for the John Lewis Silver Medal in South Australia.

M. Rezaul Islam, PhD, is a Professor in Social Work at the Institute of Social Welfare and Research, University of Dhaka, and International Academic Adviser at the Department of Social Administration & Justice, University of Malaya, Malaysia. He worked as Visiting Professor at the University of Malaya, Malaysia from 2012 to 2016. He completed his MSW and PhD from the University of Nottingham, England. His research focuses on diverse areas in social sciences including social research methodology, climate vulnerability, international migration, NGOs and community development, poverty, social inequality and social justice, which is embedded in a human rights approach and inspired by people who are vulnerable and affected by structural causes of poverty, unemployment and inequalities. Dr Islam has widely published books and journal articles from reputed international publishers. He has published around 100 journal articles, and 60 articles are from Web of Science and Scopus cited high index journals. He is currently Member of International Advisory Board of the *Community Development Journal* (Oxford University Press) and editorial Board Member of three journals: *Asian Social Work and Policy Review* (Wiley), *Local Development & Society* (Taylor & Francis) and *International Community Well-being* (Springer).

Tahmina Islam is Professor at the Department of Social Work, Shahjalal University of Science & Technology, Bangladesh. Currently, she is pursuing her PhD at the Department of Social Administration & Justice, University of Malaya, Malaysia. A member of the Committee of Concerned Citizens (CCC) of Transparency International Bangladesh (TIB), she is involved with different types of community level activities in Bangladesh. Her research interests are violence against women, acid violence, couple conflict, psychological counselling, and indigenous people. She has some national and international publications on related issues.

Maria Binti Mohd Ismail is a PhD candidate from the Department of

Administrative Studies and Politics, University of Malaya, Malaysia. Her research area is public policy focusing on the policy implementation of rural transport plans.

Welyne J. Jehom, PhD, is Senior Lecturer at the Department of Anthropology and Sociology and Head, Center of Indigenous Studies, University of Malaya, Malaysia. Her broad research expertise includes social anthropology specifically gender, development, environment, livelihood, indigenous knowledge, native, Orang Asal, resettlement and displacement.

Nafisa Kasem is a PhD candidate at the Department of Media and Communication Studies, University of Malaya, Malaysia and faculty member of the Bangladesh University of Business and Technology (BUBT). Her research interests include social media marketing, customer relationship management, service branding, and consumer behaviour.

Kanamik Kani Khan is a registered social worker and a Social Work Lecturer at the Eastern Institute of Technology, New Zealand. He has submitted his PhD thesis in Social Work at Massey University, New Zealand. He completed his Bachelors and Masters at the University of Dhaka, Bangladesh, and MPhil at the University of Bergen, Norway. His research interests are human rights, justice, and social work.

Niaz Ahmed Khan, PhD (Wales), Post doc. (Oxford), is Professor and former Chair at the Department of Development Studies, University of Dhaka; Senior Academic Adviser, BRAC Institute of Governance and Development (BIGD); and former Country Representative – Bangladesh, International Union for Conservation of Nature (IUCN). He has published prolifically (more than 170 refereed publications including some 40 in Web of Science and/or Scopus indexed journals) on such broad fields as environment, natural resource management, and social/community development.

Abraham Kuot, PhD, is Research Fellow in the College of Medicine & Public Health, Flinders University. He is a molecular biologist, geneticist and a public health researcher with 12 years of experience and career progression, resulting in proven skills in quantitative and qualitative research methodologies.

Belinda Lunnay, PhD, is an early career researcher with expertise in qualitative methodologies and in undertaking theoretically informed data analysis. She is currently Research Associate for an ARC Discovery project in the College of Medicine & Public Health, Flinders University.

Ashek Mahmud, PhD, is Associate Professor in the Department of Sociology, Jagannath University, Bangladesh. His research interests include media studies, social capital, social development, minority studies, and postmodern culture.

Hasan Mahmud, PhD, is Assistant Professor in Sociology at Northwestern University in Qatar. He explored why migrants send remittances to home in his PhD dissertation research among Bangladeshis in Tokyo and Los Angeles. His research interests include globalization, migration, development, immigrants' incorporation, sociological theories, qualitative research, and identity politics.

Sedigheh Moghavvemi, PhD, is Senior Lecturer at the Department of Operation and Management Information Systems, University of Malaya, Malaysia. Her areas of interest are management information systems (technology adoption, social media, and entrepreneurship), economics, business and management, technology management, tourism as well as consumer behaviour.

Firuza Begham Binti Mustafa, PhD, is Associate Professor in the Department of Geography, Faculty of Arts & Social Sciences, University of Malaya, Malaysia. Her field of interest includes environmental impact assessment, environmental management, environmental geography (agricultural geography, soil and land use change) and agricultural sciences and aquaculture.

Shahreen Mat Nayan, PhD, is Senior Lecturer at the Department of Media Studies, University of Malaya, Malaysia. She received the Best Journal Article Award (under the Humanities and Social Science Category) from the Malaysian Scholarly Publication Council (MAPIM) – Ministry of Education Malaysian addition to comparative and non-violent rhetoric. She is particularly interested to discover the ways in which rhetoric and/or the media can be used as tools to promote dialogue, peace, diversity and inclusiveness.

Heath Pillen is a PhD candidate examining how persons living with type 2 diabetes come to understand and challenge stigmatizing practices and discourses. He has worked for the International Centre for Allied Health Evidence.

Veronika Poniscjakova, PhD, is Teaching Fellow at the Faculty of Business and Law, University of Portsmouth, England. She completed her PhD from the University of Nottingham, England. Her research interests include qualitative research methodology, Israel, Middle East, counter-culture, civil disobedience, far right-wing ideology, and political violence.

Aqsa Qandeel is Lecturer in Sociology at the Women University Multan, Pakistan. Currently, she is pursuing her PhD at the Department of Anthropology and Sociology, University of Malaya, Malaysia. Her research expertise is qualitative gerontology.

Fathimath Shifaza, PhD, is a Senior Lecturer in Nursing at Flinders University and founder of Evidence-based Champions in the Maldives. She is a registered nurse and has 20 years of clinical nursing and midwifery experience in Australia and internationally.

Jillian Ooi Lean Sim, PhD, is a Senior Lecturer in the Department of Geography, University of Malaya, Malaysia. Her research interest is in marine biogeography, with a focus on seagrass ecosystems. She currently leads collaborative projects to study dugong feeding patterns in seagrass meadows, develop species distribution models for seagrasses in Southeast Asia, and experiment with optimal coral reef restoration techniques.

Omar Smadi is a PhD candidate, RN, MNSC. He is an ICU nurse with 20 years of clinical experience. His research interest is teaching and learning in the blended and online environment for nurses.

Kumaran A/l Suberamanian, PhD, is Professor at the Department of Indian Studies, University of Malaya, Malaysia and has authored more than 100 research papers and more than 60 books in English, Malay and Tamil. His specializations are social media networking, Tamil language, Tamil classical literature, Indian civilization, comparative study of Japanese Manyoshu songs, Tamil cultural studies, Tamil journalism, and the Tamil–Malay–English Dictionary.

Taj Sultana is Assistant Professor at the Department of Geography and Environmental Studies University of Chittagong, Bangladesh. Now she is doing her PhD at the Department of Geography, University of Malaya, Malaysia. Her field of interests includes coastal disasters, climate change, and environmental issues.

Munira Jahan Sumi is currently doing a PhD under the Faculty of Law, University of Malaya, Malaysia. She is Assistant Professor of Law at Jagannath University, Bangladesh. She has written three books on the 1971 genocide of Bangladesh. She has also published book chapters and journal articles. Her research interests include minority and indigenous rights, genocide, human and organ trafficking and issues related to socio-legal exclusion and injustice.

Alan Taylor is Vice President of the Australasian Telehealth Society and a member of the ISO TC215 Health Informatics Committee. He is researching the sustainability of telehealth services in Australia and Brazil including the role of standards, guidelines and socio-technical codes.

Haris Abd Wahab, PhD, is an Associate Professor and currently Head of the Department of Social Administration and Justice, University of Malaya, Malaysia. He has conducted studies on community work, community development, volunteerism and disability. He has extensive experience on medical social work at the Ministry of Health, Malaysia.

Hannah Wechkunanukul, PhD, has been a pharmacist for two decades and has broadened her expertise in health service and public health. Her PhD focuses on accessibility and inequity in healthcare among cultural and linguistically diverse populations.

Bushra Zaman is Assistant Professor at the Department of Social Work, Jagannath University, Bangladesh. She is currently pursuing her PhD at the Department of Anthropology and Sociology, University of Malaya, Malaysia. She worked at the Population Council, Bangladesh office. Her research interests include qualitative research methodologies, migration, livelihoods and social capital.

Sawlat Zaman, PhD, is currently working as a Lecturer in International Business and Management at Newcastle University Business School, Newcastle University, UK. Sawlat previously taught at Cardiff Business School as a University Teacher. She taught as Assistant Professor at IBA, University of Dhaka, Bangladesh. Her teaching and research expertise includes global HRM and employment relations, international business environment and corporate governance.

1. Introduction to the *Field Guide for Research in Community Settings: Tools, Methods, Challenges and Strategies*

M. Rezaul Islam, Niaz Ahmed Khan, Siti Hajar Abu Bakar Ah, Haris Abd Wahab and Mashitah Binti Hamidi

Fieldwork/data collection is one of the most important parts in the research process, and it is particularly important for social sciences research. A number of aspects that need to be considered by a researcher before starting data collection include: ethical permission from the concerned ethical body/committee, informed consent, contract with different stakeholders, field settings, time allocation and time management, field leading, data collection, contextual and cultural diversities, community settings, socioeconomic and psychological patterns of the community, political pattern, rapport building between data collectors and respondents, permission to access community, language and mode of data collection, power relations, role of gatekeepers, privacy and confidentiality issues, layers of expectations among researchers/respondents/funding organization, data recording (written, memorization, voice recording and video recording), and so on. Many aspects are very difficult to understand before going into the field. Sometimes, a researcher's previous experience about a particular community may help to gain field access, but it may be difficult to assess the field in advance due to rapid changes within people's livelihoods and other shifts in the community. The change of a political paradigm sometimes seems also to be a challenge at the field level. We believe that although technological innovation has benefited some aspects of the data collection of fieldwork in social research, many other dimensions (mentioned above) of fieldwork endure unchanged. It is true that the improvement of technology is no promise that the quality of fieldwork will improve. However, the orbit of fieldwork has always had to deal with the shifting nature of societies themselves (Porter and Grossman, 2004).

There are a number of issues that can be challenges at the field level for the data collection process, though this edited volume strongly argues that the local context is the prime and leading consideration for such challenges that researchers should take seriously. One important issue within this spectrum is ethical consideration relating particularly to 'harms and benefits' (Cassell, 1982). In many cases, particularly data collection in low-income communities through participatory research, the role of social advocacy and empowerment of the poor and the powerless is very important (Porter and Grossman, 2004). On the other hand, in developing countries, there has been an expansion in forbidden or restricted research due to the stimulation of privatization and human subject regulations (Warren and Staples, 1989). In qualitative study, such as anthropology, there has been much debate as to whether such research (mainly through observation) is a real science. This became a critical issue when Malinowski and Radcliffe-Brown strongly argued that anthropological research is also a science like experimental research (Jarvie, 1986). This volume is a breakthrough that provides many examples from diverse fields in terms of the nature and types of communities, cross-country and ethnic diversity, various community settings, cultural and religious beliefs, multiple socioeconomic and psychological patterns and so on. Contributions to this edited book – reflecting these diversities – prove that the basis for all new knowledge in the social sciences is the affective. This book will be an interesting read for the researcher in social sciences faced with adjusting to uncertainties. The new material in this book adds to our basic understanding of real-world difficulties.

The present volume provides many examples from the field of anthropology, demonstrating that affect is the centre of all of our knowledge-creation efforts. In this regard, George Devereux (1967) pointed to various ways in which researchers deal with uncertainties. The new material in this book adds to our basic understanding of the real-world difficulties experienced by diverse communities and of the ways in which human beings face many changes to their livelihoods. This volume provides many examples of the challenges researchers face during data collection, such as various misperceptions of their roles as outsider-researchers and qualms about their impacts on the lives of the communities they study. Many chapters show that development of trust is an essential component in fieldwork that can be considered as a fragile product but essential for effective interpersonal interaction (Stodulka et al., 2019).

We feel confident that this book will add considerable value to literature on research methodologies in social sciences by focusing on some practical dimensions of field research for advanced degrees in a way which has seldom been tried in earlier studies. The book extensively addresses a fundamental component of social science research methodology – namely fieldwork, more specifically the application of techniques and strategies of fieldwork in data collection including the issue of research ethics. One important feature of this book is that it explores a wide range of contextual and community settings across several countries within which the respective researchers have devised and applied context- and community-specific research approaches, data collection methods and field research instruments to suit and pursue their research objectives. In documenting the diverse experiences of the researchers in the varied contexts, this book also captures the practical challenges including ethical dilemmas faced by the researchers during the data collection process. Secondly, the authors also provide a large number of practical illustrations and examples of the strategies they adopted during fieldwork in order to overcome these challenges. Thus this book may serve as handy resource material for research students across a wide range of social and behavioural science disciplines by giving them an opportunity to learn these hands-on tips, strategies and experiences shared by fellow researchers who have already paved the way and emerged successfully! Given these strengths, the editors are optimistic that the publication may attract wide international readership.

This volume, in the main, attempts to offer some practical tips and messages in relation to fieldwork in social and behavioural sciences; the messages address such phases of empirical research as the application of research tools and techniques in data collection, the challenges commonly faced in the field, and the strategies that researchers adopt to overcome these challenges, either by using their indigenous or innovative skills or exploiting and making judicious use of the advantages already available within the standard research methodologies. The specific objectives are: (i) to examine the major challenges the researchers face during their fieldwork (data collection), (ii) to capture diverse learning across different countries and communities (local perspective and contextual aspects), and (iii) to learn about the strategies (either indigenous or within the methodological scope) the researchers followed to overcome the challenges. In general, this book will help to enrich researchers' capacity and skills, especially in the context of social science fieldwork and empirical examinations. It is often argued that social research is more effectively understood and learnt as a practice rather than through classroom briefings. This book includes 18 chapters which are written in the light of the various authors' practical field experiences.

Within its broad focus of fieldwork tools, methods, challenges and strategies in social and behavioural sciences, the book covers a very wide range of important research topics and agendas. Examples of such topics include: definitional debates of research, types and classification, philosophical aspects of research, research design and planning, research methods (for example, survey, experimental, case study, ethnographic, content analysis), data collection methods (face-to-face interview, in-depth case interviews, focus group discussions, key informants' interviews, community mapping, observation, documentation review, etc.), and data collection instruments (interview schedule, guideline, and checklist). Other issues include preparation and protocol for fieldwork, ethical issues, sampling procedures (for qualitative, quantitative and mixed-method approaches), data analysis techniques (use of SPSS, NVIVO, thematic, triangulation, etc.), research management, data management, data coding, and the qualities of social researchers. It also covers the qualities that are helpful in conducting a research project such as mental, psychological, and social factors and the need for financial as well as time management. Various ethical issues in conducting social research receive considerable attention in several chapters. The discussion also addresses research ethics from two distinct perspectives, i.e. Western and Asian, and focuses on the strategies and techniques deployed by the researchers to tackle various ethical challenges.

Secondly, the book provides many perspectives and contextual aspects related to the procedural and communal level challenges commonly faced by researchers. This is a good opportunity for the reader to examine these challenges through a wide range of examples from different communities, countries, and ethnicities. Many chapters address the issues and dilemmas of research ethics head on. The cases and examples will be of value to research students in preparing them for fieldwork and empirical data collection. Thirdly, this book has captured some practical experiences that may help research students to learn how to put into practice the method or approach that they are theoretically conversant with. It thus contributes to bridging the gaps between relevant theories and practices of social research. For example, a research student knows about the procedure, use, advantages and disadvantages of the interview method, but he or she may not yet have the practical skills to use this data collection tool in the field. A student may already have decided on the ethical guidelines that he or she will follow during data collection, but lack practical experience in how these guidelines should be followed at the field level. One more example is that a student may have knowledge about the use of ethnographic method, but not have any experience as to how it can be used among vulnerable communities in Bangladesh. This book will advise the research student on the preparation they need and pointers on how to gain practical experience as he or she uses different research tools and techniques in the field. The many examples of how to work in diverse countries and communities will surely enrich the student's research knowledge.

The book contains extensive examples of application of selected research tools in different cultural and socioeconomic contexts and communities. In a number of chapters, the authors report and analyse community experiences from Muslim and non-Muslim countries, while other chapters address the challenges arising from research among ethnic (tribal) communities. Each chapter has its own scope and limitation; the book does not follow a particular uniform template and allows the authors a degree of freedom to present their cases and experiences in a manner and format that best serve and suit the purposes of their respective chapters. Research students may learn the techniques and art of applying and adjusting a particular research tool in various contextual settings. Thus one can get diverse meanings and applications of a particular research method or tool adapted to changing contexts.

In many cases, the chapters of this book use verbatim quotations and dialogues from the field in order to give the contextual meaning and portray the real voices and vision of the research participants/respondents. Such an approach will surely help the readers, especially research students, to learn practical techniques of capturing field voices from their own research in an academically acceptable manner. This is particularly important for students who plan to use the qualitative research approach in their studies. From our experience of serving as advanced research degree examiners or reviewers, we noted that students often struggle with effective ways of depicting and capturing field observations and people's views, especially in qualitative research. This book can be a very useful guide for research students faced with these challenges.

Another important approach and feature of this book is that it follows a 'storytelling' method in delivering and understanding the meanings and perspectives of the research subjects. Research students may be particularly interested to hear the stories from different countries at various levels – community, group and individual. We believe that this is a relatively new approach to community research. Most of the chapters expand the respective stories with analysis of particular contextual settings in order to make the presentations exciting to the readers. Most textbooks or resource materials follow a traditional form of writing that typically involves the following sequence of presentation: the dictionary meaning of a concept first, then the general meaning, followed by some refereed definitions and connotations, and finally the author(s)' view on the definition. The approach used in this book – manifested in the 'storytelling' mode – will make a departure from this conventional structure and format. Here the readers will get the concepts, their application and associated examples in a systematic manner that will help them to understand and grasp the messages and meanings more easily.

This edited volume brings together 18 chapters contributed by 41 authors from around the world. Chapter 2, 'Challenges and solutions for collecting data in health research: experiences of Australian doctoral and early career researchers' by Mohammad Hamiduzzaman and colleagues begins our journey by exploring the methodological challenges in health research in Australia. They mention that the National Health and Medical Research Council stipulates a governance process that covers standards of ethical practice and the legal responsibilities of researchers in respecting privacy and maintaining confidentiality and dignity of participants. In this connection, they argue that data collection in clinical and community settings remains challenging for doctoral and early career researchers due to the complexities of research governance systems and issues with the involvement of participants in research activities. The major challenges are related to research governance, expertise of researchers, health literacy of participants, fieldwork settings, approaching and designing questions, and research fatigue. In Chapter 3, 'Challenges with opening up closed off communities: interviewing ultra-Orthodox Jewish communities in Israel', Veronika Poniscjakova explores her doctoral research (at the University of Nottingham) fieldwork challenges among counter-culture communities in Israel. She examined the religious Zionist and ultra-Orthodox Jewish communities' attitudes towards political developments and crises of political and religious nature. Her challenges were primarily related to access, trust building, and language issues. She had to identify gatekeepers to introduce her to individuals who were more open-minded. This affected representation and validity but led to a snowball effect. The chapter advises readers to identify gatekeepers, communicate with interviewees in a culturally sensitive way whilst still getting good data, and understand the participants' world.

Chapter 4, 'Ethnography research with Indonesian female factory workers: challenges and strategies in the field' by Mashitah Binti Hamidi, explores the fieldwork challenges she faced with the Indonesian female migrant workers in Malaysia's manufacturing sector. She describes that this research challenged her in her role as an 'insider' doing research in her own backyard while seeking to understand at the same time as an 'outsider'. In Chapter 5, entitled '"How can you be so naïve?" Negotiating insider status among co-ethnic migrants in global ethnographic fieldwork', Hasan Mahmud addresses the data collection challenges by using the Weberian and Symbolic Interactionist approaches, two foundations of ethnographic research, which both imply that the researchers are outsiders to the groups they study and need to access the insiders' perspective. The author describes his fieldwork challenges among Bangladeshi migrants in Tokyo and Los Angeles. He begins with Merton's discussion on the insider/outsider debate from the sociology of knowledge perspective and demonstrates its epistemological importance for fieldwork. He looks at the ethnographic conceptualization of the field in the context of globalization and how migration researchers negotiate their insider/outsider role in conducting fieldwork.

A comparative study brings more data collection challenges when working with two different communities in two countries. Rajendra Baikady in Chapter 6, 'Challenges and opportunities in conducting cross-country PhD study: experiences of data collection in India and China', faced these comparative challenges while he collected data from India and China. He examined the status of social work education in a parliamentary democracy and in a communist regime. He looked at the curriculum, teaching, learning and practices, level of indigenization of social work education and practice and civil society engagement in social work education. His study examined the ontological and the epistemological assumptions that social work is a socially constructed institutional care practice where the emergence and the development of social work are largely governed by the social, economic, political and cultural context of the country. These contexts either involve or influence the development and relevance of social work. In Chapter 7, 'Researching the garment sector in Bangladesh: fieldwork challenges and responses', Sawlat Zaman discusses the data collection challenges arising from the ready-made garment (RMG) sector of Bangladesh, where much debate and controversies exist around this industry, especially due to catastrophic disasters like Spectrum Collapse, Rana Plaza, and Tazrin Fire that call into question the sector's record on fair labour practices. She discusses access, cultural and contextual challenges experienced by her doctoral research. Data collection is particularly challenging for any researcher working in a community which is comparatively remote and with a low standard of living.

This book incorporates diverse challenges from two hard-to-reach communities in Bangladesh and Nigeria. Shofiqur Rahman Chowdhury with his supervisors M. Rezaul Islam and Haris Abd Wahab capture some of these challenges in Chapter 8, 'Gaining access to research participants for data collection in doctoral studies: evidence from a rural area of Bangladesh'. The authors explore the challenges where a faith-based Islamic NGO named Islamic Relief Worldwide provided interest-free loans and training to the rural poor community under the community empowerment domain. The challenges encountered are community threat, understanding of local culture, clarifying study objectives, and conducting uninterrupted surveys and interviews. They describe how the use of different social and institutional gatekeepers, community mapping, applying local contextual examples to clarify study objectives, and recalling positive memories were effective ways to deal with the nuances in the field and data collection. Chapter 9, 'The challenges and strategies of accessing hard-to-reach locations during fieldwork data collection: the case of northeast Nigeria' by Nasa'i Muhammad Gwadabe and Adekunle Daoud Balogun, narrates and analyses the challenges such as location and accessibility, insecurity, culture and religion, duration of data collection, researchers' fatigue and sensitive information during data collection on Internally Displaced Persons (IDPs) in northeast Nigeria.

Ashek Mahmud with his supervisors M. Rezaul Islam and Hamedi M. Adnan in Chapter 10, 'Data collection on "smartphone addiction and social capital effects" among the university students of Bangladesh: challenges and strategies for the way out' relate how they faced various ethical drawbacks, sociocultural malpractices, and structural limitations to collect data from smartphone-addicted university students in Bangladesh. In Chapter 11, 'Undercover fieldwork: a queer experience of healthcare in Bangladesh',

Kanamik Kani Khan describes his experience of PhD fieldwork with sexual and gender diverse communities who live invisibly in Bangladesh. He conducted in-depth case interviews, focus group discussions, and key informants' interviews where developing trust and gaining access to this invisible community were challenging and describes how building networks and recruiting participants were key strategies to overcome the challenges. Like Chapter 6, Chapter 12 also deals with an example of cross-country fieldwork. In their chapter entitled 'Ethical issues, challenges and solutions during fieldwork with homeless elderly people of Malaysia and Pakistan', Aqsa Qandeel and her supervisor Welyne J. Jehom discuss a number of challenges arising from fieldwork with two diverse elderly groups, including their living situations, mental conditions, and tracing of respondents, interactional hesitation with a stranger, linguistic differentiation, racial difference, unfavourable response to the interviewee, being a foreigner, mood swings, and issues of interviewee femininity. In Chapter 13, 'Field research in the conflict zone: an empirical study of the Chittagong Hill Tracts (CHT) in Bangladesh', Md. Rafiqul Islam explores the data collection challenges experienced among the ethnic community in Bangladesh. This is one of the conflictual and violent zones in Bangladesh where safety, security, silence, mistrust between communities, a culture of violence, unwillingness to share information and interference of the security forces in the context of conflict research were specific data collection challenges.

In Chapter 14, 'Research with coastal people in Bangladesh: challenges and way forward', Taj Sultana and her supervisors Firuza Begham Binti Mustafa, Jillian Ooi Lean Sim and M. Rezaul Islam describe some contextual challenges of data collection using a mixed-method approach that included complexity of site accessibility impeded by tidal floods; social issues such as personal security, lack of trust between researcher and respondents, and the problem of matching official addresses to actual physical locations; and political issues that came about because data collection coincided with the national elections of 2018, creating a volatile and politically charged situation within the study area. Munira Jahan Sumi with her supervisors M. Rezaul Islam and Ramy Bulan explore the data collection challenges arising from the Santal (an ethnic) community about their land rights in Bangladesh in Chapter 15, 'Data collection from the Santal community: a journey towards an unknown world in ascertaining the nexus between reality and dream'. Most of the challenges were rooted in the Santal's traditional livelihood practices and in understanding their local context. In Chapter 16, 'Challenges in accessing rural area and managing sub-culture differences in Kuala Krai, Kelantan, Malaysia', Maria Binti Mohd Ismail and Raja Noriza Binti Raja Ariffin explore some diverse challenges such as remoteness, local accent of the language, cultural difference, and values conflict, in a remote area in Kuala Krai, Kelantan, Malaysia.

Bushra Zaman with her supervisors M. Rezaul Islam and Rosila Bee Mohd Hussain in Chapter 17, 'Fieldwork experience: challenges and managing risks as a female researcher', explore their data collection experiences among the Bangladeshi and Indonesian labour migrants working in Malaysia. Bushra Zaman's PhD study, 'Usage of social capital among migrant workers for their livelihoods in Malaysia', examined whether social capital can bring any change in the migrant workers' livelihoods between two high labour sending countries, Indonesia and Bangladesh. She faced gender stereotyping, language barriers, safety and security issues, natural caution of migrant workers, and rejection from the key informants. In the end, leveraging the power of networking, building relationships, developing acceptance, pursuing alternative avenues to address challenges, persevering and being prepared, and following the passion and purpose of a researcher helped to minimize and manage those risks. An interesting account of data collection difficulties is presented in Chapter 18, 'Data collection on acid attack survivor women: a PhD researcher's experience from Bangladesh', by Tahmina Islam and her supervisors M. Rezaul Islam and Siti Hajar Abu Bakar Ah. The main challenges related to social and physical aspects such as the behaviour of people surrounding the acid attack survivors and the bad transport and communications system of the country. Civil society engagement and the researcher's expression of forbearance and empathy solved these problems. Finally, Chapter 19, 'Challenges, strategies, and way out techniques in conducting in-depth interviews among managers in Malaysian organizations', describes some challenges at organizational level when a PhD researcher (low power) attempts to get access and approval from the higher authorities (high power) to conduct her research. This power relation is discussed by Nafisa Kasem and her supervisors Shahreen Mat Nayan, Kumaran A/l Suberamanian and Sedigheh Moghavvemi.

In conclusion, we reiterate that this book includes chapters from diverse countries, cultures, and Muslim and non-Muslim community contexts, which capture and highlight PhD field research experiences. This reflects the global focus of this book with potential global outreach. Research methodology is an essential and compulsory subject in nearly all faculties such as arts, social sciences, business, and medical sciences commonly taught in tertiary educational institutions. Thus the potential readership of this book may be quite diverse and wide. We believe this will be a particularly valuable resource for research students since fieldwork and data collection are integral and fundamental components of any research project.

REFERENCES

Cassell, J. (1982). Harms, benefits, wrongs, and rights in fieldwork. In J. E. Sieber (ed.), *The Ethics of Social Research* (pp. 7–31). New York: Springer.

Devereux, G. (1967). *From Anxiety to Method in the Behavioral Sciences, Etc.* Paris: Hague.

Jarvie, I. C. (1986). On theories of fieldwork and the scientific character of social anthropology. In I. C. Jarvie, *Thinking about Society: Theory and Practice* (pp. 107–126). Dordrecht: Springer.

Porter, P. W. and Grossman, L. S. (2004). Fieldwork in nonwestern contexts: Continuity and change. In S. D. Brunn, S. L. Cutter, and J. W. Harrington Jr. (eds.), *Geography and Technology* (pp. 201–220). Dordrecht: Springer.

Stodulka, T., Dinkelaker, S., and Thajib, F. (eds.) (2019). *Affective Dimensions of Fieldwork and Ethnography*. Cham: Springer Nature.

Warren, C. A. and Staples, W. G. (1989). Fieldwork in forbidden terrain: The state, privatization and human subjects regulations. *The American Sociologist*, 20(3), 263–277.

2. Challenges and solutions for collecting data in health research: experiences of Australian doctoral and early career researchers

Mohammad Hamiduzzaman, Alan Taylor, Belinda Lunnay, Abraham Kuot, Hannah Wechkunanukul, Omar Smadi, Heath Pillen and Fathimath Shifaza

NAVIGATING THE HEALTH RESEARCH CONTEXT IN AUSTRALIA

In Australia, maintaining standards stipulated by research governance structures is an obligation of data collection (Sainsbury, 2016). Governance is defined as the process of ensuring institutional accountability for human research conducted under their auspices (NHMRC, 2015). Research governance standards include ethics approval (compliance to the existing legislation, regulations and codes of practices, legal contracts, financial and risk management); site-specific assessment (managing research misconduct by institutional policies and procedures); and reporting (Carter et al., 2016).

Ethical review in health research is conducted by the Human Research Ethics Committee (HREC). There are 200 HRECs in universities and independent research organizations across all eight states and territories of Australia (NHMRC, 2015). These HRECs assess each research proposal based on the National Health & Medical Research Council (NHMRC). The National Statement on Ethical Conduct in Human Research and National Health upholds the rights, dignity, and welfare of research participants as well as ensuring that the investigation is methodically sound and anticipated benefits of the research justify any potential risk of discomfort or harm (Reilly et al., 2016). The NHMRC standards support researchers to become cognizant of the legal requirements for research, for instance, the gaining of ethics approval from relevant authorities to commence data collection (Carter et al.,

2016). In an ethics application to an HREC, the researcher must introduce the project, state the research objectives, and provide information about potential participants, recruitment process, nature of interaction between the researcher and the participants, processes for determining the inclusion and exclusion of participants, and maintaining research integrity and respect for participants (Reilly et al., 2016). In addition, several documents must accompany the ethics application to ensure transparency of the research, including a Letter of Introduction, Participant Information, and Consent Form.

The NHMRC recognizes that respect for participants relates to providing them with sufficient information and freedom to make their own decisions about participating in the research project. A Letter of Introduction is prepared to introduce the interviewer and provide general information about them to potential participants (NHMRC, 2015). An information sheet provides details of the focus of the research and the possible benefits and risks involved with participation in the research. The NHMRC also emphasizes the requirement for obtaining informed consent from participants. Two principles are advised by the NHMRC (2015): consent must be voluntary, and consent must be based on sufficient information about the project. Anonymity of the participants (e.g. de-identified data collection, use of pseudonyms in reporting) and confidentiality of the information gathered are major considerations in human health research. Regular monitoring of the ethical conduct of research is the responsibility of HRECs and site-specific institutions (Sainsbury, 2016). There are also specific ethical considerations for research conducted using online platforms or digital media that warrant additional consideration, and advice on this is provided elsewhere (Lunnay et al., 2015).

Following approval by an HREC, site-specific assessment and authorization comprise the second stipulation of research governance, involving an assessment of whether a research project might feasibly be accommodated within a particular healthcare institution (Sainsbury, 2016). There are several aspects considered in the site-specific assessment, including risk management; relevant legal, regulatory, and jurisdictional resources; available budget; and administrative requirements (Dyke and Anderson, 2014). The outcome of the site assessment is an institutional authorization of a research project or a decision not to authorize a specific project in recruiting participants and data collection.

Despite mandated processes for ethics and governance review and approval, early career researchers still encounter unanticipated challenges during processes of participant recruitment and management, and in obtaining data from them. The available literature reveals several challenges include a lack of experience and confidence in choosing an appropriate research site and participants, designing and conducting interviews or surveys, resistance from participants, managing interactions between researchers and participants, and arranging a site (Malterud, 2001). A certain grey area exists between the discussion of data collection methods and contextualization of the methods to suit the phenomenon of interest (Andrew and Halcomb, 2009). As a doctoral researcher, some of the complexities involved in this contextualization only become apparent after considerable time spent in data collection and analysis. What is needed are further strategies that might be used to bridge data collection methods, as presented in their ideal form, to the realities of research encountered by novice researchers working with humans in complex healthcare contexts (see Figure 2.1).

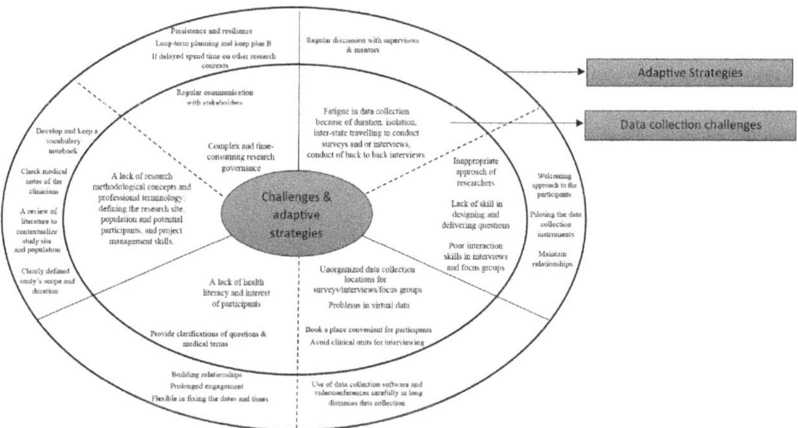

Source: Developed by authors.

Figure 2.1 *Data collection challenges and way-out strategies in early-career research*

CHALLENGES IN THE DATA COLLECTION

The findings presented in this chapter were obtained from eight doctoral and early career researchers who conducted studies on clinical education, ophthalmology, cardiovascular disease, emergency and pre-hospital care, telehealth services, alcohol consumption, dementia care, determinants of health, and education for stigma-reduction. These research studies (mixed-methods, quantitative and qualitative) included diverse cohorts that varied in geographical location, age, ethnicity, language, socio-economic status, and access. The authors' experiences of conducting data collection were in different health and social settings of Australia such as hospitals, clinics, nursing homes, community centres, academic institutions, and households. Data collection strategies used by the researchers included in-person communication and online interaction and commonly used tools included survey questionnaire, focus groups, interviews, observation, document analysis, field notes, and feedback forms. The themes that emerged were relevant to the governance, researchers' expertise, literacy of participants, fieldwork settings, approaching and designing questions, and research fatigue, which are presented in the following sections.

Complex Research Governance

The authors identified the site-specific authorization and lack of scope in timely data collection due to complex ethical review as major challenges. The HRECs participate in the national ethical approvals system, whereby approval by one committee is acceptable to other committees. However, not all states and healthcare organizations participate in the scheme, so in some multi-site research studies additional ethics applications are required and each individual researcher relative to the specific context (Smith-Merry and Walton, 2014) should identify these. Obtaining ethics approval does not guarantee permission to commence participant recruitment as approval to approach participants at each research site is also required. In clinical trials, and low risk, qualitative research governance approvals have to be granted by individual hospitals within the same healthcare organization. Thus, the same governance application must be submitted multiple times. To obtain governance approvals, a site contract and several executive approvals are necessary. The researchers, who were unfamiliar with the executive structures at a specific site, had trouble in identifying the executives who could sign the governance approval, even when assisted by local ethics committees.

For the projects that the authors were part of, ethics review and site-specific approvals often took months to obtain. In some jurisdictions, the governance approvals require the agreement of contracts that stipulated the conditions for accessing the site and participants. There were two to three phases involved in clinical trials and accessing existing data was considered as the first step to contextualize the study topic and participants. However, access to existing datasets required contacting the authorized person of a healthcare organization and developing an agreement between the researcher and the organization, resulted in delays in commencing data collection. Furthermore, many contracts set conditions on the publication of research results. As a result, it was not possible to interview participants working in some organizations. To further complicate this stage, the electronic systems managing site-specific authorizations vary between jurisdictions and are designed for research occurring at one site only and not across several sites, which means it becomes incredibly time consuming to manage multiple, concurrent applications. Such complexities in ethical review and site-specific assessment in combination with a lack of pre-existing knowledge of how to navigate these activities can act to delay the process of recruitment and data collection.

Expertise of Researchers

Professional knowledge and skills relating to data collection methods and how to use data collection tools were regarded as important factors. The authors who were involved in clinical interventions had a lack of prior knowledge on ontological and epistemological aspects of their research topic. Understanding, deciding upon, and applying a philosophical approach for a study, especially in nursing and health sciences, tended to take longer than anticipated, resulting in delays in commencing data collection. The authors conducting interdisciplinary research experienced a challenge in grasping terminologies and concepts from other disciplines, particularly across medical/therapeutic and social epidemiological/population health disciplines.

Finding a suitable research site (e.g. hospitals, clinics or community setting) was mentally taxing, especially for authors who have a different cultural background (i.e. international doctoral researchers). The author who conducted multi-site clinical trials in rural and remote nursing homes experienced a lack of interest among the managers to be involved in projects. This influenced the recruitment of organizations and study participants and quality of interaction with clinicians (as research participants) during surveys and interviews. In conducting a study on the ethnic differences in seeking medical care for chest pain among culturally and linguistically diverse (CALD) populations, one author found that there are different definitions of migrants, immigrants, CALD and ethnicity.

Arranging dates and times for conducting surveys or interviews with participants and building relationships with stakeholders were essential parts of data collection. Two authors experienced a challenge in building relationships with stakeholders as new public health researchers with limited project management experience, which contributed to irregular interactions with participants. This irregularity impacted on the participants' confidence in participating in the interviews and in the recording of interviews. For another researcher, despite having prior experience in stakeholder management and project management, he found it difficult to engage and enlist potential stakeholders to support with recruitment. As a smaller research project and one that sat outside of dominant research paradigms, the challenge was to demonstrate how this research might benefit stakeholders given conflicting priorities and timelines. One author conducted a clinical study in which some practitioners showed concern about being recorded as they thought it might have negative repercussions in the workplace. Although the authors clarified their positions in the interviews and in the use of their voices, they were challenged because of a lack of proper pre-planning in building relationships. A few authors also found it problematic to collect field notes because access to clinical units (e.g. emergency or palliative care units) depends on the clinicians' time commitments and patients' conditions.

Health Literacy of Participants

The participants' general education and health literacy impacted on the data collection. For three authors, participants' low education influenced their understanding about the reasons for conducting research as well as the study aims and objectives. Understanding the value of research for the broader society can influence the recruitment of participants and their continued participation. It was found in some studies that those who expressed their interest and participated in interviews and/or focus groups were mostly well educated and active within their community. One of the key issues with engaging participants in qualitative research was their desire to impart a polished and coherent account of their experiences. This meant that participants were performing a hermeneutic function – that is an interpretation of their own experiences – but in doing so made it unclear to what extent their accounts were a faithful account of their original experience. In doing so, data tended to move away from a description and close evaluation of personal experience to more abstract and impersonal notions of what it is like to live with illness or healthcare needs.

In addition, two authors expressed that a lack of health literacy among the participants contributed to misunderstandings in response to survey and interview questions. As the questions included clinical terms and lengthy sentences, most of the participants requested clarification of these terms. It became more difficult for the participants with low health literacy in understanding the survey response structure when the researchers were not present during the completion of surveys or the participants were asked to complete online surveys. For example, in a doctoral study on healthcare access, some participants misinterpreted the variations of measurement scale about interactions between clinicians and patients such as do not agree, partially agree, agree, strongly agree and fully agree. Such challenging experiences were continued for the authors even in organizing the location of data collection.

Fieldwork Settings

Organizing the place of interviews was identified by some authors as a barrier. When interviews and focus groups were organized at university campus or community library, the attendance rate of clinicians was low as the hospital settings were preferable for them. However, the location of hospitals, especially in rural and remote areas, presented barriers to community attendance of focus groups. For example, one author who investigated dementia care in rural nursing homes conducted focus groups in the board room of the organization and found that some staff were not confident in discussing their problems with the facilitator. Power issues between aged care workers and management biased the responses and examples to the questions gathered. It was also challenging to collect data for two authors who investigated the emergency care for patients with chronic conditions or use of personalized dementia care model. Both authors who recounted experiences of this type attempted to recruit and collect data from clinical care units; however, after the first day of data collection they realized that the clinicians perceived the completion of this questionnaire was part of their routine tasks. If the completion of the questionnaire by the clinicians continued, this perception might impact on the quality of data gathered.

For research spanning organizational and state boundaries it was not always possible for some authors to conduct in-person surveys, interviews or focus groups, and instead online surveying, video conferencing or telephone or mobile phone mediums had to be used. This virtual platform added a value in data collection; however, some participants were worried about their confidentiality and anonymity, which in a study on online nursing education resulted in a low survey response rate. One author investigated virtual health literacy and conducted virtual focus groups (i.e. video conference technology) among the older participants from eight research sites. While they consented to participate in the virtual group discussion, at the meeting time, a few women participants did not want to turn up because of a concern over the loss of anonymity.

Other limitations in the use of technology were the quality of the audio obtained and issues with communication via email. The quality of audio recording was poor in some cases, especially in rural and remote areas because of poor internet and telephone connections, which increased the transcription difficulties, limited the extent to which automatic online transcription services could be used and increased transcription costs. Although the email was discussed as an effective form of data collection, the authors found that email servers at times identified the researcher email (invitation email) as junk mail and directed it into the spam or junk folder. For example, one author who conducted a study on the applicability of a Community of Inquiry framework to online and blended nursing education in Australia stated that of the 1,201 emails he had sent, only 555 were viewed by the recipient, with the rest not reaching or not being opened. As such, sending the invitation directly from the researcher by email can be problematic if the email ended up in the junk or spam mailbox.

Approach, Questions and Questioning

Once the settings for data collection were arranged, the use of appropriate language in data collection instruments, the explanation of medical terms, and the researcher's spoken English accent emerged as important challenges to the data collection process. In the first meeting on the date of interviews or focus groups, it was difficult for some authors to approach the participants appropriately because of either excitement or anxiety. For example, one author who conducted interviews with Indigenous women in residential aged care centres mentioned that he was unaware of the cultural implications of maintaining eye contact with participants. Some Indigenous participants identified that the questioning about their identity, level of education, spiritual beliefs, and relationships with family members was culturally sensitive. These issues impacted on the participants' consideration of attendance in the post-intervention and follow-up interviews.

During the interviews, the researchers could expect being asked for clarifications by the participants about the questions and prompts used (Sivertsen et al., 2019). A dilemma was identified in the researchers' role as a moderator. Some authors conducted interviews by themselves and some of them depended on the social workers or clinical consultant for conducting interviews, which raised the issue about who would be the best person to conduct interviews. Most of the authors agreed that having poor knowledge about clinical and epidemiological terminologies impacted on the quality of questioning and the use of prompts at the right time. One author conducting qualitative interviews noted a tendency to overlook important ideas presented by participants. Only on reviewing the interview transcripts did he realize how he had failed to engage with key ideas presented by interviewees, possibly reflecting a limited understanding of the phenomenon being explored. In addition, the language in data collection instruments and accent presented certain challenges because of the Australian multi-lingual environment. Some authors found that they were unaware of the spoken languages and cultural backgrounds of participants. A few authors also mentioned that international doctoral students who conducted interviews in clinics experienced challenges in using and understanding the accent of English-speaking language, which influenced the use of timely and appropriate questions and prompts.

One qualitative researcher noted how his interviewing style changed throughout the project as he reflected on the questioning style and its effect on participant responses. In particular, he was surprised at how intrusive participants found his questioning, which acted to interrupt the flow of the interviewee's narrative. By reflecting on his own questioning style via interview transcripts (i.e. reflection on action), he found that he became more reflexive about his own conduct during future interviews (i.e. reflection in action) (Daley, 2010).

Fatigue in Data Collection

Factors that affected fatigue included the duration, conduct of back-to-back interviews, limited control over the interview sessions, and the writing of field notes. The quality of interviews and focus groups was impacted by the number of questions asked and the length of fieldwork. In one study, the author found that the clinicians felt uncomfortable completing a survey about patients' behavioural aspects because of the lengthy questionnaire. In some instances, after completing the pre-intervention surveys clinicians noted issues with the length of surveys, which meant that they failed to complete the post-intervention surveys. After collecting data for a lengthy period of time, the authors found themselves exhausted in the last interviews (e.g. three-months follow-up), especially when they were required to travel inter-state. Inter-state travelling was psychologically demanding for a few authors because of isolation from family that resulted in feeling pressure to complete the interviews and compromised the attention they could give to the quality of data.

Another issue of fatigue pertained to interviewing without appropriate break or interval. Although the authors were very careful, conducting interviews without intervals caused a fatigue that impacted the quality of using prompts in a few instances. This was also a result of a lack of control over some focus group sessions where there existed issues of dominant behaviour within the group. After managing one focus group, it became difficult to complete a second focus groups without a break of several hours.

Fatigue also occurred due to the use of different data collection instruments by one researcher at the same time. For example, one author discussed the use of four data collection tools in one study. Upon arrival at the research site, this author realized that there was limited scope and time within the data collection framework for him to take notes because of the busy schedule of the clinicians. In addition, after conducting interviews and focus groups, writing field notes on the same study topic was identified as difficult for some authors.

In summary, the challenges in data collection ranged from governance to researchers' capacity to setting to participants' health literacy (Figure 2.1). However, the authors were able to successfully complete data collection from participants based on their professionalism, research skills, and personal strategies.

STRATEGIES TO OVERCOME THE CHALLENGES

The authors used various strategies depending on the fieldwork circumstances including individual persistence and resilience, engagement in long-term planning and scheduling, having a clear understanding of the study's scope and duration, developing contextual knowledge about research setting and participants, piloting the data collection instruments, and prolonged engagement with participants and interest groups (Figure 2.1).

Individual Persistence and Resilience

Persistence and resilience were two crucial components to commence, maintaining flow and success in data collection. As the researchers experienced fatigue because of complex research governance and lengthy participant recruitment processes, according to the authors there was a need to maintain determination and flexibility to manage the data collection and participants. Some authors went through a lengthy ethics review and site-specific authorization; however, patience and critical reflection-based learning helped them to overcome this challenge. Here, the authors defined 'critical reflection' as a reasoning process that helps to refine the goal settings, using learning from real-life experiences to inform future data collection tasks. Some authors stated that their supervisors suggested that they be attentive towards setting and following data collection milestones and use appropriate management techniques to achieve the milestones. Regular communication and discussion with supervisors and other stakeholders were imperative to avoid feeling isolated in data collection. Having control over the interview or focus groups sessions was also found important to avoid unrelated topics, and potentially reduce time wasting in fieldwork. Supervisors had the potential to offer a critical voice in planning, conducting, and reflecting on data collection. This critical voice was particularly important when recruiting from hard-to-reach populations, which required special attention and flexibility in the design and communication of recruitment materials. For one author, his supervisor suggested that he consult colleagues within the department who had special expertise (for example in recruiting from stigmatized groups) or personal contacts that might be able to support participant recruitment.

Long-Term Planning

Long-term planning was critical to effectively keep fieldwork on schedule. Most of the authors confirmed that the planning with respect to research governance, site specific authorization, recruitment of participants and data collection helped them to develop an organized approach to fieldwork. In relation to the recruitment of participants and interviewing the participants, two authors emphasized the usefulness of contingency planning. For example, one author shared his experience about the use of indirect contact methods (i.e. recruitment of an organization to approach participants) in recruiting participants from the community that resulted in a low number of respondents. This author, therefore, requested an ethics modification for using social media and community forum that contributed to an increase in participants' number. Pre-planning was important for organizing surveys, interviews and focus groups, especially in the multi-site clinical trials involving pre, post and follow-up data collection phases. The authors conducting clinical trials focused on integrating project management skills such as democratic leadership, self-motivation and critical insight into each step of fieldwork, which were also identified in the literature (Namageyo-Funa et al., 2014).

Clear Understanding of the Study's Scope and Duration

All research should have a defined scope and duration. The expectation of researchers was to make substantial intellectual contributions, but a full-time doctoral researcher generally has three years (three and a half years if extended) to produce a dissertation thesis and potential publications. The authors of the paper who are international doctoral researchers in Australia emphasized the need to clearly define the fieldwork scope, and limit expectations for data collection. One author noted his open discussion with supervisors about the scope and duration of the study and the supervisors guided him to keep the study specific and focused data collection that resulted in a timely recruitment of participants and interviews. Sometimes the best decision made was to recognize that no progress could be made rapidly, and instead look at other options. For instance, when long delays in obtaining ethics approvals and participants' recruitment occurred this could indicate that time would be better spent in other research contexts. If the supervisor is unsure or relatively inexperienced in recruiting and collecting data from a particular population or with respect to a particular phenomenon/issue, it is worthwhile consulting with other researchers that possess this experience. A certain grey area exists between the description of data collection methods within research methods literature, and the contextualization of these methods to suit the phenomenon of interest (Hamiduzzaman, 2018). As a doctoral student, some of the complexities involved in this contextualization only become apparent after considerable time spent in data collection and analysis, at which point the research scope and duration may already have ballooned.

Contextual Knowledge about Research Setting and Participants

Prior knowledge about the research sites and potential participants was found helpful. Four authors suggested reviewing literature to contextualize the research sites and achieve an idea about the interview locations and nature of participants. One author recommended finding more details in medical reports of individual cases to understand the clinical data of patients and develop a medical vocabulary notebook. For example, 'onset time' of chest pain recorded in the ambulance sheet differs from the time recorded in the triage report. This author sought more details in the doctors' and nurses' notes to justify the time data. Learning the medical terminologies and their abbreviations used in Australia was found to improve communication and interviews with participants for international doctoral researchers. One author consulted with the doctor (in hospital) to help clarify the message when there was poor handwriting in the report. In another case, an author performing research into clinical education reviewed the profile pages of potential participants from university websites, which helped him to understand the background of participants. Another author wanted to obtain data from as many participants as possible; thus, this author communicated with the participants and asked about the best way of communicating via phone, email or SMS, and also allowed them to choose the date, time, and a comfortable place for interview. This author organized a meeting room in case the participants wanted to be away from their office or shared their office with someone else.

One researcher described his use of local community centres to conduct all research activities. Within South Australia, community centres are typically operated or funded by local government and offer a safe and regulated environment for performing research activities. The benefit of using community centres is that venue hire is typically inexpensive, and the centres are designed with access to marginalized populations in mind, including accessible facilities and close proximity to public transport and other facilities (e.g. shopping centres, toilets, and schools). The researcher also offered participants cash reimbursement at the signing of consent to reduce any barriers to transportation to the research venue (either by public transport or personal vehicle), that could not be achieved in the same way by offering alternative forms of reimbursement such as vouchers for other goods and services. This demonstrated a level of thoughtfulness and consideration towards members of the target population, which the researcher felt would generate respect, trust, and reciprocity between researcher and participants.

Pilot the Data Collection Instruments

Another suggestion related to piloting the data collection instruments such as measurement scales, interviews, and focus groups. Piloting the instruments provides an opportunity to understand the use of interview questions and review the questions. This piloting also enabled researchers to understand the nature of the approach required for the participants in a specific study and devising the necessary plan and steps to solve potential barriers.

Prolonged Engagement with Participants and Interest Groups

In some jurisdictions research applications may run smoothly but in others it is important to establish relationships with people within partner organizations who help the researchers navigate the internal processes within an organization. In the case of snowball sampling, having trusted and reciprocating organizational contacts and participants was invaluable for identifying other people to interview. Having a trusted friend in a partner organization provided contextual knowledge of the organization that was needed to inform interviews with participants. If the researchers were better able to understand the issues faced by the participants being interviewed, then more targeted questions could be posed during interviews.

In relation to approaching the participants, welcoming them and asking 'how they are' and 'if they are very busy at this time of the year' were found to be enablers in breaking the ice and supporting participants to become more comfortable and open in providing information. It was also important to reassure the participants about the confidentiality of the data and to clarify any questions or answers where there is suspected miscommunication. Rapport building was found operative in obtaining sensitive information; however, the suggestion of some authors was to be more careful in asking sensitive questions regarding cultural identity. These adaptive strategies provided an understanding of how and when to intervene in order to successfully complete data collection.

REFERENCES

Andrew, S. and Halcomb, E. J. (2009). Future challenges for mixed methods research in nursing and the health sciences. In S. Andrew and E. J. Halcomb (eds.), *Mixed Methods Research for Nursing and the Health Sciences* (pp. 217–224). Chichester: Wiley-Blackwell.

Carter, S. M., Braunack-Mayer, A., and Jancey, J. (2016). Health promotion practice, research ethics and publishing. *Health Promotion Journal of Australia. Health Promotion Journal of Australia*, 26(3), 167–169.

Daley, A. (2010). Reflections on reflexivity and critical reflection as critical research practices. *Affilia*, 25, 68–82.

Dyke, T. and Anderson, W. P. (2014). A history of health and medical research in Australia. *Medical Journal of Australia*, 201(S1), S33–S36.

Hamiduzzaman, M. (2018). The world is not mine: Factors and issues of rural elderly women's access to modern healthcare services in Bangladesh. Doctoral dissertation, Flinders University of South Australia, College of Nursing and Health Sciences.

Lunnay, B., Borlagdan, J., McNaughton, D., and Ward, P. (2015). Ethical use of social media to facilitate qualitative research. *Qualitative Health Research*, 25(1), 99–109.

Malterud, K. (2001). Qualitative research: Standards, challenges, and guidelines. *The Lancet*, 358(9280), 483–488.

Namageyo-Funa, A., Rimando, M., Brace, A. M., Christiana, R. W., Fowles, T. L., Davis, T. L., ... Sealy, D. A. (2014). Recruitment in qualitative public health research: Lessons learned during dissertation sample recruitment. *The Qualitative Report*, 19(4), 1–17.

NHMRC (2015). National Statement on Ethical Conduct in Human Research. National Health and Medical Research Council, Australia. https://www.google.com.au/url?sa=t&rct=j&q=&esrc=s&source=web&cd=2&cad=rja&uact=8&ved=0ahUKEwjsteHJxZzYAhULerwKHVlmDqoQFgg1MAE&url=https%3A%2F%2Fwww.nhmrc.gov.au%2Fprintpdf%2Fbook%2Fexport%2Fhtml%2F51613&usg=AOvVaw2PVYZwVUA92gLouVQNVkOb.

Reilly, T., Crawford, G., Lobo, R., Leavy, J., and Jancey, J. (2016). Ethics and health promotion practice: Exploring attitudes and practices in Western Australian health organisations. *Health Promotion Journal of Australia*, 27(1), 54–60.

Sainsbury, P. (2016). Development and oversight of ethical health promotion quality assurance and evaluation activities involving human participants. *Health Promotion Journal of Australia*, 26(3), 176–181.

Sivertsen, N., Harrington, A., and Hamiduzzaman, M. (2019). Exploring Aboriginal aged care residents' cultural and spiritual needs in South Australia. *BMC Health Services Research*, 19(1), 477.

Smith-Merry, J. L. and Walton, M. M. (2014). Research governance as a facilitator for ethical and timely research? Learning from the experience of a large government-funded multisite research project. *Australian Health Review*, 38(3), 295–300.

3. Challenges with opening up closed off communities: interviewing ultra-Orthodox Jewish communities in Israel

Veronika Poniscjakova

CONTEXT: HAREDI COMMUNITIES IN ISRAEL

To fully understand the challenges with researching these communities, this section provides an overview of the Haredi belief system and lifestyle. Haredim are strictly religious, they rigorously adhere to the *Halachic*[1] rules. They are committed to *Halacha* and *mitzvot*[2] in the most fundamental, literal, pious, and stringent way and their lives are focused mostly around synagogue life (Ben-Yehuda, 2010). They also relate to traditional Jewish society of late nineteenth-century Eastern Europe (Ben-Yehuda, 2010), and they are dedicated to the unchanged tradition of Judaism and its values (Finkelman, 2014). Moreover, they view themselves as students who defend themselves against and oppose the secular, mainstream culture that they describe in demeaning terms (Ben-Yehuda, 2010). Since they oppose the mainstream culture, they try to stay away from it. Thus, from a sociological view, their principal distinctive feature is self-segregation, resulting in a separate and all-encompassing society (Foscarini, 2014) that is composed of separate residence, workplace, and education frameworks. Haredim have a separate education framework to isolate them from the danger of people and values they reject (Finkelman, 2004). Males and females are separated in this system and the state does not intervene in the curriculum (Ben-Yehuda, 2010). Haredim live in Haredi-only neighbourhoods or Haredi-only cities to protect the community from the outside, as exposure to modern culture could distract them from the strict observance of *Halacha* (Finkelman, 2004). Defined geographic spaces play a vital role in moulding social processes within Haredi communities (Ben-Yehuda, 2010, p. 18). Separation is evident also in the segregation of the sexes, a mandatory dress code for men and women, and language and jargon (Foscarini, 2014). All these help isolate Haredim from people and the values they reject (Finkelman,

2004). Apart from separation from secular Jews, it separates them also from non-Jews, whom they perceive as unreliable and hostile (Don-Yehiya, 2014). However, it should be noted that these characteristics are not uniform across all the Haredi groups.

I hoped to research the 'hard core' of these communities; however, as this chapter will note, the characteristics of these communities had made it virtually impossible. As noted above, these groups do not interact with outsiders to their communities, and thus, being an outsider presented the main challenge. This includes not only the barrier between Jewish and non-Jewish communities (that I am a part of), even secular Jews are viewed negatively and Haredim do not often interact with them. Moreover, as one of my interviewees suggested, even Haredim themselves may not be able to secure interviews with the members of their own community. Despite being a Haredi Jew herself, Chava said she had struggled to conduct interviews in the community for her PhD (Interview, Chava,[3] 29 May 2017). Secondly, there is a strict separation between genders in Haredi society. For instance, one of my interviewees told me he had never spoken to a woman he had not been related to until he had married one via a *shidduch*[4] (Interview, Yirmiyahu, 14 June 2017). As a woman, this had an impact on whom I was going to be able to interview. These two challenges, as well as less serious ones, such as the language barrier, were the most difficult to address, ultimately pushing the doctoral project in a different direction, and thus affecting the choice of research design and research methods.

CHALLENGES AND STRATEGIES TO OVERCOME THE CHALLENGES ASSOCIATED WITH QUALITATIVE RESEARCH

In addition to the communities-specific challenges that will be covered in the next part of this chapter, challenges associated with qualitative research projects are noted here as well, and in my case they were closely interlinked. Most qualitative research projects suffer from issues such as validity and generalizability stemming from a small sample size. In addition, there are often challenges with conducting research fieldwork abroad, for instance with regards to ensuring safety and following ethical guidelines laid down by universities or funding bodies (Merriam, 2014).

There are certainly many merits to using interviews as a primary research method. Interviews are a method for accessing people's attitudes and values that cannot be observed in questionnaires; interviews provide the ability to access what happens in the world, what people do in real life (Silverman, 2006). Qualitative interviews seek to understand the subjects' life experiences in great depth, coherence, and density (Gu, 2012). Therefore, interviews are the most advantageous method for research that deals with communities' attitudes and values that one is seeking to explore in depth. The choice of qualitative interviews proved to be effective, as I was able to speak to the members of the communities and better understand their viewpoints, for instance regarding the Israel–Palestine conflict. The interview questions I created consisted of both closed and open-ended questions. The closed questions were useful to understand and compare trends between and within different religious streams, while open-ended questions, as Silverman rightly points out, helped to get a better understanding of interviewees' views, their interpretation of events, experiences, and opinions (Silverman, 2006).

Whilst interviews are effective for in-depth study of communities, there are issues with regards to validity, reliability and generalizability of interview data. As Silverman points out, interview data do not give us access to facts (Silverman, 2006). As such, it should be highlighted that the objective of qualitative projects is to take the subject's perspective (Bryman, 2003). Therefore, even in cases when a participant said something factually incorrect, whether on purpose or not, it should be itself considered as data. An example of that is for instance a participant saying, without providing any factual evidence or source, that Palestinians do not exist as a nation or that Palestinians do not want to live in an independent state (Interview, Daniel, 7 June 2017). Bryman also points out the issue with external validity or generalizability in the case study approach, such as this one, as a single case cannot be representative of the entire group and findings may not be applicable more generally to other cases (Bryman, 2012).

This study consisted of 21 participants; therefore it cannot be considered a representative sample of the population. However, despite the small sample size, the number is big enough to be indicative of trends among the communities. Ideally, to maximize the validity of the research design, it would have been useful to interview people of different gender, age, and education (Reeves et al., 2008). In this case, however, this was not possible due to access issues. Yet, even given the small sample size, an indication of 'trends' can be useful. For instance, in their study, Guest et al. determined that at least 12 interviews were sufficient to ensure research validity (Guest et al., 2006). On the other hand, Warren's position is that for a qualitative interview study to be published, the minimum number of interviews should be between 20 and 30 (Warren, 2002 cited in Bryman, 2012). In contrast, Dukes recommends three to ten participants in a phenomenological study (Dukes, 1984) and Ray recommends between 8 and 12 people (Ray, 1994, cited in Sim et al., 2018). Therefore, 21 interviews should provide sufficient insight into the nature of Haredi communities. However, it should be noted that in this case the people who agreed to be interviewed are not fully representative of their own community for one important reason – that they were willing to be interviewed in the first place. As noted earlier, 'hard core' (representative) Haredi communities do not interact with outsiders.

Furthermore, there was a challenge with visiting places that could have been valuable for undertaking both interviews as well as non-participant observation. I was limited in this respect as the locations within Israel where the research was undertaken had been to a large degree influenced by two main factors: the likelihood of securing interviews and presence of gatekeepers, and secondly, the University's and home School's Ethics committee's directives. The latter required me to follow the United Kingdom's Foreign Office travel advice website that did not recommend travelling to the Occupied Territories and certain other parts of Israel. This meant, ultimately, that I was unable to visit purely Haredi cities such as Beitar Illit and Modi'in Illit in the West Bank. Therefore, it was necessary to find an alternative option. I decided to focus on the three biggest cities in Israel instead, which helped me develop a better understanding of the Haredi population, as well as the Israeli society as a whole, and observe different population dynamics.

I chose to spend most of my time in Jerusalem, considering its demographic dynamics: 32 per cent of Jews living in Jerusalem identify as Haredi (Grave-Lazi, 2016) where they maintain their traditional lifestyles, segregated from the other segments of the society (Alfasi and Fenster, 2005, p. 354). This is much higher than Israel's average of 9 per cent (Pew Research Center, 2016), which in theory should increase my chances of securing more interviews. At the same time, with numerous Haredi neighbourhoods, it was a valuable place to conduct the non-participant observation. In addition to Jerusalem, I spent two weeks in Tel Aviv and four days in Haifa to observe different dynamics.

I originally hoped to visit other cities in Israel as well, for instance, Bnei Brak and Beit Shemesh, which have predominantly Haredi populations. However, an absence of local contacts prevented me from visiting these places, particularly due to occasional outbreaks of violence in Israel. As the home School pointed out, the fieldwork location in Israel presented a challenge. Even though ultimately my safety was not compromised at all during the fieldwork, there were several outbreaks of violence, including stabbings and shootings. To mitigate risks, volatile areas were avoided and use of public transport was minimized, and I became familiarized with Israel's emergency procedures, such as finding shelter in case of rockets fired from outside Israel into Israeli territory.

CHALLENGES AND STRATEGIES TO OVERCOME CHALLENGES ASSOCIATED WITH RESEARCHING HAREDIM

Interviewing Haredim raises a number of issues, as already highlighted, most importantly, access issues. As these communities live closed off from the rest of the population and their level of interactions with outsiders is minimal, I struggled with identifying people willing to be interviewed. In addition, I was restricted by my lack of Hebrew/Yiddish language proficiency. Moreover, when I did conduct interviews, I had to ensure I was culturally aware. There were also some challenges with conducting non-participant observation.

As noted above, Haredim tend to live in alienation from the mainstream population, and thus the 'hard core' members of the communities I had hoped to interview were off-limits. As such, this meant compromises on my side and adjusting my research scope. As highlighted earlier, rather than interviewing the 'hard core' of the communities, I had to identify more open-minded individuals. Whilst this affected generalizability of findings, and establishment of trends across different strata of the Haredi population, it was realistically the only way of getting glimpses into the Haredi world.

As already highlighted, one of the concerns prior to and during the fieldwork was access and trust-building. As noted, these communities do not talk to outsiders, and interactions between men and women are not welcome in the Haredi communities. Therefore, to gain access to the communities, I had to identify contacts – gatekeepers willing to introduce an outsider to the communities. This proved extremely difficult; despite contacting many people, some did not respond at all, some promised they would help but then failed to do so, and only a fraction of people were willing to be interviewed in the end. There were limitations to who was willing to be interviewed. Indeed, as Norman points out, attributes such as nationality, gender, age or religion can impact trust (Norman, 2009, p. 83). Whilst the interviews snowballed after the initial ones, as I always ended the interview asking participants if they could recommend any other people potentially open to be interviewed, some did help, but some did not. For instance, Jacob said he could not introduce a non-Jewish, Slovakian girl to his friends or neighbours, as this would raise suspicions. Ultimately, he was worried this would ruin his children's *shidduch* (Field notes, Israel, 5 June 2017).

The most useful contact was the one developed within academia. I developed a contact at a local university who introduced me to people from my chosen population pool. Overall, contacting academics, as well as other well-connected individuals such as journalists can be an excellent tool. On the other hand, it should be noted that this also presented a methodological challenge, as most people who were interviewed were not a representative sample of their own communities as they had received a secular education at some points in their life and thus interacted with outsiders more than a regular Haredi member would do, as opposed to the 'hard core' members who study only within their Haredi educational frameworks. Those who were interviewed were more open than their communities, partly as a result of more exposure to secular education. When being interviewed, some participants made sure to explain how their views differ from their own community's. The sampling method worked on an opportunist and snowball basis, which was the easiest way, and the most reliable way to secure interviews. Bryman (2012) suggests that the problem with snowball sampling is that it is very unlikely that the sample will be representative of the population, which happened to be the case with my research. There was selection bias, as the interviewees did not reflect the composition of the Israeli society.

As mentioned, to accelerate the snowballing process, I asked the interviewees to introduce me to other potential interviewees. Whilst some refused to do so, some interviewees were more than helpful, although this did not automatically mean their contacts were willing to be interviewed. For instance, one of my (secular) contacts felt confident that some of her few Haredi friends and former students would be willing to be interviewed if she asked them (Field notes, Israel, 4 July 2017). However, after a few days, it became obvious that her friends and former students were not willing to be interviewed (Field notes, Israel, 12 July 2017). Again, this can be attributed to access issues due to my background. Indeed, Whiting (2008) suggests that participants often respond more favourably to interviewers who are similar to themselves, whilst my outsider status was apparent. To mitigate this to a certain extent, prior to coming to Israel, I spent eight months taking Hebrew evening classes. Whilst I was not proficient in the language and unable to undertake interviews in Hebrew, acquiring at least a minimum proficiency in the local language could help mitigate possible ethical issues and barriers to trust development (Norman, 2009). I did find that basic knowledge of Hebrew helped me to build rapport with people and gain access to the communities, thus mitigating the above-mentioned access issues. At the same time, however, interviewing only people who spoke English meant excluding a great number of people who did not speak English. Moreover, even though all the participants were Israeli, many of them were not born in Israel, and therefore this was also a source of selection bias.

Even when I was able to interview more open-minded individuals, and build some rapport, thanks to some basic knowledge of Hebrew and an excellent understanding of the local culture, I did not automatically gain the trust of all my interviewees. For instance, Rivka agreed to be interviewed after having been asked by one of my other participants. Whilst she did agree, she made it clear to me it was a favour to her friend. The fact that she did not trust me could be observed after the end of the interview. During the interview, she said she never interacted with outsiders like me (Interview, Rivka, 4 July 2017). After the interview, she told me she had parked her car a minute away from the place of the meeting. By coincidence, not intentionally, I went the same direction as Rivka did after the interview, without Rivka being aware of it. Rivka walked for ten minutes, and she did not have a car parked a minute away. She clearly wanted to meet in a place away from her own community so that she would not be seen in the company of an outsider (Field notes, Israel, 4 July 2017).

Nevertheless, I felt lucky to interview people like Rivka, who can be considered as among the more 'hard core' of the Haredi communities. It seemed easier to find Haredi women willing to be interviewed, as opposed to Haredi men, due to gender access issues. In Jewish religious circles, particularly the Haredi ones, contact between men and women is restricted. As Stadler notes, the realm of the Haredi world has always been the province of male ethnographers. When Stadler conducted her study dealing with the Haredi yeshiva world, she noted that encounters between researcher and informant posed "a potential threat to the community's basic definitions of masculinity and femininity and its sacred order" (Stadler, 2007, p. 23). Moreover, studies have shown that participants often say different things to male and female researchers (Murphy and Dingwall, 2003). As such, one's gender can pose obstacles to securing interviews. This was true in my case – being a female researcher presented a challenge and therefore the likelihood of securing interviews with men was lower. In addition, unlike in Stadler's study, there was never a male mediator present at the interviews I conducted – I did not have one – and was perceived as a complete outsider, a non-Jew. An example similar to this case is Dalby's (1983, cited in Guest et al., 2012) study of geisha culture. That study could only have been conducted by a female fluent in Japanese, and willing to undertake some geisha training, and no male researcher could have done that (Guest et al., 2012). A similar barrier was present in my case. Only a male member of their own communities would be able to conduct in-depth interviews with the Haredi men who never interact with women and outsiders. On the other hand, I was able to meet women that male researchers may not be able to talk to. Overall, there are some challenges, such as the researcher's gender, that cannot be mitigated. Therefore, this should be taken into consideration and any research design limitations and flaws in this respect should be acknowledged.

Regardless of the interviewee's gender, it was imperative to stay culturally aware and be cognizant of the limits during interviews. For instance, this included dressing according to the Jewish laws of modesty. Thus, when meeting a Haredi interviewee, I wore a shirt with long sleeves and covered neckline, and a skirt with a hemline below the knee, and shoes concealing my entire feet. It was also imperative not to shake someone's hand, particularly men, as that is not allowed in Haredi circles. To illustrate, upon meeting Shlomo, he did not offer to shake hands. When asked to sign the consent form, and offered a pen, he instead searched his bag to find his own (Field notes, Israel, 1 June 2017).

I utilized non-participant observation that gave me insight into the social dynamics and situations that showed relationships within communities as well as towards outsiders. It allowed me to record activities and the physical settings in which activities, such as the treatment of outsiders or reactions to governmental activities, take place and thus enabled information about the behaviour of individuals or groups to be obtained (Lemke and Bellows, 2012). There were limitations with non-participant observations as well, however. I could not spend a long time period observing in the streets, as this would have raised suspicions in a community who could tell who the outsiders are. Moreover, my previous point about cultural awareness is also applicable to non-participant observation. For instance, even when walking around Jerusalem or travelling on the bus in casual clothes (yet still modest, but not according to rules of Jewish modesty), Haredi women did not dare to sit next to me. However, when wearing a long skirt and long-sleeved blouse, women were willing to sit next to or even talk to me (Field notes, Israel, 25 June 2017).

NOTES

1. *Halacha* is a Jewish religious law.
2. *Mitzvot* (plural) are religious tenets.
3. All the interviewees' names have been anonymized.
4. *Shidduch* is a marriage match.

REFERENCES

Alfasi, N. and Fenster, T. (2005). A tale of two cities: Jerusalem and Tel Aviv in an age of globalization. *Cities*, 22(5), 351–363.

Ben-Yehuda, N. (2010). *Theocratic Democracy: The Social Construction of Religious and Secular Extremism* [e-book]. New York: Oxford University Press.

Bryman, A. (2003). *Quantity and Quality in Social Research* [e-book]. London: Routledge. http://site.ebrary.com/lib/uon/detail.action?docID=10062941.

Bryman, A. (2012). *Social Research Methods* (4th edn.). New York: Oxford University Press.

Dalby, L. (1983). *Geisha*. Berkeley, CA: University of California Press.

Don-Yehiya, E. (2014). Messianism and politics: The ideological transformation of religious Zionism. *Israel Studies*, 19(2), 239–263.

Dukes, S. (1984). Phenomenological methodology in the human sciences. *Journal of Religion and Health*, 23(3), 197–203.

Finkelman, Y. (2004). Review of *Haredim Yisraelim: Hishtalvut BeLo Temi'ah? [Israeli Haredim: Integration without Assimilation?]* by Kimmy Caplan and Emmanuel Sivan. *Modern Judaism*, 24(3), 296–300.

Finkelman, Y. (2014). The ambivalent Haredi Jew. *Israel Studies*, 19(2), 264–293.

Foscarini, G. (2014). Ultra-orthodox Jewish women go to work: Secular education and vocational training as sources of emancipation and modernization. *Annali di Ca' Foscari*, 50, 53–74.

Grave-Lazi, L. (2016). Ultra-Orthodox comprise a third of population of Jerusalem, says CBS. *The Jerusalem Post*, 1 June [online]. http://www.jpost.com/Israel-News/Ultra-Orthodox-comprise-a-third-of-population-of-Jerusalem-says-CBS-455608.

Gu, C.-J. (2012). Interviews. In S. J. Gold and S. J. Nawyn (eds.), *Routledge International Handbook of Migration Studies* (pp. 506–521). Abingdon: Routledge.

Guest, G., Bunce, A., and Johnson, L. (2006). How many interviews are enough? An experiment with data saturation and variability. *Field Methods*, 18(1), 59–82.

Guest, G., Namey, E. E., and Mitchell, M. L. (2012). *Collecting Qualitative Data: A Field Manual for Applied Research*. London: Sage.

Lemke, S. and Bellows, A. C. (2012). Qualitative and mixed methods approaches to explore social dimensions of food and nutrition security. In K. Albala (ed.), *Routledge International Handbook of Food Studies* (pp. 318–328). Abingdon: Routledge.

Merriam, S. B. (2014). *Qualitative Research: A Guide to Design and Implementation* (3rd edn.). San Francisco, CA: Jossey-Bass.

Murphy, E. and Dingwall, R. (2003). *Qualitative Methods and Health Policy Research*. Hawthorne, NY: Aldine de Gruyter.

Norman, J. (2009). Got trust? The challenge of gaining access in conflict zones. In C. L. Sriram, J. C. King, J. A. Mertus, O. Martin-Ortega, and J. Herman (eds.), *Surviving Field Research: Working in Violent and Difficult Situations* (pp. 165–176). Abingdon: Routledge.

Pew Research Center (2016). Israel's religiously divided society. *Pew Research Center*, 8 March [online]. http://assets.pewresearch.org/wp-content/uploads/sites/11/2016/03/Israel-Survey-Full-Report.pdf.

Ray, M. A. (1994). The richness of phenomenology: Philosophic, theoretic and methodologic concerns. In J. M. Morse (ed.), *Critical Issues in Qualitative Research Methods* (pp. 117–133). Thousand Oaks, CA: Sage.

Reeves, S., Kuper, A., and Hodges, B. D. (2008). Qualitative research methodologies: Ethnography. *BMJ*, 337 [online]. http://www.bmj.com/content/337/bmj.a1020.

Silverman, D. (2006). *Interpreting Qualitative Data: Methods for Analyzing Talk, Text and Interaction* (3rd edn.). London: Sage.

Sim, J., Saunders, B., Waterfield, J., and Kingstone, T. (2018). Can sample size in qualitative research be determined a priori? *International Journal of Social Research Methodology*, 21(5), 619–634.

Stadler, N. (2007). Ethnography of exclusion: Initiating a dialogue with fundamentalist men. *Nashim: A Journal of Jewish Women's Studies & Gender Issues*, 14, 185–208.

Warren, C. A. B. (2002). Qualitative interviewing. In J. F. Gubrium and J. A. Holstein (eds.), *Handbook of Interview Research: Context and Method* (pp. 83–101). Thousand Oaks, CA: Sage.

Whiting, L. S. (2008). Semi-structured interviews: Guidance for novice researchers. *Nursing Standard*, 22(23), 35–40.

4. Ethnography research with Indonesian female factory workers: challenges and strategies in the field

Mashitah Binti Hamidi

MELAKA: AN OVERVIEW

The following observation by Narifumi (1998) shows the significant changes that Melaka's social-economic development has had on Melaka's geographical and demographic landscape:

> In 1970, when I started my fieldwork at Pernu, eight kilometres to the southeast, Melaka was still a sleepy, quiet town with no international-standard hotels and few attractions beside the historic remains and old streets. Industrialisation moved slowly in spite of the image of a state stagnating economically. … Not until 1977 were forts like A Famosa, St John, and Linggi gazetted as historical sites. Many monuments and historic reconstructions were officially opened or reopened in the latter part of 1980s and the early 1990s for example Historic Museum of Melaka and Stadhuys. … When I revisited the community in 1984 and 1985, I noted that rice farming and rubber tapping are definitely declining, both in the area they occupy and in the number of persons engaged in these occupations. … [M]ost of the younger generation seek job opportunities outside the village … Educated youth prefer white-collar jobs in teaching, government services and companies to blue-collar jobs, for which the market, they say, has been reduced by an inflow of cheap labour from Indonesia and Philippines. … Many females now get salaried jobs as teachers, government workers, secretaries, and work even as factory workers. … In 1997, the drastic change of Melaka was keenly felt and Melaka had become sinisterly more like Kuala Lumpur in many respects: with new shops, shopping complexes, hotels and factories [that] seemed to have sprung up like mushrooms after the rain.

Narifumi's observations depict the changes to the urban built environment and to young Malaysians' occupations, which occurred in response to the development of the state in the last quarter of the twentieth century. In particular, they portray the impact of industrial development on Melaka's shift from agriculture to industrialization and the important implications for Melaka's socio-economic circumstances.

Melaka is the third smallest state after Perlis and Penang in Peninsular Malaysia, covering an area of 1,664 km^2 (642 $miles^2$). The state is divided into three districts: Central Melaka (314 km^2), Alor Gajah (660 km^2), and Jasin (676 km^2) with a population of 830,900 in 2011. Melaka sits on the south-western coast of the Malaysian Peninsula opposite Sumatra, with the Malaysian states of Negeri Sembilan to the north and Johor to the east. Melaka is situated roughly two-thirds of the way down the west coast, 148 km south of Kuala Lumpur, the capital of Malaysia and 245 km north of Singapore and it commands a central position on the Straits of Melaka (Figure 4.1). The standardized Bahasa Malaysia spelling is 'Melaka' while 'Malacca' is the historic settlement name and remains in active use in the press and in tourism industry literature.

Figure 4.1 *Map of Peninsular Malaysia*

Melaka is known as an historic state and is a World Heritage Site.[1] Melaka was a destination for travellers and explorers well before the evolution of contemporary mass tourism. Trade and labour migration is not new to Melaka;

since the fifteenth century, Melaka has played an economic role as a premier international port by establishing reliable facilities for warehousing and trade. Early Islamic traders held sway over the port until the colonial era transformed the region in a series of European conquests. The Portuguese onslaught in 1511 overthrew the Sultan, and the Dutch ousted the Portuguese in 1641. The British took over Melaka in 1795 and incorporated it into the tripartite administrative territory called the Straits Settlements, along with Singapore and Penang. Immigration from India and China increased under the British as labourers were brought in to transform the fledgling colonies. Five hundred years of colonial history is inscribed in the built environment of Melaka town that attests to the historic presence of three European societies and two immigrant cultures. From a postcolonial perspective, however, the colonial period effaced Melaka's Malay and Islamic origins. Nevertheless, Melaka is indisputably the nation's heart of Islam as it is the centrepiece of the country's colonial history (Sandhu and Wheatley, 1983).

During the 1960s, the main generators of income growth were agriculture and the Commonwealth Forces Training Centre at Terendak (Currie, 1983). An important impetus to the founding of the industrial estates was the withdrawal of the Commonwealth Forces from their training centre at Terendak camp, 14 km from Melaka town in 1970. The retrenchment of its civilian employees also affected the retail and services sector of Melaka town. The Commonwealth Forces Training Centre was, according to Currie (1983, p. 367), "the most important generator of income outside agriculture and the government sector" in the state. After the withdrawal of the Commonwealth Forces, the unemployment rate rose sharply and at one stage amounted to 25 per cent of the existing labour force (Naerssen, 1980). Given the lack of natural resources within the state, these circumstances forced the government to look for possibilities to attract manufacturing industries.

The search for new industrial opportunities coincided with Malaysia's broader shift from import-substitution to export-oriented industrialization. The major expansionary phases of industrialization in Peninsular Malaysia occurred during the Second Malaysia Plan (1971–1975) and the first half of the Third Malaysia Plan (1976–1980). Government industrialization strategies included a range of incentives, beginning with a programme for export-oriented firms under the Investment Incentive Act of 1968 (Anazawa, 1985; Currie, 1983). In 1973, the incentive was extended to other labour-intensive export-oriented industries and the concept of free trade zone (FTZ) (later referred to as special economic zone or SEZ) introduced in an attempt to encourage labour-intensive export-oriented industries to invest in Malaysia. FTZs provide a range of tax concessions as well as exempting all establishments within the zone from paying import and export duties. With the financial support of the Federal

Government, Melaka's State Development Corporation opened up a number of new industrial estates and special economic zones.

In the 1970s, two manufacturing industrial areas in Melaka, namely, Tanjong Kling and Batu Berendam, obtained FTZ status and were the only such zones outside the Klang Valley and Penang at the time of their establishment (Naerssen, 1980). In addition, five areas were designated for development as industrial estates by the Melaka State Development Corporation. The development of new economic zones wrought significant changes to Melaka given its relatively small geographical area. Most of these areas were in Central Melaka District and the land was reserved for the manufacturing sector only.[2] In Central Melaka, rubber estates and paddy lands were replaced with manufacturing and various tertiary activities (Currie, 1983). Even outlying areas, such as Alor Gajah and Jasin Districts, which remained overwhelmingly rural in the 1970s and were dominated by rubber and dairy production, were gradually converted to free trade zones and industrial parks.

Prior to the opening of these estates, there were few manufacturing jobs in Melaka. In the early 1970s, there were around 3,100 workers in manufacturing industries (Malaysia Department of Statistics in Naerssen, 1980) and in 1978 this number had risen to an estimated 12,500. The reason for this fourfold increase was that new firms started production in several industrial estates, particularly between 1974 and 1975. According to Naerssen (1980), recognition of the importance of Melaka's manufacturing sector began with its remarkable 12 per cent contribution to the GDP of Peninsular Malaysia in 1970, which grew to 14 per cent in 1975. In 2012, Melaka topped the list of Malaysia's GDP with the highest growth of 7.2 per cent (in 2011: 4.0 per cent) spurred by manufacturing, services and construction sectors (Department of Statistics, 2013). Naerssen (1980) also gives several reasons for this growth, arguing that Melaka is attractive to investors due to its proximity to raw materials, markets, transportation facilities, labour, availability of fuel, power and water, services and ancillary industries. Investors rate low wages, government incentives and political stability as further important features making Melaka an attractive manufacturing location (Naerssen, 1980).

Of particular interest to this study is the relatively long-term employment of women in Melaka's manufacturing sector. According to an early study by Currie (1983), one of the characteristics of the Melaka industrial estates was that women were employed in about 75 per cent of the jobs. According to a 1970 census, women took up more than 80 per cent of the available jobs in the free trade zones (Currie, 1983). Most of the women were young and lived at home, and some 60 per cent of these women were bumiputera[3] (in this context, Malay) and principally originating from the areas around Melaka.

Tourism is the other major economic activity in Melaka. It had attracted 8.2 million tourists to Melaka by 2010 (Melaka State Government, 2012). In the early 1980s, Currie (1983) had predicted the potential of this sector for Melaka, but noted that it depended on "the restoration and opening of historic sites". In line with this projection, the Melaka State Development Corporation promoted tourism and declared Melaka to be a "heritage state" in 1989 (Narifumi, 1998). The promotion of both tourism and industrialization has resulted in clashes over the cultural, economic and environmental values of land. Coastal reclamation projects, for example, have proved detrimental to shrimp fisheries and negatively impacted on livelihoods in Melaka (Cartier, 1998). They have also destroyed historical sites, such as the natural flow of the Melaka River and the Portuguese community's beachside neighbourhood. Despite the growing number of tourist attractions, manufacturing dominates the small and cramped landscape in Central Melaka.

Figure 4.2 *Map of Central Melaka*

As shown in Figure 4.2, industrial areas are centred along the edges of the city proper in the suburbs of Melaka and several technology industrial areas have been gazetted, while others have been organized according to sector such as automotive, composite, halal food hub, electrical goods and electronics, and furniture. At the time of writing, Melaka had 22 industrial areas, which were developed by the private sector or the Melaka State Development Corporation (Data Asas Melaka, 2009). Among them are Ayer Keroh (various industries), Batu Berendam (electrical goods and electronics) and Serkam (halal food hub). Thirty-one companies operate in FTZ areas and another 228 companies operate in various industrial estates (Data Asas Melaka, 2009). The international corporations operating in Melaka included National Semiconductor

(United States), Infineon Technologies (Germany), Panasonic Semiconductor Discrete Devices (Japan), and Roxul Asia (Denmark) among many others.

Jasin and Alor Gajah Districts continue to be promoted as historical attractions with the museums and monuments of the pre-independence period being developed and repaired for tourism purposes as opposed to opening the land up for industrial zones.[4] The facilities and infrastructure in these districts is underdeveloped in comparison to Central Melaka. One limitation of the industrial estates that do operate in the Jasin and Alor Gajah Districts is the poor development of the public transport system, especially to and from Central Melaka (Narifumi, 1998). This was verified during my fieldwork when Indonesian informants who worked in these more remote areas of Melaka reported that a distinct difference between locations was the accessibility to social amenities and public transport.

This study incorporated three industrial areas of Melaka where a large number of Indonesian women were working in export-oriented factories, namely, Central Melaka, Alor Gajah and Jasin Districts. In Central Melaka, my research focused on the Melaka Tengah area which consists of Batu Berendam I and II Free Trade Zones and the Ayer Keroh and Cheng industrial estates. In Alor Gajah District, I conducted research in the Alor Gajah Industrial Zone and Masjid Tanah industrial estate. In Jasin District, I conducted research in Merlimau industrial estate.

OUTLINE OF FIELDWORK AND METHODOLOGY

This writing is based on fieldwork, which occurred between January and August 2011. During that time, I conducted face-to-face interviews with 49 informants, consisting of 30 Indonesian women who were currently working as labour migrants and 19 informants who had a professional involvement with labour migration at that time. To understand how women from varying backgrounds experienced transnational migration and worked in the manufacturing sector, I sought to interview a range of women: single, married, separated and divorced, first-time and repeat migrants. Out of the 30 Indonesian women migrants, 27 worked in Melaka, with the remaining three consisting of one working in Kuala Lumpur and two in Selangor factories. The different locations resulted from the snowball sampling technique that I used. It sometimes happened that an informant in Melaka would refer me to her friend who worked in a factory in either Kuala Lumpur or Selangor. The female migrants in Melaka worked in a number of districts. Fourteen worked in Central Melaka, in Batu Berendam I, Batu Berendam II, Serkam and Ayer Keroh industrial areas. A further six informants worked in Alor Gajah district in two prominent industrial areas there, namely Alor Gajah Industrial Park and Masjid Tanah. In Jasin District, five informants were all directly recruited by the same export-oriented factory operating in the Merlimau area. The places of residence of these 27 workers were also scattered across Melaka. Only seven informants were located within walking distance of their factories (less than three kilometres). Most informants therefore commuted to work by the shuttle bus services provided by their factory or labour outsourcing agent.

I also conducted interviews with 19 migration stakeholders. This group consisted of the following: four staff or managers of human resources departments in four factories; three labour outsourcing agents or staff members; three government officials (two Malaysian and an Indonesian Labour Attaché); three representatives of civil society (an in-house union leader, an Indonesian expatriate involved in a welfare organization for female Indonesian labour migrants, and a Malaysian trade union organizer); and six local people from a variety of social settings. The informants provided a broader perspective on the processes and context of female labour migration in Melaka. Ten, or nearly two thirds of these informants held high-level or decision-making positions in their organization. These included the Indonesian Labour Attaché, human resources managers and a director of a government department. The retrospection of the former migrants provided additional insights into how migration and manufacturing employment shapes the lives of female migrants. The remaining informants occupied lower-level positions as clerks, a hostel warden and a shuttle service driver. This range of information was helpful for understanding different perspectives on labour migration, including the perspectives of former migrants, of concerned members of civil society, as well as those from the bottom and the top of migration-related institutions and structures.

The majority of these 19 informants were aged in their early 40s to late 50s, three were around 30, and the remaining five were in their 20s. Thirteen of these 19 migration stakeholders were male: the Labour Attaché, two directors, four human resources managers, two civil group representatives, a karaoke owner, a technician at a factory, a hostel warden and a bus driver. Of the six women I interviewed, one worked as an officer at JTK (the Malaysian Labour Department), one worked for a labour outsourcing agency and one was involved in a welfare organization for female Indonesian migrants. A further three were local residents: a former factory worker, a shop assistant in Melaka Sentral bus terminal and a security guard at a foreign workers' hostel. The nationality and ethnic background of these informants also varied. The majority of the Malaysian informants were Malay (12 out of 19), with the remaining Malaysians comprising two Indian Malaysians, one Chinese Malaysian and a Kadazan Malaysian (from Sabah in East Malaysia). A further three informants were non-Malaysians, including two Indonesians (from Java) and one Singaporean Chinese. The location of these 19 interviews ranged from Melaka to Selangor, the federal administrative centre of Putrajaya, and the capital city of Kuala Lumpur.

This research was conducted by employing ethnographic research methods. As Glick Schiller (2003) noted, the strength of ethnographic methods is their ability to not only build upon previous observations and generate hypotheses from them, but also to produce new research material, questions and hypotheses from ongoing observations. Ethnography is thus especially useful for exploratory research, which generates questions that can later be examined systematically, and in this way promotes new theorization (Mahler and Pessar, 2006). Recruitment methods in ethnographic research are related to the specific research question being asked in order to get more information through interviews and observation. Taking an ethnographic approach can require extra effort on the part of the researcher as she must be prepared to participate in the many varied social settings that make up people's lives. In such a way, it is the accumulation of research across a range of micro social settings that provides a qualitatively rich understanding of women's lives (Haraway, 1991).

My own approach was based on the contention that women's agency and the gendered nature of migration could not be understood solely through an analysis of policy prescriptions and other documentary forms of evidence, but rather through the everyday practices that ethnographers observe during fieldwork (see, for example, Rudnyckyj, 2004). By formulating and identifying the everyday practices and activities of migrants and other relevant actors, the level of agency of Indonesian female workers can be determined in comparison to other migrants or local counterparts.

Snowballing techniques were used to identify potential informants. For example, after each interview session, I asked the participants to recommend acquaintances who might be willing to talk to me. In the end, this method proved to be very fruitful as I found it all but impossible to get permission to interview women at work. Only one company allowed me to walk around the factory and talk with an Indonesian labour migrant who worked as a store-keeper in the factory's store. This informant talked about her routine, expressed her concerns about work safety, and discussed her relationships with her co-workers and the factory's management. From this short conversation, I made another appointment to meet her later at her hostel for a longer conversation. During the second meeting, she criticized the treatment she received as a migrant from the management and the local Malaysian supervisor and was eager to tell her stories and communicate her sense of injustice. In other interactions with Indonesian migrants, I used the same strategy of slowly building rapport in order to obtain their trust. This meant that I would meet with women on more than one occasion and often in different locations before I attempted to interview them on a more in-depth level.

Due to the lack of access to women through their place of work, I had to be creative in order to connect with Indonesian women. This often meant hanging around places where Indonesian migrants gathered, such as street eateries, bus stops and sidewalks outside factories in order to make contact with women who had finished their shift or were waiting for a shuttle bus to transport them home. Interviews were also at times conducted in quite public places, as well as in their hostels. This contrasted with interviews with the other informants (such as officials, human resources personnel and labour outsourcing agents), where most of the interviews were held at their place of work, and only a few conducted in public areas.

In the end, however, this barrier to interviewing women at their place of work turned out to have its advantages. In visiting various locales, such as malls, bus stations, restaurants and karaoke centres frequented by Indonesian female migrants, I was able to gain a fuller understanding of the lifestyle changes with which manufacturing employment is associated. Specific to the goals of this study, it provided a first-hand glimpse of how women spent their time after work and how public space associated with the social activities of these women was gendered and Indonesianized – often with negative associations.

This is in line with Weber's notion of *Verstehen* or interpretation, which seeks to gauge the reasons behind social actors' activities and what they strive to achieve through them. Such an approach encourages the researcher to "use our ordinary capacity to speak, listen, read and write in order to uncover or reconstruct the intentions, values, rules, and symbolic meanings social actors use in their lives, their institutions and their activities" (Bessant and Watts, 2002, p. 53).

Participant observation was also conducted in a number of group activities. I was invited to a monthly religious event at an Indonesian women's hostel during which they performed recitations of the holy Quran involving Indonesian men and women. I also joined popular 'off-shift' activities such as singing and dancing in karaoke centres, eating bakso (a popular Indonesian food) at stalls, browsing at the night market and also visiting the women's Facebook pages. In these activities, I was an observer and a participant in the sense that I was present in the scene of the setting as a social being: watching, observing, talking and sometimes taking part in the activities of the migrants and the people in the community around them (Zaman, 2008).

All the interviews were conducted by me in Malay or English. As Malay-Indonesian words sometimes have different meanings and some of the Indonesian women had strong local dialects, I asked for further explanations of anything that I did not understand. Most of the interviews lasted for around an hour, though some were shorter in duration and others, especially with officials and civil society representatives, lasted up to two hours. I also relied on material gathered during the fieldwork in the form of newspaper articles, government publications, booklets from labour brokers, and NGO blogs and websites. The interviews were informal and open-ended, and where necessary, second interviews were conducted to confirm or elaborate upon information. These follow-up interviews were carried out either in person, or by telephone and email. Upon my return to Australia, some of my Indonesian informants kept in touch with me via text messaging and occasional phone calls. Their willingness to maintain contact with me created a channel for asking follow-up questions that emerged during the course of writing my PhD thesis.

Interviews were tape-recorded when the permission was granted by the participant; otherwise, I recorded their responses by hand. Subsequently, I transcribed the tapes and handwritten notes. I then performed a narrative analysis based on coding and categorizing the interviewee responses using NVivo 8, a qualitative data analysis software program. I also integrated into this narrative analysis the research notes gathered from participant observations, newspaper and journal articles relating to women's participation in transnational labour migration, as well as photographs and videos that I took during the fieldwork. This level of coding allowed me to analyse the data across a broad spectrum of issues as well as sources (from interviews to graphic sources). By centralizing all the data sources into NVivo 8, I was also able to uncover themes and patterns that I had failed to consider at the beginning stage of the study.

ETHNOGRAPHY AT HOME

I lived in Melaka as a teenager from the age of 17 when I pursued a matriculation[5] programme at Masjid Tanah until I left to study at university at the age of 20. My parents still live in Melaka (indeed, not far from Melaka Sentral bus terminal), as does my brother and his family. I am also a Malaysian doing research in Malaysia. So a consideration of my positionality is an important element of this 'ethnography at home'. Madden (2010) argues that doing ethnography at home requires the consideration of two important characteristics: the emic (the insider's position) and etic (the outsider's position).[6] According to Madden (2010), ethnography has tended to privilege the emic perspective as the most important lens through which to access "the 'folk' or 'native' or 'insider' point of view". He suggests, however, that the outsider's view should not be disregarded as this will help the researcher to understand the concerns that brought them to the field (Madden, 2010). In general, being an outsider tends to imply that the researcher has little knowledge of the setting prior to immersion in participant observation and, conversely, being an insider means that the researcher already has some knowledge of the setting (Bonner and Tolhurst, 2002). In this study, I was both insider and outsider depending on the angle of viewing. I am an insider in relation to Melaka but an outsider in relation to the lives of the migrant women I researched. However, extending Madden's insight that the outsider's point of view should not be disregarded, I would also suggest that the insider-outsider point of view is also of value to our research. In the following discussion, I describe how it was that my position 'within' and 'between' (inside and outside) the research location became a primary navigational tool in this study. Specifically, this section seeks to reflect upon the ways in which my social positioning affected my interactions with informants in the field and ultimately the collection and interpretation of data.

Personally, this topic challenged me in my role as an 'insider' doing research in my own backyard while seeking to understand at the same time as an 'outsider' the experience of female migrants from Indonesia working in the manufacturing sector. The only reference points I had was my recollection of a family member's experience of hiring Indonesian maids, and their perception that Indonesian maids were demanding and that they changed their personalities during the time of employment. In the worst case, one maid who had been employed for more than two years was alleged to have stolen valuable items from the family. Another negative image that preceded this research was that of 'Minah Indon', the term used by locals to refer to Indonesian women and their supposed sexy appearance and immoral attitudes. This prejudice was related to my memory of another family member becoming involved in a relationship with an Indonesian girl, leading to a reaction of panic and hysteria by his parents. I held these experiences and perceptions in my ethnographic apparatus, like other local citizens who perceived Indonesian female workers as problematic, loose and immoral.

It is important to recognize these ideas and representations, as this issue of how Indonesian women respond to such public representations has in fact become a central theme in my research. Clearly, there is plenty of evidence that such negative stereotypes are both widespread and have an impact on Indonesian women's experiences. Yet, there is also a subjective element within this ethnographic study because, as a human being, I bring with me a prior set of social constructions about myself and others. This acknowledgement, however, does not mean that I do not also strive to achieve a level of objectivity in my research. Some level of objectivity is critical in order to engage closely with the research subjects, and to excavate the meaning of their lives, feelings and experiences. After getting to know the situation of these Indonesian women through our conversation, interviews and observations, I became sympathetic towards the struggles they faced in their lives in Indonesia and Malaysia. From this, I developed my own form of "personal-political reflexivity" (Madden, 2010, p. 22), one that aims to record their struggles but in a way that also brings to light the women's own resourcefulness and agency.

Neutrality is clearly an unrealistic approach within the complexity of fieldwork (Patel, 2010, p. 21). Nevertheless, this does not have to come at the cost of objectivity. Important here is to acknowledge both the subjectivity and objectivity of our cognitive frames in order to gain reliable and meaningful data, new perspectives in the approach to research and more understanding towards the research in hand. In this regard, I agree with the view expressed by Madden (2010, p. 23):

> In my own work I engage in reflection on the subjective and objective elements of my methodological approach, I reflect on the politics of location and on the influence my social and historical identity has on the creation of the text, and I do all these things simultaneously. Such reflexivity is simply an essential part of managing the influence of 'me' on the research and representation of 'them'.

There is an additional issue relating to objectivity and subjectivity in a study that is primarily focused on the lived experiences of women. Haraway (1991, p. 188) is not alone in observing the extent to which the feminine subject is not given sight. Women, she argues, are viewed primarily through a lens of being observed, described or conquered. Essentially, they become objects explained away by a so-called objective, detached, scientific gaze. Yet instead of aspiring to achieve total vision/objectivity in relation to our research subjects, Haraway reclaims the value (and inevitability) of the partial perspective. From this perspective, what may be conceived as a limitation of the present study (a focus on Indonesian women's perspective of transnational labour migration rather than integrating information from different nationalities or men's perspectives of gendered migration agency) can also be seen as strength.

An important insight during this process of self-reflection was to see that along with my informants, I was also located in this study at the intersection of nationality, ethnicity, class, gender and age, among other axes. Born and raised as a third generation of migrants from Indonesia, my upbringing as 'native' Malay and Malaysian led me to sometimes obliterate my family roots from multiple racial intersections. The descendant of Indonesian grandparents on my father's side and Chinese great-grandparents on my mother's side, much of this family history has been obscured by my classification as 'Malay-Muslim' bumiputera. During childhood, I never questioned the existence of the large number of Indonesians in Malaysia as I assumed they had migrated like my grandparents a long time ago. When I was at university and could better understand the everyday gossip, issues and conflicts between Malaysia and Indonesia from the media, I was interested to understand the history and contemporary details of the Malaysian and Indonesian relationship.

As my postgraduate studies were funded by the Malaysian Government and I was a staff member at the University of Malaya, I chose a topic related to my academic field, Industrial Sociology, so that I could focus on questions that were relevant to industrial or workplace sociology, and which also reflected my personal interests. Hence, this study of female Indonesian labour migrants in Malaysia's manufacturing sector represents a conjunction of research interests and personal knowledge, and perhaps explains why I did not seek to study other groups of workers, such as service sector or domestic workers.

Conducting research at home enabled me to access an established network as I positioned myself as insider who had local knowledge while being an outsider in relation to the Indonesian women. I was not only positioning myself in relation to these multiple selves but also constantly being positioned by those with whom I was engaged in the research process. My reflexive work, therefore, was to examine how my multiple and interrelated social positioning affected how I presented myself and how I might be perceived in the field.

As an academic at the oldest public university in Malaysia and a student researcher from an Australian university, I was warmly welcomed by the officials and some corporate entities. On the other hand, one of the drawbacks of introducing myself with this background was that some companies (especially subsidiaries to international corporations) resisted interviews for the reason that I might expose the company's confidential information and jeopardize their relationship with clients. I was also denied access to the factory compounds as these areas were restricted to outsiders.

In addition to my professional background, my personal identity was also a factor that was relevant to my sameness and the otherness to Indonesian informants. As a middle aged woman (in my early 30s), I was always welcomed by the Indonesian women of the same age or older. As a wife and a mother, and also a temporary migrant even though in a different context, some conversations developed in interesting ways when I talked about family, children and migration matters because on some occasions we shared similar opinions, interests and experiences. The otherness between myself and Indonesian migrants was more strongly felt in my social interactions with younger women, and was most acute in the case of teenage Indonesian women, who had just arrived a few months previously. These young women would distance themselves from me and often my requests to women under 25 years to participate in this study ended in rejection. In one incident, a young woman I interviewed at Melaka Sentral bus terminal said "I thought you were the police" after I had approached her following her remittance of money to Indonesia. When I interviewed older women and asked their advice on how to approach young migrants, one told me that I should not have a problem because I am local and the Indonesians are all legal and documented. Fortunately, in this case, despite her initial suspicion, the interview with the young woman at Melaka Sentral bus terminal went smoothly after I explained who I was and communicated my intentions. To protect the identity of the participants and the companies where they worked, pseudonyms are used throughout the study. Identity was a key source of concern for a number of participants.

My visibility as an urban, middle-class female Malay Malaysian was also an issue when I tried to engage with respondents in public. Wearing the tudung (headscarf) showed that I was a local Malay and my greeting to women in the Malay language invited strange feelings. One of the informants told me "Malaysian do not like us, I was wondering why kakak [literally, older sister but used as a polite term to refer to a Malay woman a few years older] came and talked to me". This kind of fear or prejudice toward locals constricted my ability to access more informants. This problem has arisen for other scholars, such as Pei-chia Lan (2006). During her fieldwork in Taiwan, young Muslim women from Java distanced themselves from the ethnographer. In that study, the social hierarchy and cultural gap made the process of recruiting Indonesian domestic workers in Taiwan more difficult compared to Filipina counterparts and demanded more effort and time (Lan, 2006, p. 10). To construct a more intimate atmosphere with the Indonesian women in this study, I gradually learned how to gain a lot of information just by 'hanging out'. As Bernard (1994, p. 152) wrote: "Hanging out builds trust, and trust results in ordinary conversation and ordinary behaviour in your presence".

Despite these difficulties, my background as a local Melakan also helped to minimize disadvantages during the fieldwork. I had a vast reserve of local knowledge as well as relatives, friends and acquaintances who had contact with Indonesian women working in local factories and who were prepared to assist me. I developed various strategies including the approach I call 'walk-in recruitment' to try to get interviews. After a series of rejections from Indonesian and local informants in the first couple of weeks of fieldwork, and after considering that none of the state government agencies could provide adequate information or statistics about the factories that employed Indonesian women or even women of any nationality, I decided to use basic information obtained from the internet. This yielded specific information about the number of companies operating in each of the industrial zones in Melaka. Armed with that information, I went to every mentioned district and asked the factory's security guard about the possibility of Indonesians being employed at their factories. Being from Melaka helped with such 'walk-in recruitment' and indeed I was surprised by how helpful many guards were. In this way, I gained a lot of useful information especially in regard to contacts with the human resources department within these factories and with employees.

The above discussion illustrates that one important criterion in judging the validity of research data is through a consideration of the positionality and reflexivity of the ethnographer. Indeed, through the reflexive process of examining my own positionality during fieldwork, I reached a transformed understanding of my research subjects, even though it did not change my standing as to who I was.

NOTES

1. Declared along with George Town, Penang by UNESCO on 7 July 2008.
2. In 2009, out of 166,300 hectares, 7,034 hectares (4.23 per cent) were urban and industrial. Source: Data Asas Melaka, 2009, p. 2.
3. Bumiputera literally translates as 'son of the soil' and in Malaysia is used to refer to groups considered indigenous to Malaysia. The largest group of bumiputera in Malaysia are the Malays, but there are a number of other indigenous ethnic groups in Peninsular and East Malaysia, such as the Semai, Kadazan, Iban and Bidayuh.
4. Tanjung Tuan Lighthouse, Kota Belanda Fort Supai and the Tomb of Dol Said are among the historical attractions in Alor Gajah. In Jasin, the notable attraction is the Tomb of Tun Teja.
5. The Malaysian Matriculation Programme is a one- or two-year pre-university preparatory programme, or equivalent to an A-level programme.
6. The terms 'phonemic' and 'phonetic' are taken from linguistics. They depict the situation of the researcher as an insider (emic) or outsider (etic).

REFERENCES

Anazawa, M. (1985). Free trade zones in Malaysia. *Hokudai Academic Papers*, 15, 91–148. http://hdl.handle.net/2115/30723.

Bernard, H. R. (1994). *Research Methods in Anthropology*. London: Sage.

Bessant, J. and Watts, R. (2002). *Sociology Australia* (2nd edn.). Sydney: Allen & Unwin.

Bonner, A. and Tolhurst, G. (2002). Insider-outsider perspectives of participant observation. *Nurse Researcher*, 9(4), 7–19.

Cartier, C. (1998). Megadevelopment in Malaysia: From heritage landscapes to "leisurescapes" in Melaka's tourism sector. *Singapore Journal of Tropical Geography*, 19(2), 151–176.

Currie, J. I. (1983). The economy of Melaka today and tomorrow. In K. S. Sandhu and P. Wheatley (eds.), *Melaka: The Transformation of a Malay Capital, c.1400–1980* (pp. 351–379). Oxford: Oxford University Press.

Data Asas Melaka (2009). *Melaka Basic Data 2009*. Melaka: Jabtan Ketua Menteri Melaka.

Department of Statistics, Malaysia (2013). GDP by state: National Accounts 2005–2012. Putrajaya: Department of Statistics, Malaysia.

Glick Schiller, N. (2003). The centrality of ethnography in the study of transnational migration: Seeing the wetlands instead of the swamp. In N. Foner (ed.), *American Arrivals: Anthropology Engages the New Immigration* (pp. 99–128). Santa Fe, NM: School of American Research Press.

Haraway, D. (1991). *Simians, Cyborgs, and Women: The Reinvention of Nature*. New York: Routledge.

Madden, R. (2010). *Being Ethnographic: A Guide to the Theory and Practice of Ethnography*. London: Sage.

Mahler, S. J. and Pessar, P. R. (2006). Gender matters: Ethnographers bring gender from the periphery toward the core of migration studies. *International Migration Review*, 40(1), 27–63.
Melaka state government official portal (n.d.). Tourism promotion division. http://www.melaka.gov.my/en/kerajaan/sektor-pembangunan/bahagian-promosi-pelancongan#sthash.u3zn5GQ9.dpuf.
Naerssen, A. van (1980). Location factors and linkages at the industrial estates of Malacca town. *Institute of Southeast Asian Studies Singapore, Research Notes and Discussions Paper*, vol. 16.
Narifumi, T. (1998). Touristic impressions of social transformations in Melaka. Economic Planning Unit research paper. Melaka: Prime Minister Department.
Patel, R. (2010). *Working the Night Shift: Women in India's Call Center Industry*. Stanford, CA: Stanford University Press.
Pei-chia, L. (2006). *Global Cinderellas: Migrant Domestics and Newly Rich Employers in Taiwan*. Durham, NC: Duke University Press.
Rudnyckyj, D. (2004). Technologies of servitude: Governmentality and Indonesian transnational labor migration. *Anthropological Quarterly*, 77(3), 407–434.
Sandhu, K. S. and Wheatley, P. (eds.) (1983). *Melaka: The Transformation of a Malay Capital, c.1400–1980*. Oxford: Oxford University Press.
Zaman, S. (2008). Native among the natives: Physician anthropologist doing hospital ethnography at home. *Journal of Contemporary Ethnography*, 37(2), 135–154.

5. "How can you be so naïve?" Negotiating insider status among co-ethnic migrants in global ethnographic fieldwork

Hasan Mahmud

LITERATURE ON QUALITATIVE FIELDWORK

Researcher's Position in the Field

Merton (1972) was first to identify an epistemic claim in research by a particular group to the 'monopolistic' – or at least, a 'privileged' – access to particular kind of knowledge. He saw the development of this doctrine by Black intellectuals who tried to establish their monopolistic access to knowledge about Blacks (e.g. Black history, Black family, Black psychology, and the like) in America. From generalization of this claim it followed that Blacks understood Blacks better, which was extended to an indefinite number of other marginal groups and collectivities (e.g. women, ethnic minorities, immigrants, gays, and lesbians, etc.). Thus, Merton recognized the emergence of a new credentialism of ascribed status whereby an insider gets access to real knowledge by his/her socialization into the group under study. In contrast, the outsider is structurally barred from comprehending alien groups, statuses, cultures and societies due to the lack of such socialization. The claim further assumes that even if the outsider is adequately trained and manages to get access, his/her interest will be characteristically different from that of the insiders. Merton saw ethnocentrism as an inevitable outcome of this doctrine. He criticized it for being "deceptively simple" and "sociologically fallacious" (1972, p. 24). For individuals essentially hold multiple statuses instead of just one. For instance, one can be a Black, a female, an immigrant, etc. simultaneously, as these identities are not mutually exclusive. Therefore, determining membership only by a single status eventually excludes some insiders from others, for instance, Black women from Black men, or Black immigrants from Black Americans, etc.

Merton also recognized an 'outsider doctrine' in social sciences emanating from the Baconian conception of science, which held that one could access true knowledge only by stepping outside of one's group affiliation. Therefore, he insisted that both the insider and outsider doctrines have their "distinctive assets and liabilities" (1972, p. 33). To utilize the assets, while overcoming the liabilities, Merton proposed to abandon the quest for the researcher's group affiliation. He wrote: "We no longer ask whether it is the insider or the outsider who has monopolistic or privileged access to social truth; instead, we begin to consider their distinctive and interactive roles in the process of truth-seeking" (1972, p. 36). Merton argued that one would need to go beyond a mere acquaintance and to acquire "an empirically confirmable comprehension" of the conditions and processes in society (1972, p. 41). He also stressed the importance of theory and methods in transcending one's status as an insider or outsider. However, Merton warned about the risk of sociological euphemism – the tendency in the use of analytical concepts (e.g. social stratification, social exchange, reward system, dysfunction, symbolic interaction, etc.) of ignoring "the intense feelings of pain and suffering that are the experience of some people caught up in the social patterns under examination" (1972, p. 38).

Merton's criticism of the insider/outsider dichotomy as a structural problem and his solution to overcome it by engaging in an intellectual trade-off between the insider and outsider researchers immediately gained acceptance among scholars. Thus, Willie (1973, p. 1270) wrote: "a proper understanding of insiders and outsiders must rely upon studies of outsiders by insider investigators and studies of insiders by outsider investigators along with studies of each group by its member". However, Merton did not go beyond biological determinism and overlooked the possibility of changes in the researcher's identification through interactions with their subjects, such as an insider regarded as an outsider for particular biographic distinctions, or an outsider given temporary membership through specific strategic interactions. For instance, Osili (2007) described how he was accepted as an insider among a group of Nigerian migrants in Chicago he did not know before. In contrast, he found himself as an outsider in his community in Nigeria, where he was born and raised. Merton's emphasis only on the perspective of the researchers and ignoring the interactional dimension of the relationship between researchers and their subjects have eventually limited the scope of his argument (Griffith, 1998). To fully comprehend the interactionality between the researcher and the people under study, we need an adequate understanding of the conception of the ethnographic field and the researcher's positionality in the continuously unfolding global field.

Ethnographic Field

The notions of insider and outsider imply a confined place/space against which the researcher's position is considered. For Merton, this boundary consists of the researcher's biographic features like race, ethnicity, sexual orientation, etc. However, classical anthropologists viewed this as a spatially demarcated autonomous place and container of local culture (Coleman and Collins, 2006). This conception of the ethnographic field as spatial encapsulation and bounding of culture was popularized by Malinowski (1922) and his followers with two central analytical practices: first, the assumption of internal consistency and the external difference that permit comparison between the part and the whole; and secondly, constituting the problem of context by providing anthropology an epistemological means to uphold its scientific status (Coleman and Collins, 2006). This way of configuring the field site has consequences for how participant-observers position themselves in their fields. For instance, Burrell (2009) observes that the ethnographer – by entering the field site – works to transition himself or herself from an outsider to insider, becoming accepted as a quasi-member of the society under study on an equal footing to others of similar social standing. The ethnographer's ability to observe and interpret the experience as an insider affects the ethnographic knowledge thus produced. At the same time, she or he needs to avoid a complete conversion to maintain the ability to analyse social processes as an external observer.

Several anthropologists, however, raised a question about the traditional conception of the field site as a confined space containing a whole culture (Gupta and Ferguson, 1997; Hannerz, 2003; Marcus, 1998; Marcus and Fisher, 1986). By referring to the increasing scale and complexity of culture in the era of globalization, Marcus and Fisher (1986) called attention to the problem of "how to represent the embedding of richly described local cultural worlds in larger impersonal systems of political economy" (1986, p. 77). They argued that the field as a small bounded space containing a culture of a village is increasingly less accurate. Marcus (1995) proposes his notion of 'an ethnography in/of the world system' through 'follow the person', 'follow the object', and 'follow the metaphor', among other configurations – all lending an overarching cohesion to 'multi-sited' ethnographies. Similarly, Gupta and Ferguson (1997) outlined methodological and epistemological strategies that foregrounded questions of location, intervention, and the construction of situated knowledge. They emphasized that ethnographers need to look at the field as a mode of study that cares about and pays attention to the interlocking of multiple socio-political sites and locations.

Scholars in other disciplines also began to reconceptualize the ethnographic field as emergent from and localized expression of a distinct institutional apparatus. That is, "the professional universe of the ethnographer, constituted by her social origins, affiliations, dispositions, gender, and above all her position within a microcosm of fellow anthropologists" (Bourdieu, 2003, p. 283). This implies that an ethnographer's field is all-encompassing, so much so that she or he never leaves the field. The comparison between 'home' and 'the field' made by Gupta and Ferguson (1997) also captures this: they defined home as a relational position in which the researcher feels 'at home' while the field is where the researcher does not find the comfort/ease of being at home. In this sense, a researcher may find her- or himself out of the field even amid fieldwork (e.g. when she or he returns to the private room and sits by the table writing field notes), or maintaining a close connection to events in the field from a long distance (e.g. ethnographic fieldworks in cyberspace). Thus, Fitzgerald's assertion seems more reasonable that "the field of ethnographic inquiry is not simply a geographic place waiting to be entered, but rather a conceptual space whose boundaries are constantly negotiated and constructed by the ethnographer and members" (Fitzgerald, 2006, p. 3).

The sociological conception of the 'field' as a conceptual space demarcated by permeable and malleable boundaries constructed through social interaction has gained acceptance among recent ethnographers (Burrell, 2009; Duneier, 1999; Ergun and Erdemir, 2010; Grahame and Grahame, 2009; Gregory and Ruby, 2011; Hamdan, 2009). By introducing the metaphor of performance, Coleman and Collins (2006, p. 12) define the field as "constructed through a play of social relationships established between the ethnographers and informants that may extend across physical sites, comprehending embodied as well as visual and verbal interactions". Therefore, the field may be viewed as embedded in an ongoing process of 'becoming' through social interactions, rather than as something fixed in time and space. Such a conception of the field requires researchers to have the ability to move back and forth between insider and outsider roles.

The Researcher in Ethnographic Field

The conventional ethnographic perspective regards the researcher as essentially an outsider who must get access and become an insider (Becker, 2001; Malinowski, 1922). While the distance embodied in the researcher's outsiderness contributes to maintaining objectivity, her/his access to the insider perspective enhances the accuracy of the data. These two criteria – objectivity and accuracy – thus uphold the status of ethnography as a scientific endeavour. Nevertheless, these two are often found mutually contradictory: greater access to the insider's perspective allows for acquiring rich and detailed data, but at the cost of higher risk of bias, whereas distance allows for maintaining objectivity, but may impede attaining the ethnographic depth.

Ethnographic studies since Malinowski emphasize going to the field among natives, who are unfamiliar to the researcher. These also highlight the need to develop close ties with a few individuals among the natives. We find this in *Street Corner Society* (1955), where Whyte actively constructed friendship with Doc, or in *Sidewalk* (1999), where Duneier sought collaboration with Hakim. Again, like Malinowski, both Whyte and Duneier left their respective social settings and stepped into fields – Whyte in an urban slum in Boston and Duneier on the sidewalk in Downtown Manhattan – where they both were strangers and which were mostly unknown and misunderstood in the mainstream society. However, unlike Malinowski, who observed the natives without deeply participating (Emerson, 2001, p. 7), both Whyte and Duneier participated for several years in the daily lives of their subjects in their actual social settings. One common aspect that underlies most of the classic ethnographic studies is the researcher's ability to become an insider through empathetic interactions.

Ethnographers see definite advantages in insiderness as it allows researchers to discover a new perspective, a hidden meaning, or a unique understanding (Labaree, 2002). The possession of a common set of interests, concerns, and social values (e.g. shared experiences) is seen as offering insiders special lenses to understand the social reality of the community, which are generally unavailable to the outsiders. Some recent ethnographic studies identify problems of getting access encountered by insiders (Anderson, 2003; Lee, 2007; Osili, 2007). Hence, they modify the claim of unproblematic access. The underlying assumption remains the same: insiderness facilitates greater access at the beginning of one's research, to particular groups within the community, and critical information (Pustulka et al., 2019; Voloder and Kirpitchenko, 2016). The idea is that insiderness significantly reduces the need for preliminary negotiation that an outsider must conduct to gain access to the community and to work with key informants, as Geertz elaborated in his study on the Balinese cockfight.

Insiderness is also seen as allowing for a better understanding of how information is gathered, synthesized, stored and disseminated within the community, and may potentially contribute clues as to why information is possessed or distributed by some stakeholders but withheld from others (Ergun and Erdemir, 2010; Waters, 1999). Access to information can be facilitated by the fact that insiders, as unobtrusive observers, are more capable of taking advantage of 'privileged eavesdropping' (Becker, 2001). Researchers attach unique value to insiderness as it provides a vantage point facilitating understanding of emotive dimensions of behaviour, which is often unavailable for outsiders to interpret. They also believe that insiderness provides an avenue for interpreting culture-specific cues in interviews and other forms of communication that are facilitated by a shared knowledge of normative rules, values and belief systems, such as non-verbal cues and the use of unique terminology (Ergun and Erdemir, 2010; Gregory and Ruby, 2011; Voloder and Kirpitchenko, 2014; Zinn, 2001). Finally, researchers emphasize the ability to utilize the insider status in discovering greater clarity of purpose and understanding of one's work through a deeper understanding and knowledge of the experiences of those being researched (Emerson and Pollner, 2001; Zinn, 2001).

Whether coming from the outside or from within the group under study, ethnographers' access to the insider's perspective allows them to learn and describe what Merton called "the intense feelings of pain and suffering that are the experience of some people caught up in the social patterns under examination" and what gets mired under "sociological euphemisms" (Merton, 1972, p. 33). Duneier (2006) illustrates this by revisiting a well-known study on heat waves in Chicago. Duneier shows how Klinenberg (2002) – due to his reliance on premeditated theory and official data and having "no data on individuals who passed away" – failed to capture the true social conditions affecting death (Duneier, 2006, p. 680). As opposed to Klinenberg's conclusion about death caused by an individual's old age and social isolation, Duneier's ethnographic fieldwork reveals, even after a decade of the incidence, that the victims were not necessarily old and lone individuals, but were suffering from extreme poverty, unemployment, and alcoholism. Thus, he argues that ethnography's ability to find "actual people whose lives correspond to the theories that sociologists employ to explain the social world" (2006, p. 687) makes ethnography a distinct method of social investigation.

Negotiating Insider Status in the Field in Migration Research

Despite Merton's widely accepted criticism, the belief that insiders have easy access to the field remains alive, especially among migration scholars. For instance, Rumbaut (1999) observes that half of the immigration scholars in the United States are themselves, immigrants. However, the migration scholars who share distinct biographical features with the groups they studied reveal this belief as unfounded in practice, at least partially. For instance, Kushow selected co-ethnic Somali migrants with an expectation – in his words – "that my insider status would give me fairly instant access to informants and interview subjects, that my insider knowledge would allow me to see the Somali situation more clearly, and that my local knowledge would transfer to superior interview questions" (2003, p. 594). However, once in the field, Kushow discovered himself as a kind of 'suspicious outsider', especially – to his surprise – regarding Somali political and cultural matters, which he thought of himself as quite knowledgeable about. Besides, as opposed to the idea that knowledge about the home community facilitates easy access to immigrant groups (Fitzgerald, 2006, p. 5), Kushow found that his insider knowledge about clan dynamics in Somalia hampered his access to Somali migrants (2003, p. 595). Furthermore, his gender as a male cut himself off from the female Somali immigrants due to the traditional gendered social organization of the group.

These challenges are not typical only of ethnography among im/migrants, but also in all ethnographies. For instance, Elijah Anderson reflects on his experiences in his study of Jelly's bar and liquor store in Chicago's south side ghetto (Anderson, 2003). As an educated black man who had no apparent reason for hanging out in a lower class setting, Anderson entered the field as a problematic newcomer. He was not accepted as an insider from the beginning. He had to move through a series of insider and outsider identities – from occasional customer to regular, from acquaintance to friend and 'cousin', from problematic newcomer to undisguised researcher, etc. Other researchers studying their groups also find their identity as a researcher pushing them towards outsiderness (Gregory and Ruby, 2011; Osili, 2007).

In contrast, the researcher's outsider status may facilitate greater access. As Waters – a white professor studying the West Indian immigrant second generation at school – wrote: "Being an outsider who was visiting from Massachusetts rendered me more interesting and less threatening to the students" (1999, p. 357). Therefore, having some common biographic features with those one studies does not guarantee access to the field as an insider, nor does its absence hinder access altogether. One must be able to situate oneself strategically and observe individuals in their respective social world (Goffman, 2001).

As discussed above, ethnographers are seen as outsiders regardless of their background characteristics and also as entering a field generally unfamiliar to them (Emerson, 2001). While entering the field, their shared biographical features (e.g. ethnicity, citizenship, gender, etc.) may be strategically exploited to facilitate access. Thus, Zinn utilized her own identity as a Latina to cultivate close relationships with Latina mothers through the shared experience of sewing and got access to their private family settings. Similarly, Stevanovic-Fenn (2012) utilized her experience of living in Bangladesh and knowledge of Bengali to make meaningful conversation resulting in 'gratifying' interactions with Bangladeshi immigrants in New York and welcoming entry into the field.

Although getting closer to informants is necessarily viewed as a positive attribute in acquiring the insider's (emic) perspective (Becker, 2001), getting too close is viewed as tarnishing the outsider's (etic) perspective necessary for objective/scientific analysis of data. The role of a researcher stands in sharp contrast with that of an insider, as Kondo (2001) explains. She faced this challenge of balancing her identity as a researcher and as a member of those she studied. Therefore, it is essential to maintain a balance between getting close and not too close by keeping a distance necessary for the scientist's gaze.

One of the common ways for ethnographers to approach entry to the field is to place oneself in the daily routine of the people one studies (Anderson, 2003; Duneier, 1999; Goffman, 2001). The entry points are very consequential as these inevitably affect ethnographers' fieldwork by facilitating their access to specific individuals and events while limiting access to others (Duneier, 2011, p. 3). Therefore, ethnographers' initial contacts act as both resources and constraints in the field. Ergun and Erdemir (2010) provide a fascinating account of negotiating the insider position. As Ergun was accepted by the locals as 'one of them' because of her shared ethnic origin, she could declare that she was not there to evaluate any political party without hurting her informants in both the government and the opposition. By contrast, Erdemir had to express that he shared political affiliation with that of the Alevis because of his informants' perception of him as an outsider. Thus, he would express social democratic and republican values of the left-wing politics, disapproval of Sunni repression on the Alevis, etc. Still, Erdemir maintained his neutrality at a different level – he took side with the Alevis regarding their opposition to the nationalist Sunni authority. However, Erdemir avoided taking any side (i.e., expressing an opinion in a convoluted and unintelligible manner) regarding intra-Alevi factionalism prevalent during his fieldwork. This strategy allowed Erdemir to present himself to the Alevis as an ally, while also express his neutrality in case of their internal factional politics.

Unlike outsider researchers who may use their naïveté about local politics as a mask to avoid expressing political affiliation, researchers with an insider or partial insider status find this strategy useless. The insider researcher is expected to share the informants' views about the righteousness, justness, or legitimacy of the causes and/or the wickedness or illegitimacy of the informants' opponents. The failure to share the informant's political view is likely to damage the trust and credibility of the researcher. Therefore, both Ergun and Erdemir had to position them with their informants' political views. Their different initial acceptance affected their strategies: Ergun was seen as right-wing and/or nationalist (since all Turk nationalists have right-wing political views) and also anti-leftist (due to her US education). So, her informants assumed her to have similar political opinions and rarely questioned it. Since her informants' assumed perception of her was helping her maintain rapport, she did not divulge her real unorthodox political views. However, Erdemir's plain unorthodox political view (e.g. secular and social-democratic political orientation) was the bridge between him and his informants. Therefore, he would willingly express his alignment with the Alevis' anti-nationalist, anti-Sunni political stance and would also demonstrate it by drinking alcohol with them, or singing leftist songs, or answering trivia questions about communism.

Ethical Considerations in Ethnographic Fieldwork

Since negotiating insiderness in fieldwork is always purposeful, this mostly involves ethical dilemmas. Of these, two are most common: one is to represent the insiders' perspective in which researchers are expected to refrain from imposing their perspective on the people they study (Emerson, 2001; Fine, 1994). The other dilemma is to ensure that researchers do not incur any harm to people they study, which requires them to maintain an 'unobtrusive' presence in the field (Fine, 2003). To address the first challenge, ethnographers adopt an analytic description with underlying assumptions that "an ethnographic description can never be exact" and also that such "descriptions of the same social scene will vary" (Emerson, 2001, pp. 28–29). Therefore, they identify and convey the meanings their subjects attach to actions in the empirical world.

A popular style of analytic description is 'thick description', which provides "our constructions of other people's constructions of what they and their compatriots are up to" (Geertz, 2001, pp. 59–60). This necessarily involves an interpretive understanding and representing the subtleties and complexities of local meaning. However, there is no technique to grasp all the nuances of meaning, which generates biased results to varying degrees. What ethnographers do is to try to eliminate as much bias as possible. This may be approached by emphasizing what people do rather than what they say (Goffman, 2001), triangulating data from multiple sources (Duneier, 1999), collaborating with key informants in data analysis and writing (Whyte, 1955), recruiting research assistants from the natives (Gregory and Ruby, 2011; Waters, 1999) and so forth. By introducing the concept of 'inconvenience sampling', Duneier (2011) adds another innovative technique to reduce bias by identifying, before leaving the field, whether the findings have implications for people unstudied and limiting knowledge claims by excluding them, or stay more in the field to include their perspective.

In making ethnographic representation of people, ethnographers not only face the challenge of textualizing what they learn in the field but also encounter an expectation of a certain type of representation from the groups they study, especially if the group identifies the researcher as one of them. Thus, one of Kushow's informants suggested that he "should write about the good things, about how the Somali community in Canada is very clean and not involved in criminal activities like selling drugs, about our beautiful culture, about how Somalia before the war was a great country, and finally about the problems that we have with Canadian immigration" (2003, p. 595). Similarly, Ergun and Erdemir (2010) were repeatedly asked to take sides with their informants in justifying their own political views. What all these ethnographers did was tactically refuse to adhere to those requests, and thus maintained the scientific standard of their data and analysis.

REFLECTIONS FROM THE FIELD

Fields of Research

In my dissertation I explored why migrants send remittances, and conducted ethnographic fieldwork among Bangladeshi migrants in Tokyo and Los Angeles (LA). I selected these fields based on my theoretical interest in comparing migrants from a single origin country in different destination countries characterized by temporary migration (in Japan) and permanent settlement (in the USA). The differences in the destination state's immigration policy affected migrant selectivity, their relationships to the family and community as well as the state, all of which shaped their life experiences including sending remittances.

Most Bangladeshis entered Japan as tourists and overstayed their visas or entered under the pretext of college students and would engage in income-earning activities illegally. By contrast, nearly all Bangladeshis entered the USA as legal permanent residents eligible to work full time, or with proper intent to study, who found employment after graduating from universities. Finally, Bangladeshis migrated to Japan alone, regardless of their marital status. They would return to Bangladesh to raise family, whereas their counterparts in LA would bring their families to the USA and settle permanently. Consequently, the Bangladeshi community began with a few hundred immigrants in LA in the late 1980s and grew to over 50,000 immigrants by 2010. By contrast, the number of Bangladeshis in Japan continued to dwindle from over 50,000 in the early 1990s to less than 10,000 by 2013. In addition to the nature of the contexts and migration processes, my shared social and cultural background with potential informants influenced my decision to select these two field sites for the study.

Entry to the Field

I adopted a global ethnographic approach (Burawoy et al., 2000) involving two field sites in Tokyo and LA. My fieldwork in Tokyo involved 14 months of ethnographic fieldwork, including three months in the summer of 2012 and eleven months from October 2013 to July 2014. I also conducted 42 in-depth case interviews. At the beginning of my fieldwork, I conducted a questionnaire survey on a convenient sample of 120 migrants.

My first challenge was to locate the negligible number of Bangladeshi migrants in a mega-city of over 13 million people. By looking into immigrant niches in Tokyo, I found a good number of Bangladeshi-owned ethnic shops in Shin-Okubo (Korea Town), Ikebukuro, Akihabara, Akabane, and a few other areas with notable migrant populations. I also found these migrants in several mosques in Tokyo city and neighbouring areas. Besides frequently visiting these places, I utilized the networks of friends and acquaintances I made during my previous stay in Tokyo to find potential informants. I found it challenging to recruit informants. However, once someone agreed to be interviewed, he or she would often suggest further interviewees. Thus, I also used the snowball method to recruit my interviewees.

My fieldwork in LA involved approximately two years of ethnographic fieldwork between the summer of 2011 and mid-2013, 45 in-depth case interviews, and a purposive survey including 200 questions. My fieldwork centred in the Bangladeshi neighbourhood, known as 'Little Bangladesh' near the Down Town. I identified research participants at various locations in the community, including four ethnic stores and two mosques. Besides, I contacted many at community events and celebrations like the Bangladesh Day Parade, the Bangla New Year celebration, etc. Some of my friends and community leaders also introduced me to people. In addition to interviewing, I participated in various community events to build rapport as well as to observe these immigrants' interactions, including remittance practices. I would spend several hours every weekend at the ethnic stores, particularly the one with a money-transferring service. The owner of the agency agreed to allow me to sit there and would deliberately ask people about the reasons for their remittance so that I might learn from their conversation. I also came across anecdotal information about these immigrants' remittances in informal gatherings at community events and the ethnic stores.

Negotiating Insider Status in the Field

I expected easy entry to the field as a Bangladeshi student. I already had been living near Little Bangladesh's neighbourhood in LA before I started my dissertation research. I made a few friends among Bangladeshi immigrants with whom I would start impromptu conversations, take sides in political debates and discussions, etc. Some of them also invited me to dinner parties. Thus, I thought I had acquired a considerable degree of insider status in the community. However, as soon as I started asking questions regarding their remittances, I realized that I was no longer an insider. Most would squarely refuse to talk as soon as requested to participate in my study, which surprised me, for Stevanovic-Fenn (2012) reported Bangladeshi immigrants as very enthusiastic in talking about their remittances. I also noticed that those I came to know through my regular visits to the ethnic stores, mosques, or community events began to avoid me once I started asking people to participate in my study. Later in my fieldwork, one respondent told me that his roommate believed I was spying on behalf of the CIA about the immigrants' remittances. Distrust about my research among the immigrants was so pervasive that even those I befriended would ask me: "How can you be so naïve? As a Bangladeshi, you, of course, know why we send remittances home."

To overcome the initial barrier in rapport building and recruiting interviewees, I gave up my belief of being an insider in the community and assumed the position of an outsider. Then, I would apply most of the conventional strategies to seek entry to the field. My strategies included putting myself into the daily life of these immigrants: frequenting common gathering places during particular times of the days and weeks so that I could meet more people, participating in casual conversations with strangers, offering them information whenever they needed, showing interest in the topics of their choice, etc. These techniques helped create my image as a researcher within a few months, and I began to find some immigrants interested in my research. I noticed that these techniques were relatively more effective on strangers than on those I already knew. However, my friends among the immigrants would agree to participate in my research without my prodding.

The uneasy feeling that a non-Bengali, white, female researcher (e.g. Stevanovic-Fenn) was warmly received by Bangladeshi immigrants, whereas I – a native Bangladeshi – had to approach them as an outsider never left me during my fieldwork. Because of sharing the same origin, I was welcome in most ethnic stores, gatherings, community events, and even residences of many Bangladeshi immigrants. However, I would feel a certain degree of outsiderness once I started my research. My first field notes were full of entries about my disappointments. Knowing about my frustration, a friend among the immigrants explained to me how sensitive the issue of money and family relations was in our culture. In Bangladeshi culture, it is a social norm that the children, especially the grown-up sons, should take care of the parents and dependent siblings (Ballard, 1982). Thus, sending money home became an informal mechanism to judge one as good or bad in the community – somebody who regularly sent money to home would be regarded as a good son. In contrast, the one who would not remit would be regarded as bad (Stevanovic-Fenn also found this in her study). I realized that my Bangladeshi identity was the main reason for many of the potential respondents to refuse cooperation. Perhaps, they feared being judged based on their remittance practices. Besides, they might have thought that I would be able to detect misinformation and embellishment they might use to give me a better perspective of them about how caring they were to their families. However, Stevanovic-Fenn was a stranger with perceivably limited cultural knowledge about Bangladeshis so that she did not pose the kind of threat I did as a native Bangladeshi. Perhaps her informants found it relatively easy to do face-saving, which would be difficult with me. This was supported by the fact that assuming an outsider identity helped me to recruit strangers for interviews far more than the immigrants

I already knew. This was perhaps because the strangers would not anticipate meeting me further, which would take away their hesitation to talk to me about their remittances. But my acquaintances knew they were likely to meet me again, which may have stopped them from opening up to me.

My entry to the field in Tokyo was relatively easy and quick. This was partly because I had already conducted interviews and ethnographic fieldwork among Bangladeshis. They entered Japan as Japanese language students (popularly known as *nihon-gakusei*, or language students) in Tokyo for my MA thesis. The owners of three ethnic shops, a Bangladeshi instructor of a driving school, a Bangladeshi travel agent, and a few community leaders helped me to contact potential interviewees. However, the absence of a co-ethnic immigrant neighbourhood and the widely dispersed location of Bangladeshi migrants was a challenge for me at the beginning. I would have to travel extensively across Tokyo city, often to be disappointed as my targeted informant was unavailable. Besides, these migrants worked excessively long hours, making them less available for interviews (Mahmud, 2014). However, one of the biggest challenges for me was that several of my informants expected information about migrating to the USA and Canada and assistance in processing paperwork. I did not know much about immigration processes in the USA and Canada at that time. Nevertheless, they would think I did not want to help them, and therefore I made an excuse. This resulted in my losing a few key informants in my previous study who refused to take part in my study this time. To overcome this, I learned the necessary information about the immigration processes in the UK, Canada, and Australia and would provide information to those who asked for it. Given their extremely time-constrained daily schedule, I would maintain an open schedule for myself so that I could meet my informants at their convenience and availability. I would sometimes meet someone as early as 4 a.m. and as late as 11 p.m. I would often accompany them during their train rides between work and residence. I would also conduct multiple short interviews with a particular informant instead of a longer one. Finally, I volunteered to arrange a few community events and thereby was able to develop a rapport with community leaders and activists, who offered valuable information and support in my fieldwork. Thus, I actively participated in community activities like an outsider and gradually transitioned to become an insider partially by gaining acceptance among community members.

REFERENCES

Anderson, E. (2003). Jelly's place: An ethnographic memoir. *Symbolic Interaction*, 26, 217–237.

Ballard, R. (1982). South Asian families. In R. N. Rapoport, M. Fogarty, and R. Rapoport (eds.), *Families in Britain* (pp. 179–204). London: Routledge & Kegan Paul.

Becker, H. S. (2001). The epistemology of qualitative research. In R. M. Emerson (ed.), *Contemporary Field Research* (2nd edn., pp. 317–330). Prospect Heights, IL: Waveland Press.

Bourdieu, P. (2003). Participant objectivation. *Journal of the Royal Anthropological Association*, 9(2), 281–294.

Burawoy, M., Blum, J. A., George, S., Gille, Z., and Thayer, M. (2000). *Global Ethnography: Forces, Connections, and Imaginations in a Postmodern World.* Berkeley: University of California Press.

Burrell, J. (2009). The field site as a network: A strategy for locating ethnographic research. *Field Methods*, 21(2), 181–199.

Coleman, S. and Collins, P. (eds.) (2006). *Locating the Field: Space, Place and Context in Anthropology.* New York and Oxford: Berg.

Duneier, M. (1999). *Sidewalk.* New York: Farrar, Straus & Giroux.

Duneier, M. (2006). Ethnography, the ecological fallacy and the 1995 Chicago heat wave. *American Sociological Review*, 71, 679–688.

Duneier, M. (2011). How not to lie with ethnography. *Sociological Methodology*, 41(1), 1–11.

Emerson, R. M. (2001). *Contemporary Field Research: Perspectives and Formulations* (2nd edn.). Prospect Heights, IL: Waveland Press.

Emerson, R. M. and Pollner, P. (2001). Constructing participant/observation relations. In R. M. Emerson (ed.), *Contemporary Field Research: Perspectives and Formulations* (2nd edn., pp. 239–259). Prospect Heights, IL: Waveland Press.

Ergun, A. and Erdemir, A. (2010). Negotiating insider and outsider identities in the field: “Insider” in a foreign land; “outsider” in one’s own land. *Field Methods*, 22(1), 16–38.

Fine, G. A. (2003). Towards a peopled ethnography: Developing theory from group life. *Ethnography*, 4(1), 41–60.

Fine, M. (1994). Working the hyphens: Reinventing self and other in qualitative research. In N. K. Denzin and Y. S. Lincoln (eds.), *Handbook of Qualitative Research* (pp. 70–82). Thousand Oaks, CA: Sage.

Fitzgerald, D. (2006). Towards a theoretical ethnography of migration. *Qualitative Sociology*, 29(1), 1–24.

Geertz, C. (2001). Thick description: Towards an interpretive theory of culture. In R. M. Emerson (ed.), *Contemporary Field Research: Perspectives and Formulations* (2nd edn., pp. 55–75). Prospect Heights, IL: Waveland Press.

Goffman, E. (2001). On fieldwork. In R. M. Emerson (ed.), *Contemporary Field Research: Perspectives and Formulations* (2nd edn., pp. 114–158). Prospect Heights, IL: Waveland Press.

Grahame, P. R. and Grahame, K. M. (2009). Points of departure: Insiders, outsiders, and social relations in Caribbean field research. *Human Studies*, 32, 291–312.

Gregory, E. and Ruby, M. (2011). The ‘insider/outsider’ dilemma of ethnography: Working with young children and their families in cross-cultural contexts. *Journal of Early Childhood Research*, 9(2), 162–174.

Griffith, A. I. (1998). Insider/outsider: Epistemological privilege and mothering work. *Human Studies*, 21, 361–376.

Gupta, A. and Ferguson, J. (eds.) (1997). *Anthropological Locations: Boundaries and Grounds for a Field Science*. Berkeley & Los Angeles: University of California Press.

Hamdan, A. K. (2009). Reflexivity of discomfort in insider-outsider educational research. *McGill Journal of Education*, 44(3), 377–404.

Hannerz, U. (2003). Being there … and there … and there! Reflections on multi-site ethnography. *Ethnography*, 4(2), 201–216.

Klinenberg, E. (2002). *Heat Wave: A Social Autopsy of Disaster in Chicago*. Chicago, IL: University of Chicago Press.

Kondo, D. K. (2001). How the problem of "crafting selves" emerged. In R. M. Emerson (ed.), *Contemporary Field Research: Perspectives and Formulations* (2nd edn., pp. 188–202). Prospect Heights, IL: Waveland Press.

Kushow, A. M. (2003). Beyond indigenous authenticity: Reflections on the insider/outsider debate in immigration research. *Symbolic Interaction*, 26(4), 591–599.

Labaree, R. V. (2002). The risk of 'going observationalist': Negotiating the hidden dilemmas of being an insider participant observer. *Qualitative Research*, 2(1), 97–122.

Lee, C. K. (2007). *Against the Law: Labor Protests in China's Rustbelt and Sunbelt*. Berkeley: University of California Press.

Mahmud, H. (2014). 'It's my money': Social class and the perception of remittances among Bangladeshi migrants in Japan. *Current Sociology*, 62(3), 412–430.

Malinowski, B. (1922). *Argonauts of the Western Pacific*. Prospect Heights, IL: Waveland Press.

Marcus, G. E. (1995). Ethnography in/of the world system: The emergence of multi-sited ethnography. *Annual Review of Anthropology*, 25, 95–117.

Marcus, G. E. (1998). *Ethnography through Thick and Thin*. Princeton, NJ: Princeton University Press.

Marcus, G. E. and Fisher, M. (1986). *Anthropology as Cultural Critique*. Chicago: University of Chicago Press.

Merton, R. K. (1972). Insiders and outsiders: A chapter in the sociology of knowledge. *American Journal of Sociology*, 78(1), 9–47.

Osili, U. O. (2007). Understanding migrants' remittances: Evidence from the U.S.-Nigeria Migration Survey. https://www.imi.ox.ac.uk/events/amw-2008/papers/osili.pdf.

Pustulka, P., Bell, J., and Trąbka, A. (2019). Questionable insiders: Changing positionalities of interviewers throughout stages of migration research. *Field Methods*, 31(3), 241–259.

Rumbaut, R. (1999). Immigration research in the United States: Social origins and future orientations. *American Behavioral Scientist*, 42(9), 1285–1301.

Stevanovic-Fenn, N. (2012). Remittances and the moral economies of Bangladeshi New York immigrants in light of the economic crisis. Doctoral dissertation, Columbia University.

Voloder, L. and Kirpitchenko, L. (eds.) (2014). *Insider Research on Migration and Mobility: International Perspectives on Researcher Positioning*. Farnham: Ashgate.

Waters, M. C. (1999). *Black Identities: West Indian Immigrant Dreams and American Reality*. Cambridge, MA and London: Harvard University Press.

Whyte, W. F. (1955). *Street Corner Society: The Social Structure of an Italian Slum* (2nd edn.). Chicago, IL: University of Chicago Press.

Willie, C. V. (1973). On Merton's insiders and outsiders. *American Journal of Sociology*, 78(5), 1269–1272.

Zinn, M. B. (2001). Insider field research in minority communities. In R. M. Emerson (ed.), *Contemporary Field Research: Perspectives and Formulations* (2nd edn., pp. 159–166). Prospect Heights, IL: Waveland Press.

6. Challenges and opportunities in conducting cross-country PhD study: experiences of data collection in India and China

Rajendra Baikady

RESEARCH CONTEXT

The present comparative study was conducted with the understanding that China and India are two countries in the world that share the most characteristics in common. Both are the most populous countries in the world and both are located in Asia. Both are proud of their individual long civilizations that go back some 5,000 years, but both suffered invasions and colonial rules. Both India and China won their independence in the late 1940s and advocated the principles of peaceful coexistence; the moral ideas of Chinese and Indians are similar. When considering social work education, in both countries social work has a long history and a strong background, and the problems faced by China and India in standardizing social work education are not very different as regards to curriculum issues, problems of standardization, and uniformity in the practice and education across each country. In the researcher's view, this comparative study of India and China will help to understand the development of social work education and the challenges of social work education in these two countries with different socio-political structures. There is a need for the social work discipline to study from others and to learn things which make a difference in other social work settings, and to understand the faculties of social work and the students, academicians and institutions that need to develop a good relationship and collaboration to develop the profession. In this regard, the present study examines the differences between India and China's political settings in relation to the development of social work education and its challenges.

India is a decentralized democratic country, where the rights and the duties of the citizens are guaranteed and safeguarded by the constitution. The concepts of social justice, equality and equal opportunity are meaningful in terms of the concept of freedom of expression and speech. As a democratic republic India guarantees freedom of speech and expression, and as a result, social justice and social advocacy are part of social work training and practice in India. In contrast, China is a socialist communist country, where economic and productive power is exercised by the central government, and the Communist Party of China controls every aspect of people's lives. Social work as a service profession is thus under government control. Given these conditions it is interesting to understand the teaching, learning and the practice of social work in China in comparison to the rest of the world. This researcher did not find any specific research study carried out earlier on this topic in relation to India and China. Two useful comparative studies that were available to the researcher were Sewpaul and Haruhiko's 'A comparison of social work education across South Africa and Japan in relation to the Global Standards for Social Work Education and Training' (2011) and Chien-Chung Huang and Edwards' *Comparative Study of Social Work Education in China and US* (in Chinese, in press). Meeuwisse and Swärd (2007) noted that comparative studies of social work are a neglected field, but demands for them are increasing. With this understanding the present study covers broad areas related to social work education in India and China. The study will analyse the differences and the similarities of social work education in India and China with respect to teaching, learning and practice. In addition to this the researcher analyses the status of social work education and its development in India and China from a political perspective. This study may help social work educators, practitioners, scholars, students, and associate members of professional organizations in India and China to gain insight into the present status of social work education and its development. Further the present study is an important effort to understand the international social work perspective. As noted by Healy (2001), during the early development of the profession of social work the primary tasks were to forge ties within the profession and learn from practitioners in other countries. Caragata and Sanchez (2002) observed that social work in both wealthy and poor countries faces similar social challenges as a result of globalization.

Nader Ahmadi (2003) argued that international social work can play a considerable role in the development and stabilization of democracy and promoting concepts such as social justice, human rights and equality. Through the opportunity to learn from other countries international social workers can more easily understand the social-political and national and international law relating to social service and human service practice. The comparative studies in social work education and practice are expected to bring insight about shared problems in different societies and could eventually lead to insight about, and even a demand for, shared efforts in solving common social problems. It is expected that by sharing and learning from each other's experiences international social work could contribute to setting new global human values and ethics. Further by conducting international studies in social work one can gain understanding of human problems in a wide variety of contexts and try to find solutions to specific countries' problems. Cross-national and cross-cultural learning experiences may help in defining problems and finding solutions in other contexts. In addition, cross-cultural learning experiences may also inspire and enrich national and local social work practices within local, national and international contexts. Finally, international comparative studies contribute to enhancing the profession's scholastic knowledge and its practice in an international context (Ahmadi, 2003).

At present in the globalized world, the role of universities and NGOs is rapidly increasing in social development and social welfare. As a result, many NGOs are engaged in carrying out international social work in developing countries in areas such as disaster management, poverty alleviation, educational development and employment generation. Civil society organizations and NGOs across the globe are already addressing the negative consequences of globalization, liberalization and privatization. At the global level a number of NGOs are engaged in providing social services in areas such as sex trafficking, drug abuse and crime, child and women's welfare, and social work with marginalized populations and disadvantaged groups. At the international level, organizations such as UNDP and UNICEF provide social work services to many people in need. Hessle (2001) notes that in the last five years, universities and schools of social work are acting as links between people and governments. Thus, universities, educational institutions and local actors, such as local governments, local social services agencies and NGOs are becoming increasingly interactive at local, national and international levels. Further in many developed countries social work researchers are working closely with the government and providing cooperation to the government machinery in solving social issues and problems. Even in developing countries government agencies consult both national and international schools of social work and researchers for help in forming and developing their country's social legislation and social welfare policies. In this respect there is a need to study these aspects of social work and government collaboration and how government is becoming a supporter to the social work profession and practice.

As noted by Johnson (1996), comparative studies within the international context are important as schools of social work across the world have started to internationalize their social work programme, curriculum and the learning environment in recent years. In this regard, schools of social work across the globe have started outreach to other countries through exchanging students, practitioners and faculty; offering special courses on international social work or integrating topics of international importance into course content; placing students in international field practice; undertaking international collaborative research; and doing volunteer work in international communities. Comparative international studies are expected to contribute to the development of both the contexts which are under study. There are many advantages of working across borders and international research and projects. The limitations of individual capacity to devise and implement solutions and the applicability of ideas are two major challenges of working across borders. However, emerging global social problems need a more international approach to be dealt with effectively. Issues such as HIV/AIDS, international crime, migration and environmental issues are everyone's concern because of their very nature of moving across borders. Thus, international social work practice and education are becoming more relevant as countries can no longer 'solve' their social problems in isolation.

The present study of India and China will focus on social work education and the similarities and differences in teaching and learning social work in two different social, economic and political contexts. The study aims to motivate and encourage social work educators and schools of social work in building cordial academic and research collaboration within the two national contexts to contribute in the development of social work. It is hoped that the present study will contribute to the development of social work in China in particular and India and the rest of the world in general. The study will bring an outsider perspective to Chinese social work and the challenges it faces, which is very important in the development of social work as rightly noted by Wu (1991); international cooperation will play a very important role in promoting social work education in China. However, there is a need for social work educators in China to fully recognize the importance of academic exchange and welcome opportunities to share ideas and experiences with academics and practitioners from outside China. Although both faculty training and research activities and international cooperation have made some progress in social work education and practice within China, there is still a need to welcome international comparative study between the different social, political and cultural contexts.

CHALLENGES IN DATA COLLECTION AND STRATEGIES ADOPTED TO OVERCOME THEM

In this part of the chapter I will discuss various challenges that I faced during the data collection process in both India and China. For the purpose of clarity and connectivity I will discuss the strategies that I adopted during my data collection process along with each challenge faced. This will help readers to get more detailed and concrete understanding of the topic under discussion.

Geographically Scattered Field for Data Collection

As the field for data collection was huge and geographically scattered in both India and China, conducting data collection and the selection of respondents and schools of social work was a challenge. Further the social work institutions in China have a different history than that of India. I chose the institutions based on purposive sampling. Hence I had the feeling that I may have missed out on a few key informants who should have been interviewed for the study. The names of these people were suggested by others who were interviewed. But, given the limitations of time and money, I could not visit distant places for isolated individual interviews.

Language

The difference in language was the greatest challenge in this study. While I decided to conduct the study in English, constant and rigorous attention was needed to ensure that all voices were heard and all data were understood. As the researcher was unfamiliar with the Chinese language I chose to interview social work educators and students who were able to communicate and discuss in English. As English is not very familiar to many of the students and educators I had the feeling that I may have missed some of the information during the interview as the respondents were unable to express it fluently. But because of the time and the financial constraints and the lack of opportunity to learn Chinese, this difficulty could not easily be overcome. Translators and the translation service were not used because of the financial constraints as well as the challenge related to the accuracy of the transcription by translators. All the interviews were conducted personally by the researcher. All were personal one-to-one interviews.

Availability of Respondents

The data collection in India and China took place across six months each. The researcher qualified for financial support from a foundation (INLAKS) and the Indian Council of Social Science Research (ICSSR) which helped the researcher to undertake a six-month study visit to Shandong University and during this visit the data required for the study were collected. However, despite the six months' duration and repeated visits to the study sites, I was unable to meet all educators in the institutions. Some of the social work educators in some schools of social work were unavailable for interview during my data collection visit. Due to financial and time constraints I could not visit those schools again for individual interviews. Further the six-month data collection visit to China was a very short period to understand the culture, economy and the political aspects of the country for a comparative study.

Another issue in reaching the respondents for interview was the nature of the research topic. Both in India and China many educators were reluctant to give an interview or to discuss the topic as the study was related to social work education and its comparison in two different political systems. Given that the title of the study was 'Comparing social work education in a parliamentary democracy and in a communist regime ...' many educators were hesitant to participate. This was evident from one senior educator's comment in India: 'I am afraid if I say something and you write something ... I don't know anything about Chinese social work'.

In order to deal with this issue the researcher approached all educators through their head of department and after obtaining permission from the head of the department in the respective study site, contacted each of the respondents through their email address. In the first contact the researcher introduced himself and also gave a clear explanation of the study and expected support by the educators. The objectives and the aim of the study were also explained in the initial email. As an agreement to the invitation, educators were asked to choose an appointment on a day and date convenient for them. At the first meeting the researcher explained the study aim and the objectives and also clarified doubts if there were any for the respondents. The researcher also said that if the respondent wished to see the interview transcription before data analysis then that would be made available to the participant.

Ethical Dilemmas

Ethical issues are commonly faced by cross-cultural researchers and project teams. Issues related to cultural lenses, use of instruments and potential biases of investigators are the common challenges faced by researchers in cross-cultural studies. A number of ethical and methodological challenges faced by researchers in cross-cultural research have been examined and discussed extensively (Beach and Eriksson, 2010; Kim, 2000; Liamputtong, 2008; Niblo and Jackson, 2004; Sobal, 1998; Sullivan and Cottone, 2010). In this study there were three major ethical issues that the researcher confronted during the data collection and fieldwork. The first was in relation to the confidentiality of the information relating to the research respondents. The names of the institutions of study were an important variable in the analysis of the data. Hence the name of the institutions was coded as A, B, C, D, or E. Only the researcher knew the codes and the corresponding institutions. The names of the institutions in the report and the results were coded in this way. The names of the research participants were not mentioned anywhere in the study report. The names of the respondents immediately after the interview were coded with serial numbers and once again the names corresponding to the serial numbers were known only to the researcher. As a researcher I endeavoured not to influence the respondents by my own ideological stance. In the process of data collection, I aimed to stay ideologically neutral and gave equal importance to all the respondents and the information. I tried to be very impartial and non-selective in conducting the interview. I took care that my personal bias did not influence the data collection process. Throughout my data collection I tried to remain non-judgemental and strived not to influence the interviewee or the interview process.

Cultural, Economic and Political Differences

As noted earlier, India and China share many characteristics. Both are extremely populous and both are located in Asia. However, there are numerous differences in terms of economic achievements, political system and cultural aspects. Social work as a service profession is influenced by both culture, economy and the political system of the country in which it operates. In this study it was important that the researcher understands the unique political and economic context of the two different study sites and its influence on the development and growth of social work. Marshall and Batten (2003) noted that one of the essential ethical considerations for cross-cultural research is understanding, valuing and respecting the culture of participants and the researchers. Further Marshall and Batten (2003, p. 139) note that despite multiple and complex cultural and contextual differences that exist among and between the researchers and participants there is a very little emphasis in ethical codes and research paradigms addressing these issues. Researchers have also found a gap between the ethical guidelines provided by the university and the situational realties faced by the researchers in their own cultural contexts (Honan et al., 2013).

The challenge for the researcher in this study was to understand the similarities and the differences between two distinct socio-economic, political and cultural contexts and find comparable parameters for the study. The central point of the study is social work education and its growth and the state's support in its development and growth. The researcher in this study examined extensive literature related to social, economic, political and cultural aspects of both India and China. Further, as the researcher is not Chinese, and was an outsider, in order to examine the research topic with deeper understanding and knowledge he attended extensive lectures provided by the host department in China and also undertook several informal discussions with peer learners and the educators within Chinese universities. Travel within the country and participation in class seminar discussions helped the researcher to understand various aspects related to Chinese society. Further clarifications and experience were gained through discussions with his co-supervisor at the Chinese university.

LESSONS LEARNT BY THE RESEARCHER

As the study was a comparison between two countries, understanding the culture and socio-political condition in both contexts and making a comparison of these aspects was a practical challenge for me. The data collection process helped me to understand the cultural differences and the socio-political aspects of China and thereby to make a comparison of these aspects with the Indian experience. While discussing evaluation, grading and their opportunities with students, I felt like I am a fellow learner with them.

At that point in time, controlling my emotions was a great challenge for me. Gradually I learnt how to focus on my task and started concentrating on my interviews. Hence some interviews took me more time than others. Another important lesson that I learnt was that, when data are collected using qualitative methods, the reflections of research participants should be analysed in the context of their background and involvement with the subject under consideration. Also, things such as body language, voice pitch, and facial expressions all constitute an important part of the data. In addition, patience on the part of the researcher to facilitate in-depth interactions by continuously rephrasing the questions for research participants is of utmost importance.

Finally, the data collection process taught me patience and perseverance. Undertaking a comparative study with limited resources and understanding a new culture and national context were a challenge for me at the beginning. Contacting the educators and the students in a completely diverse culture was a challenge but gradually I started adjusting to the situation and the data collection process in China taught me about adopting a professional approach, using time management and the importance of analysing the information carefully. Conducting interviews with the students and the educators who are not native speakers of English was challenging in the beginning but after some interviews I learnt how to make them understand the topic and the issues under consideration and how to involve them in the discussion. In general, the fieldwork in India and China helped me to improve myself personally and professionally.

REFERENCES

Ahmadi, N. (2003). Globalisation of consciousness and new challenges for international social work. *International Journal of Social Welfare*, 12, 14–23.

Beach, D. and Eriksson, A. (2010). The relationship between ethical positions and methodological approaches: A Scandinavian perspective. *Ethnography and Education*, 5, 129–142.

Caragata, L. and Sanchez, M. (2002). Globalization and global need: New imperatives for expanding international social work education in North America. *International Social Work*, 45(2), 217–238.

Chien-Chung Huang and Edwards, R. L. (in press). *Comparative Study of Social Work Education in China and US* [in Chinese]. Beijing: Social Sciences Academic Press (China).

Healy, L. M. (2001). *International Social Work: Professional Action in an Interdependent World*. New York: Oxford University Press.

Hessle, S. (2001). Vad är internationellt socialt arbete? [What is international social work?]. *Socionomen*, 2, 60–63.

Honan, E., Hamid, M. O., Alhamdan, B., Phommalangsy, P., and Lingard, B. (2013). Ethical issues in cross-cultural research. *International Journal of Research & Method in Education*, 36, 386–399.

Johnson, W. H. (1996). International activity in undergraduate social work education in the United States. *International Social Work*, 39, 189–199.

Kim, U. (2000). Indigenous, cultural, and cross-cultural psychology: A theoretical, conceptual, and epistemological analysis. *Asian Journal of Social Psychology*, 3, 265–287.

Laczniak, R. N. (2015). The *Journal of Advertising* and the development of advertising theory: Reflections and directions for future research. *Journal of Advertising*, 44(4), 429–433.

Liamputtong, P. (Ed.) (2008). *Doing cross-cultural research: Ethical and methodological perspectives* (Vol. 34). Springer Science & Business Media.

Marshall, A. and Batten, S. (2003). Ethical issues in cross-cultural research. In W.-M. Roth (ed.), *Connections '03, Conference Proceedings* (pp. 139–151). Victoria, BC: University of Victoria.

Meeuwisse, A. and Swärd, H. (2007). Cross-national comparisons of social work: A question of initial assumptions and levels of analysis. *European Journal of Social Work*, 10(4), 481–496.

Niblo, D. M. and Jackson, M. S. (2004). Model for combining the qualitative emic approach with the quantitative derived etic approach. *Australian Psychologist*, 39(2), 127–133.

Sewpaul, V. and Haruhiko, S. (2011). A comparison of social work education across South Africa and Japan in relation to the Global Standards for Social Work Education and Training. *International Journal of Social Welfare*, 20, 192–202.

Sobal, J. (1998). Cultural comparison research designs in food, eating and nutrition. *Food Quality and Preference*, 9(6), 385–392.

Sullivan, C. and Cottone, R. R. (2010). Emergent characteristics of effective cross-cultural research: A review of the literature. *Journal of Counseling & Development*, 88(3), 357–362.

Wu, Q. (1991). An exploration of the vocationalization and professionalization of social work. In N. Chow et al. (eds.), *Status-Quo, Challenge and Prospect: Collected Works of the Seminar of the Asian-Pacific Region Social Work Education* (pp. 71–75). Beijing: Peking University Press (in Chinese).

7. Researching the garment sector in Bangladesh: fieldwork challenges and responses

Sawlat Zaman

STUDY CONTEXT

Industry Background

As an industry, the readymade garments (RMG) sector started its journey back in 1978. Only 22 or so export-oriented garment factories were operating in Bangladesh in 1979 (Rashid, 2006). The sector's growth has earned Bangladesh now the second-largest apparel supplier's position after China (Dhaka Tribune, 2018a; Textile Today, 2018). The RMG sector employs more than four million workers in approximately 4,560 garment factories (Statista.com, 2018; BGMEA, 2019) though there is speculation that the real number may be more than 6,000. Most of the workers in these factories are female and therefore the sector is said to have contributed especially to women's economic empowerment through employment (The Daily Star, 2018). This industry also employs a significant number of people who work as office staff for various jobs in merchandising, finance and accounts, commercial (marketing), stores, logistics, and other departments. Foreign expatriates working in this sector are mainly from India and Sri Lanka; there are also a few expatriates from China, Philippines and South Korea. The presence of more than 200,000 foreigners (The Daily Star, 2015) in the RMG sector is yet more evidence of the sector's success in the global market. However, no official record exists as to the exact number of office staff working in the garment sector of Bangladesh.

I went to Bangladesh in 2011 to collect data and it took me more than five months to complete data collection. This fieldwork took place almost two years before the Tazrin fire disaster in 2012 that killed 123 people (The Guardian, 2012) and the Rana Plaza collapse in 2013 that took the lives of 1,132 people (ILO, 2019). However, for a long time even before these disasters, the garment sector of Bangladesh often received heavy criticism on issues of cheap labour (low wages), worker abuse, and health and safety of workers due to lack of fire safety or building safety; many factories were located in multistorey, unsafe buildings built without planning permission by the concerned authority.

When the Spectrum building collapse happened in 2005, it cost the lives of 64 workers and more than 80 workers were severely injured (Clean Clothes Campaign, 2013). The Spectrum collapse is still used as a 'case study' of industrial disasters in modules on employment relations or industrial relations in many Western universities. In brief, time and again the sector has caught the attention of world media and labour or union activist groups on mistreatment of workers, low pay, and safety issues despite its contribution to the economy. The literature search also indicated that major academic publications by local Bangladeshi researchers are also primarily focused on factory workers and their socio-economic well-being. I therefore chose to look into these supplier firms and their management practices around office employees other than factory workers.

Country Context

Developing an understanding of a research context can be done through a literature search. Broadly, a country can be placed somewhere between high and low context (Hall, 1976). Researchers such as Hall and Hall (1990) offered a spectrum of national cultures ranging from 'high context cultures' to 'low context cultures'. A country with a high context culture in a typical sense would place a high value on interpersonal relationships and where individuals and group members demonstrate a very close-knit community. A typical low context culture would show more of an individualistic society which is not so close-knit and where relational aspects are less emphasized. If we consider any research in a high context country, this has implications both in terms of the investigating approach and for the data found. Bangladesh is a high context country; a realization and understanding of this comes perhaps more naturally if the researcher is from the same country.

However, for a non-native researcher, one way to begin to understand the social and especially cultural context of a country could be by looking at Geert Hofstede's (1991, 2011) model of cultural dimensions. Despite criticism by researchers such as McSweeney (2002), Hofstede's (1991, 2011) work can be an important tool for a researcher to have a 'head start' to understand an unknown country and its context followed by further literature research. According to Hofstede's country-wide cultural dimensions analysis (Hofstede-insights.com, 2019), Bangladesh represents a high context culture. As a country, Bangladesh scores low as an individualistic society (it is highly collectivist), scores high in power distance (there is a higher acceptance of unequal power distribution by individuals and institutions in the society), and is a moderately masculine society driven by competition, achievement, and success (Hofstede-insights.com, 2019).

During my fieldwork, I had to rely primarily on my social networks to collect data. My approach in communicating with participants was context-driven, details of which are given below. Being a Bangladeshi, I was already familiar with its society, culture, norms and expectations. My background thus helped significantly in gaining access to interviewees and managing participants' expectations in interviews. At the same time, it meant that I needed to be careful to avoid being influenced by preconceived ideas or assumptions.

CHALLENGES AND RESPONSES IN FIELDWORK

The garment factories that I visited were primarily located in Dhaka, greater Dhaka, Narayanganj, and Savar (including the Dhaka Export Processing Zone or DEPZ). I also interviewed several of my participants over the phone since they were located in Chittagong city and I could not travel there. I mostly travelled to the factory offices to interview my participants but some I met at locations convenient for them. Before I discuss the challenges encountered in fieldwork it is important to understand the kind of preparations made beforehand. This involved exploring and investigating relevant materials to help understand the study context and gaining knowledge of the subject matter.

Getting Prepared to Study the Under-Researched

Before this fieldwork I had never stepped inside a factory and like any Bangladeshi I was at best vaguely acquainted with media-driven information on garment businesses and some controversies around labour conditions. As discussed in the section above, with limited documentary sources available on the RMG sector the following three preparatory strategies were adopted to get familiar with my research interest.

- *Preparatory strategy number one*: study all available materials even if not directly relevant to know about the context of the study.

A literature search on the subject helped in getting some contextual understanding of the subject of interest such as major controversies surrounding the industry, and conflict of interests between employers and factory workers. This also proved useful in understanding and managing reservations observed in participants in sharing information during an interview. I prepared a good forwarding letter explaining the purpose of the study and assuring the research participants and participating organizations that no 'sensitive' questions would be asked or needed to be answered if participants found them so. I also carried a supporting letter from my PhD supervisor in case it was needed.

- *Preparatory strategy number two*: look for alternative sources to understand the research subject.

When the literature search revealed limited academic papers and hardly any information on management practices at the garment factories, I searched for the next best alternatives such as peripheral sources that might shed insight on my study context. For example, I looked at the online job portals in Bangladesh especially bdjobs.com that was already well known in the local job market. I looked at recruitment advertisements posted on bdjobs.com for a three-month period and did a content analysis of those recruitment advertisements. This exercise proved beneficial in developing an understanding of the kind of qualifications such as academic background, skills, and experiences employers looked for. Content analysis of recruitment advertisements also helped develop my confidence in asking the right questions while interviewing. I also got a rough idea about different functional departments that such businesses may have. I also examined some relevant historical evidence from secondary sources to understand people's cultural orientation surrounding the industry.

- *Preparatory strategy number three*: do pilot interviews.

It is argued that pilot interviews help in enabling sensitization of the researcher to avoid a 'communicative blunder' during later interviews (Wengraf, 2001). Hence the third strategy that I adopted to prepare was conducting pilot interviews over the telephone before fieldwork. Conducting a few pilot interviews helps to refine, develop, and polish questionnaires used later to conduct interviews during fieldwork. Researchers doing primary data collection can benefit immensely from this procedure. Other than getting intended 'data' it further helps in having a sense of what to expect and how to better phrase or pose questions and end with a successful interview. I also found through pilot interviews that semi-structured questionnaires allowed my participants to answer complex issues more flexibly (Saunders et al., 2003). I could also minimize the likelihood of receiving only socially desirable answers (Fontana and Frey, 2003) from participants, which is a common disadvantage of structured survey questionnaires.

Getting Access

The primary challenge that I faced during fieldwork as a researcher was getting access to interview managerial employees in different garment businesses. The experience of getting access was not always pleasant, often proved frustrating due to the uncertainty involved, and it was very time-consuming.

In this study, I relied on what researchers such as Bourdieu (1986) called 'social capital' to gain access. Applications of social capital have been identified at an individual, community, or organizational level (Inkpen and Tsang, 2005). Individuals and people acting as a group can benefit from social relationships and ties in the form of better personal access to information. In a high context social-capital driven society, social or personal networks can prove to be very important to gain access to organizations that work in a stressed environment and are difficult to access. According to Lin (1999), social networks are the social relationships between individual actors, groups, organizations, communities, regions, and nations that serve as a source to produce positive returns. Literature evidence shows that societies that emphasize collective values tend to prefer more personal or relationship-oriented recruitment sources, for instance, employee referral or networking at job fairs. The Chinese practice of 'guanxi' uses the personal network of extended family and other developed relationships and connections to gain cooperation (Tayeb, 2005). In my case, social connections helped me get access to interview employees in garment businesses and their owners.

For the 22 organizations that I visited, I originally approached more than 60 such businesses to gain access through people I knew. I got help from my family members and relatives, my friends from school or local community and my colleagues, my parents' colleagues, and my students who would introduce me to someone who in turn knew someone else who could help in getting an interview. Often reaching my participants via networks would include more than two connections. For example, I would approach person A who would introduce me to person B and then B would connect me to person C. Every time I got access to an interviewee, I would then again do online research to acquire possible advance details on the organization, such as the kind of products they manufacture. I found that most of the company website information was directed to their clients but in some cases there would be some more detail on the organization.

I found gaining access to multiple interviewees from the same organization to be more difficult and challenging; some interviewees, especially those who acted as 'gatekeepers', even asked "Why do you want to know the same questions from other people?", or said "I have already told you everything and you will get the same from others". I would usually respond by explaining to them the weight and credibility of a research outcome gained through a greater number of interviews. I would request them to consider "Which one would you believe if you were to read a report based on one person or one that is based on responses from ten or twenty people?" Some participants as a result agreed to help by introducing other people from his or her organization.

Networking or use of references is also a typical characteristic of high context societies where social connection and status are important. My professional identity or status as a then faculty member of the University of Dhaka and my PhD studentship at one of the top-ranked UK research universities helped significantly in getting acceptance. I also carried my visiting card and exchanged cards with my participants. All these helped in building trust and confidence to gain access to these otherwise very sensitive businesses due to the speculation under which they operated. However, when I approached my participants to help me get in touch with people from other organizations, only one participant agreed to introduce me to some other employees; the rest seemed completely uninterested.

My interviewees were always very careful about issues of security and confidentiality. Sometimes I had to send a text message to the interviewee giving my name and the name of my contact (reference person) that the interviewee knew. After that I would make a phone call to schedule an interview date and time. Fear of negative publicity makes these garment organizations wary of anyone approaching them for interview or research. It is also commonly known that these businesses are often threatened with extortion and kidnapping, especially over the phone. Many of my participants shared that they do not pick up people unknown to them in fear of security. On a couple of occasions, I was even asked if I was a journalist.

Managing Uncertainty

Difficulty in reaching saturation level in data collection

After planning and preparing for an interview, when it comes to doing the actual work, I found that the next challenge was accessing a sufficient number of interviews to reach a certain level of saturation in data collection (Saunders et al., 2018). Especially in the first couple of months, I made poor progress. I was able to access only 20 per cent of my total interviewees though I was continuously trying for more. At one point, for three straight weeks I could not manage a single interview, but I kept trying. To make better use of such time, I spent time organizing the data I had collected, transcribing and translating (Bengali to English) those data and making notes.

I also found from a few initial interviews that, on specific days such as the first and the last days of the week (Sunday and Thursday in Bangladesh) my participants were busier. This left me with only three days a week to try to set interview appointments. Long gaps in my interview schedule also happened due to political (opposition parties) strikes, national holidays, or the income-tax period when the businesses are extremely busy with tax audits. There were other unforeseen issues due to which I had to come back midway to interview, such as an accident in that factory or an external audit company came for sudden factory inspection. In one case, I had to use stairways to reach the thirteenth floor of a high-rise building as the lifts were not working only to find that my prospective participant was out of the office. The authority shut down the lift service as there had been a huge fire that destroyed its fifth and sixth floor a few days before my visit and I could still smell the smoke.

My participants were always very busy – something to be expected in a busy production floor or offices located in factories where a lot of activities are running simultaneously. One example of how busy factory managers could be is the fact that they could never give a schedule beforehand and some of them explicitly said that "We can at best tell you our today's and tomorrow's schedule but beyond that, it is difficult to say when we will be free". Thus I had to make sure that when I rang someone, my transport and interview kit (consisting of a notebook, pen, charger for mobile and a recorder) were ready. There were instances when I had to move within a few hours of making a call as the participants confirmed that they would be free in the afternoon or evening on the same day.

Once an appointment was made, there was always the issue of planning my transport arrangements. Private transport like car rental was required which depleted my research fund considerably. Most of the factories are in remote places and a direct public transportation service was difficult to find or deemed unreliable in terms of reaching a destination in time to meet the appointment agreed upon.

Anybody who has visited Bangladesh and especially the city of Dhaka will know about the out-of-control traffic congestion that plagues the city every day (Financial Express, 2018). Hence, reaching the destination to attend these hard-earned interview sessions was not easy and proved to be quite strenuous. Once, for a one-hour interview I journeyed for eight hours to reach an office that would be otherwise an hour-long round trip on a traffic-free road. If I add to that the humidity and heat of summer season in Dhaka (the average temperature was 36–38 degrees Celsius with 80–90 per cent humidity), the experience became physically laborious and exhausting. Road safety in Bangladesh is also a major issue and on average, 3,000 road accidents occur in Bangladesh each year, causing around 2,700 deaths and 2,400 injuries (Dhaka Tribune, 2018b). Public transportation is poorly managed and considered unsafe as most of the drivers operating public buses do not have a licence or training. Besides, public transport in Bangladesh can be risky with the latest data indicating a very high percentage of women (94 per cent) in Dhaka being subject to some form of sexual harassment according to a study conducted by a well-known non-governmental organization, BRAC (2018). I was therefore always accompanied by someone from my family not just because of unsafe roads but also because I used rent-a-car service providers; drivers of these companies could not be completely trusted with a lone female passenger.

On a positive note, culturally Bangladesh and Bangladeshi people are known to be very hospitable and some practices such as offering guests at least a cup of tea are office etiquette. I was offered a cup of tea in all the offices I visited, which was also a reflection of the local culture in hospitality. In general, interviewees were very polite, showed much respect, and tried their best to answer the questions posed. Some of the garment firms even offered a tour of their factories. Case study organizations offered lunch, which was very considerate of them as most of these factories were in remote areas and did not have any decent places to eat. During lunch, I chatted with some of the interviewees which also helped to build rapport in an informal setting.

Getting quality, information-rich interviews

After conducting a few interviews in the field, I realized that though achieving interview access was a challenge, getting an information-rich interview was even more challenging. Essentially, the very first thing I needed to explain to my interviewees was that "My focus is to research how you recruit and manage your office staff and not factory workers". This was crucial in setting my participants' mind at ease to some extent as they seemed to be constantly worried about being questioned about their labour practices. The other tool used to gain the confidence of the participants was to share with them a checklist of topics that would be asked and this helped to create an understanding between me and my interviewees. On average each interview lasted between 30 and 45 minutes. However, the duration of an interview can be a poor predictor of the quality of information shared. I had one interview with the owner of a garment business that took place at a prominent social club in Dhaka city. The participant in question shared two hours of her time but her conversation included barely ten minutes' worth of responses that could be tied to only some of the interview topics.

I also found after a couple of interviews that I could never stick to the order of the questions originally listed. Most of the time the interviewees would talk about a range of issues that I was not necessarily interested in. Sometimes it was hard to follow some participants' comments as they seemed to have some difficulty in coherently explaining issues even though they were responding mostly in Bengali (local language). Keeping the flow of the discussion focused indeed proved to be very difficult. Some researchers (Miller and Glassner, 2004) claim that participants sometimes resort to familiar narrative constructs that lack meaningful insights into the subject of interest. In my case, most of the time the participants would voluntarily start discussing labour issues and the measures they have undertaken or the troubles they are facing. Such shortcomings in interviews were minimized by conducting a greater number of interviews and spending more time on fieldwork. Though I was sympathetic to any genuine concerns they had, I would try to politely draw their attention back to the checklist of interview topics. To me as a researcher, this was an indication of the edgy and tense environment under which these factories operate due to the generalized controversies around the RMG sector.

Moreover, these interviews mostly took place in factory-based offices where people were at work and could hardly be compared to timed, calm therapeutic sessions. There were sounds of machinery, busy people coming in and out of the offices, and interruptions were to be expected. Sometimes I had to prioritize my questions (which ones to ask first) based on the situation at hand, especially where the participants were too busy or seemed reluctant to give much time or information. If the situation seemed favourable, I would ask them a few more questions and perhaps ask for any secondary documents they may like to share with me (which would contain some demographic information on the company). I always ensured that where possible, I would ask them if I could reach them over the phone for some follow-up questions.

REFERENCES

BGMEA (2019). BGMEA at a glance. http://www.bgmea.com.bd/home/about.

Bourdieu, P. (1986). The forms of capital. In J. Richardson (ed.), *Handbook of Theory and Research for the Sociology of Education* (pp. 241–258). Westport, CT: Greenwood Press.

BRAC (2018). 94% women victims of sexual harassment in public transport. http://www.brac.net/latest-news/item/1142-94-women-victims-of-sexual-harassment-in-public-transport.

Clean Clothes Campaign (2013). Spectrum collapse: eight years on and still little action on safety. https://cleanclothes.org/news/2013/04/11/spectrum-collapse-eight-years-on-and-still-little-action-on-safety.

Dhaka Tribune (2018a). Bangladesh to set export target of $39 billion for FY19. https://www.dhakatribune.com/business/2018/08/08/bangladesh-to-set-export-target-of-39-billion-for-fy19.

Dhaka Tribune (2018b). Road safety in Bangladesh: Causes and remedies. https://www.dhakatribune.com/special-supplement/2018/10/19/road-safety-in-bangladesh-causes-and-remedies.

Financial Express (2018). Traffic jam in Dhaka: Gone out of control. https://thefinancialexpress.com.bd/views/traffic-jam-in-dhaka-gone-out-of-control-1523031013.

Fontana, A. and Frey, J. H. (2003). The interview: From structured questions to negotiated text. In N. K. Denzin and Y. S. Lincoln (eds.), *Collecting and Interpreting Qualitative Materials* (2nd edn., pp. 645–672). Thousand Oaks, CA: Sage.

Hall, E. T. (1976). *Beyond Culture*. New York: Anchor.

Hall, E. T. and Hall, M. R. (1990). *Understanding Cultural Differences*. Yarmouth, ME: Intercultural Press.

Hofstede, G. (1991). *Cultures and Organizations: Software of the Mind*. London: McGraw-Hill.

Hofstede, G. (2011). Dimensionalizing cultures: The Hofstede model in context. https://scholarworks.gvsu.edu/orpc/vol2/iss1/8/.

Hofstede-insights.com (2019). What about Bangladesh. https://www.hofstede-insights.com/country/bangladesh/.
ILO (2019). The Rana Plaza accident and its aftermath. https://www.ilo.org/global/topics/geip/WCMS_614394/lang--en/index.htm.
Inkpen, A. C. and Tsang, E. W. K. (2005). Social capital, networks, and knowledge transfer. *Academy of Management Review*, 30(1), 146–165.
Lin, N. (1999). Social networks and status attainment. *Annual Review of Sociology*, 25, 467–487.
McSweeney, B. (2002). Hofstede's model of national cultural differences and their consequences: A triumph of faith – a failure of analyses. *Human Relations*, 55(1), 89–118.
Miller, J. and Glassner, B. (2004). The 'inside' and the 'outside': Finding realities in interviews. In D. Silverman (ed.), *Qualitative Research: Theory, Method and Practice* (2nd edn., pp. 125–139). London: Sage.
Rashid, M. A. (2006). Rise of readymade garments industry in Bangladesh: Entrepreneurial ingenuity of public policy. http://notunprojonmo.com/wpcontent/uploads/2011/06/READYMADE-GARMENTSINDUSTRY.pdf.
Saunders, B., Sim, J., Kingstone, T., Baker, S., Waterfield, J., Bartlam, B., Burroughs, H., and Jinks, C. (2018). Saturation in qualitative research: Exploring its conceptualization and operationalization. *Quality and Quantity*, 52, 1893–1907.
Saunders, M., Lewis, P. and Thornhill, A. (2003). *Research Methods for Business Students* (3rd edn.) Harlow: Pearson Education.
Statista.com (2018). Number of garment factories in Bangladesh from 2010 to 2018 (in 1,000s). https://www.statista.com/statistics/987697/bangladesh-number-garment-factories/.
Tayeb, M. H. (2005). *International Human Resource Management: A Multinational Company Perspective*. New York: Oxford University Press.
Textile Today (2018). Bangladesh remains 2nd largest RMG exporter accounting 6.5 percent market share. https://www.textiletoday.com.bd/bd-remains-2nd-largest-rmg-exporter-accounting-6-5-percent/.
The Daily Star (2015). Foreign employees on the rise in Bangladesh. https://www.thedailystar.net/business/foreign-employees-the-rise-bangladesh-194584.
The Daily Star (2018). Empowering Bangladesh's female garment workers. https://www.thedailystar.net/opinion/project-syndicate/empowering-bangladeshs-female-garment-workers-1575067.
The Guardian (2012). Bangladesh textile factory fire leaves more than 100 dead. https://www.theguardian.com/world/2012/nov/25/bangladesh-textile-factory-fire.
Wengraf, T. (2001). *Qualitative Research Interviewing*. London: Sage.

8. Gaining access to research participants for data collection in doctoral studies: evidence from a rural area of Bangladesh

Shofiqur Rahman Chowdhury, M. Rezaul Islam and Haris Abd Wahab

RESEARCH CONTEXT

This study collected data from Kalikagaon, a village of Sukhanpukuri Union (smallest rural administrative and local government units) Thakurgaon Sadar Upazila (second lowest tier of regional administration) of Thakurgaon District, located in the north-western region of Bangladesh. The village extends from 88°35′34.52″E to 88°39′25.32″E Longitude and 26°6′5.24″N to 26°3′40.59″N Latitude. Figure 8.1 shows a map of the village. Though there is no written document on the naming of Kalikagaon village, the researcher discovered from informal conversation with the local people that the village name came from the name of a Hindu temple Kalimondir located at a local market called D-Hat Bazar. Elderly people referred to a landlord called Bombay Chowdhury of West Thakurgaon who had the *zamindari* (landlordship) in this area and built a temple under the name of Kali (the Hindu goddess) and offered Puja (worship) here. Kalikagaon consists of many paras (neighbourhoods) and the naming of each para has its individual history. For example, the local name of sweet making craftsmen is Vujari that relates to the Vujaripara. Similarly, Babupara comes from the name of the landlord Kamini Babu and Bangalipara originated from the local community leader Abbas Ali Bangali.

According to the Bangladesh Population Census Survey 2011, the total number of population of Kalikagaon was 5,637 including 2,768 females and 2,869 males. From the signboard of the Water Aid Bangladesh posted in the local union office, it is shown that there are 1,480 khanas (households) in Kalikagaon village. The economy of Kalikagaon is agriculture-based and there are seasonal labour migration trends among the people. In recent past,

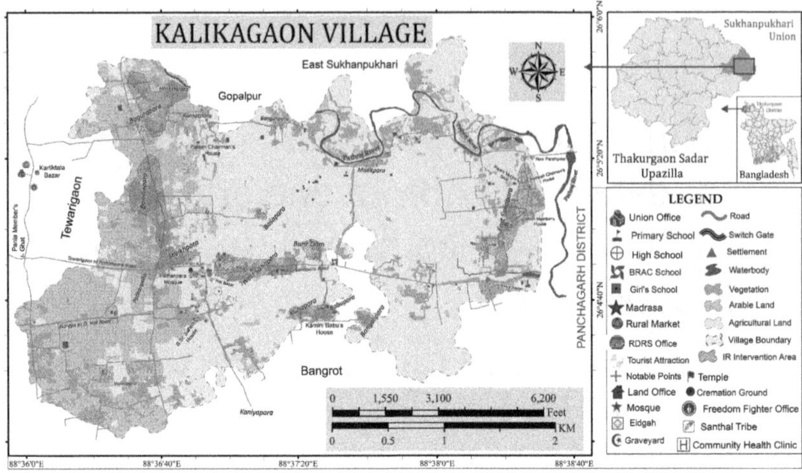

Source: Adapted from Google Earth, CEGIS Mouza Shapefile and the fieldwork study.

Figure 8.1 Map of Kalikagaon

the people of Kalikagaon village had to face Monga like other north-western regions of Bangladesh. *Monga* is a term used locally to explain acute seasonal food crises particularly after the plantation of Aman (locally called Hewti) paddy that occurred from August to the last week of November. However, crop diversification, seasonal migration, and the government's 40 days employment programme have minimized the curse of Monga. Earlier, there was only one paddy production (Hewti) every year. Now people in this area are producing Aus (locally called Chyana paddy) peanut, potato, and corn, etc. This study observed different types of land possession found in this village such as *Bondok* (mortgaged) land, Mulia (rented), and Adi (crop sharing) land.

Social problems like dowry provision, early marriage, and poverty are common in Kalikagaon village. The local name of dowry provision is called Demand and this is so common that no one considers it as illegal but became the common term. Similarly, some other problems were revealed by participants to the researcher, such as the incidence of affairs and marriage among teenagers without informing their parents. Fear of the parents and the dowry costs for adult daughters' marriages is the influencing factor for early marriage in Kalikagaon village. It was reported that a lot of female students, including Madrasha (religious school) students go to school by riding a bicycle which is rare and exceptional from the other regions of Bangladesh. The people of Kalikagaon village arrange various social and recreational events. For example, people arrange the opera programme (locally called *Palagan*) in winter, and the Bengali New Year music programme; religious gatherings such as Songkirton, Austoprohor, Horinum, Kartik puja, Ganesh puja, and Shradhanshan (funeral programme) are arranged by the Hindu community; and Shab-e Barat, Milad Mahfil, Waz Mahfil, Tamdari, and Khatna (circumcision of boys) are arranged locally by the Muslim community. Moreover, the Hindu community observes their festivals such as Durga Puja, Sorossati Puja, Janmashtami, Barney fare, Kali fare, etc. and the Muslim community observes Eid-ul fitre and Eid-ul Azha with a festive mood.

Among the population,115 households are rich, 421 are middle class, 844 are poor and 100 households are ultra-poor. Recent records show that the current population stands at 6,416 including 3,112 females and 3,304 males. Among 3,112 females, 257 are children, 734 are juvenile and 2,121 are adults. On the other hand, there are 297 male children, 887 juveniles and 2,120 adults. The official record of the Sukhanpukuri Union shows that there are 4,190 voters in Kalikagaon where the Hindu voters number 1,600 including the indigenous Santal community.

Islamic Relief Worldwide, a UK based international faith-based NGO, launched the project 'Actions for People's Rights and Livelihood' (APRIL) at Kalikagaon in April 2015 including 265 women "to establish a responsive community and institutions targeted at the ultra-poor and marginalized people's social and economic development process, [so that] rights and entitlement are protected and supported" (APRIL Project Proposal, 2015–2018). It selected Kalikagaon village following a poverty and vulnerability analysis using a score code such as code 1 for most vulnerable, code 2 for vulnerable, and code 3 for good. The score of Kalikagaon was third among the villages having the lowest score.

For the APRIL project, Islamic Relief collected prior information from various formal and informal sources. These were the local union council chairman, secretary, family planning officer, sub-assistant agriculture officer, NGO staff, Grameen Bank staff, high schools, Madrashas (religious schools), local elites, and the union information centre. Finally, it organized the selected women beneficiaries into nine groups and provided cash grants, income-generating training, and leadership training so that they themselves can operate these groups and create livelihood options. Moreover, it also introduced them to various local service providers to ensure their entitled rights. The selected women of this village were from the Muslim, Hindu, and the indigenous Santal community.

CHALLENGES OF DATA COLLECTION AND THE STRATEGIES FOR SOLUTION

This study faced a number structural and socio-cultural challenges to build a trustworthy relationship with the community people to collect the required data. It started from accessing the village and continued until the end of researcher's stay including clarifying study objectives, understanding of local culture, conducting an uninterrupted survey, and in-depth case interviews and arrangement of focus group discussions (FGDs) with community leaders. The following sections provide a detailed description of the challenges and the strategies for dealing with them followed by the researcher to overcome the constraints for the data collection successfully (see Table 8.1).

Introductions to the Research Participants

The study area was located in the north-western region of Bangladesh and the first author of this book chapter was not familiar with the study community previously since his hometown was located in Sylhet, the north-east region of Bangladesh. The primary challenge of the researcher was to build a trustworthy relationship with the respondents and ensure there was no threat from the local leader and/or the people. Moreover, during the data collection, the country was observing lot of terrorist attacks in different places by so-called religious extremist groups. The law enforcing agencies of the country told people to report on the tenants as well as any outsider's presence to the local police administration if found suspicious. The researcher had to stay in a hotel at Thakurgaon town for the first week to get official documents from the IR local office. As an outsider, this was not really safe as there was a possibility of harassment due to frequent police raids in search of extremists and criminals.

The researchers opted for three methods to gain access to the IR community. First, the researchers made official contact with the local law enforcing authorities including the Superintendent of Police (SP) of the Thakurgaon District and Officer in Charge (OC) of Thakurgaon Sadar Upazila. The researchers briefed them about the study objectives and sought physical security assurance. Secondly, the researchers communicated with the public representatives of Sukhanpukuri Union and briefed them about the study objectives. In that case, the first author's position as a faculty member of a public university of Bangladesh enabled him to find quick acceptance among the elite people of the area. To give an example, the researchers got accommodation facilities free of charge from the former chairman of the Sukhanpukuri Union. In addition, he helped forge contacts with the community decision makers and socially reputed persons. In that case, the researchers were introduced to local actors

Table 8.1 Challenges and strategies of data collection

Challenge	Strategy
Understanding of local language and culture	Staying within the village
	Regular visiting to local market
	Offering prayer in the mosque and interacting with village people
	Conversation with IR field staff
	Interacting with local gatekeeper
Solving respondents' expectation for material help	Using IR field staff
	Using socially reputed person
	Using ex-village motivator
Resolving misconception of non-interviewed person	Attending group meeting
	Visiting house at leisure time
	Using ex-village motivator
	Selecting participants' convenient place
Arrangement of FGDs	Selecting participants' convenient place
	Providing transportation costs wherever necessary
	Giving several reminders to the participants particularly in the morning and one hour before on scheduled date
	Giving information about the time to be spent and refreshment
Accuracy of data	Following multi-interview approach
	Empowering respondents through providing some examples
	Cross-checking with neighbours
	Observation
Contact with the respondents	Staying within the community
	Using a bicycle
	Fixing mutually adjusted times
Conducting continuous / spontaneous interview	Briefing study objectives using local examples
	Giving chocolate / biscuits to children or siblings
	Alteration of sequences of questions to ensure uninterrupted responses
Maintaining commitment and devotion to data collection by the researcher	Attending community festivals
	Considering the community situation as a reminder of childhood memories
	Passing leisure time in D-Hat Bazar (local market)
	Participating in sports activity and receiving hospitality from the community people

Source: Prepared by authors.

who wielded various forms of social power such as positional, reputational, community decision making and social participation. Thirdly, using the institutional gateway, this study directly contacted the respondents through IR field staff, attended their regular group meetings and briefed them on the study objectives with the help of the field staff. The representation in Figure 8.2 provides a visual picture of the researchers' access to the community.

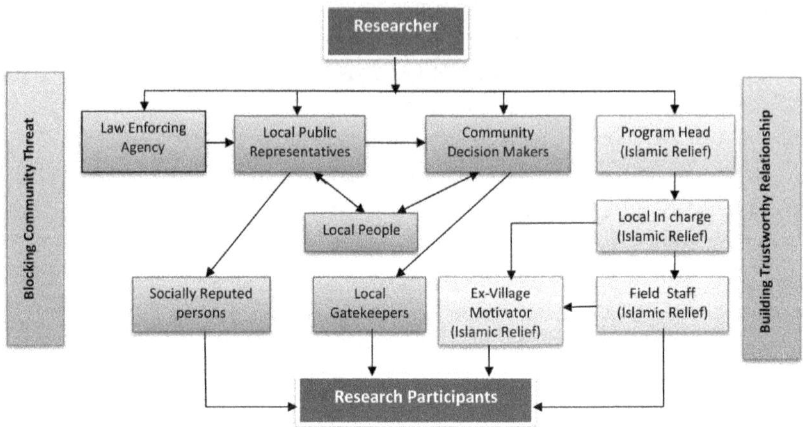

Source: Prepared by the authors.

Figure 8.2 Accessing research participants using different pathways

Moreover, with the help of village people, the researchers developed a community map that gave them an opportunity to interact with the local people and to establish a trustworthy relationship. Arrangement of community mapping was possible as the village people were passing leisure time due to no harvest season prevailing in the study area. The local people were very familiar with community mapping as a lot of NGOs were working in Kalikagaon and community mapping was a frequently used tool. This study prepared seven community maps in seven *paras* (neighbourhoods) where IR programmes were operating. This study selected the IR group meeting place for community mapping and also provided some refreshments for the participants. Local people drew the map (Figure 8.3) which was later finalized using AUTOCAD software. For clear understanding, a finalized version of one map is shown in Figure 8.4.

Clarifying Study Objectives

Initially, the studied community considered the researchers as IR high officials and expected to get some material help. Moreover, being an outsider to

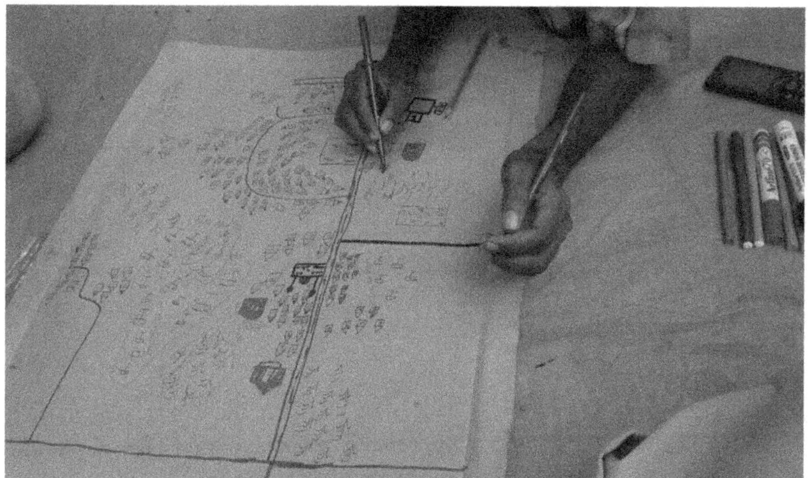

Source: Prepared by community people.

Figure 8.3 *Community map*

the community, the village people were also initially very curious about the researchers' movements. The common questions the researchers faced were "Who are you? Why have you come here? Where are you staying and how long will you stay?" The researchers took some time to make people clear about the purpose of their visit and avoid misconceptions. Initial interactions with the community people at D-Hat Bazar, Kartiktola Bazar, and Chunia Para Bazar (local market) were made possible by movement around the village by bicycle and offering prayer at the different mosques at different times which gave an opportunity to find some people who understood the study objectives and helped the researchers to reach the respondents easily. In addition, the researchers, fortunately, found one student from the University of Dhaka studying at the Department of International Relations who was a resident of this village and came home to enjoy the vacation. He helped this study through giving an explanation to the villagers about the study objectives which was very effective to build a trusting relationship with the community people.

Moreover, considering that Thakurgaon is famous for an early variety of potato production (The Daily Star, 2014, 2017; The Daily Observer, 2015), the researcher briefed the respondents about the study objectives using an example of local potato production as follows:

> I have come to know that once upon a time you faced severe *Monga* (the yearly cyclical phenomenon of poverty and hunger). People in this area could only produce

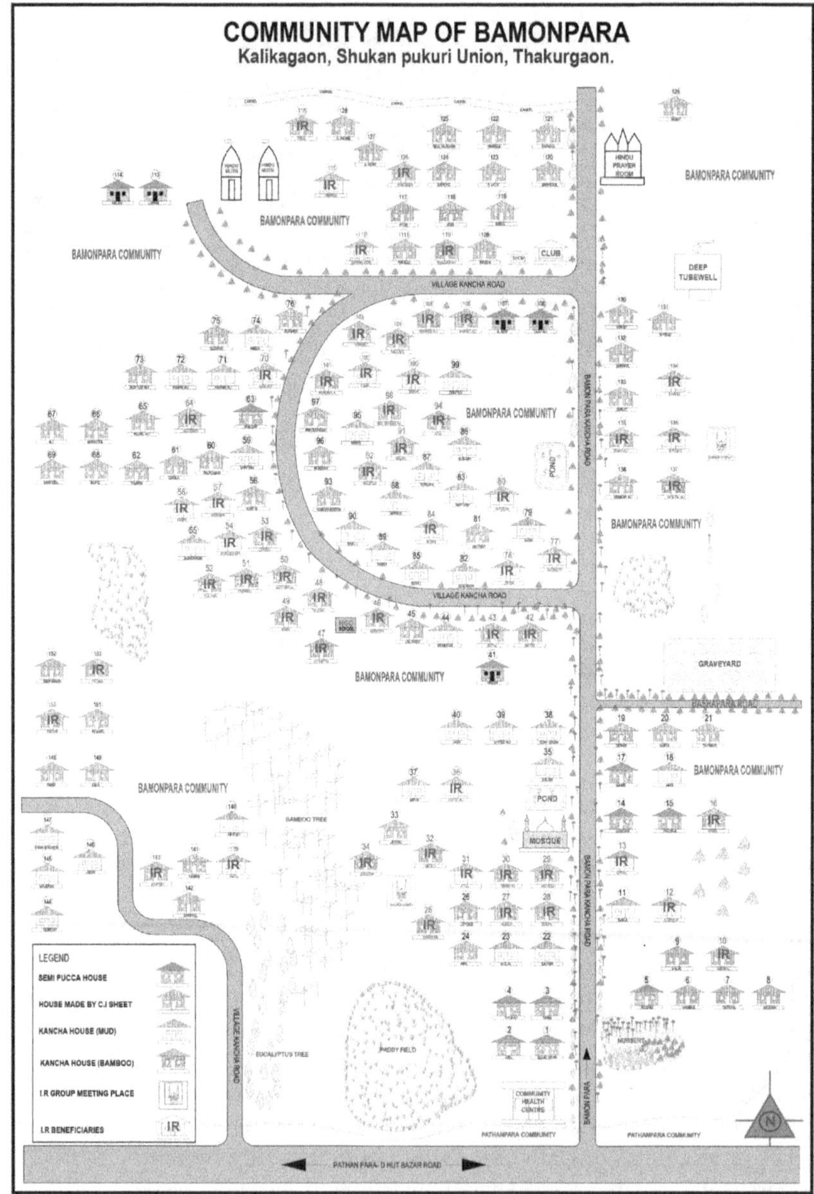

Source: Prepared by the authors with the assistance of community people.

Figure 8.4 *Community map of Bamonpara*

> *Hewti dan* (one type of rice) once in a year and had to pass their daily life with hardship, even eating *Pata shak* (leaf spinach of jute). Now the situation has changed. Now you people have different types of agricultural production such as *Chyna dan*, *Hewti dan* (two types of rice), and a variety of potato, peanut and corn in your area. Local people produce early variety (short duration) of potatoes such as *Granola*, *Cardinal Diamond* and *Sarpo mira* every year and businessmen from other districts come to Thakurgaon to purchase potato. Farmers of other districts are encouraged to follow your farming method as an example. How do people from other areas know your farming method? The fact is that someone came here; talked to some of you, found the techniques you commonly use and finally informed the people of other areas of Bangladesh. So is the case with me. Before the coming of Islamic Relief here, you also had seen the activities of other NGOs like Grameen Bank, BRAC, MANOBIK, ASHA, PROSIKA etc. Islamic Relief claimed that they are following a different strategy to help poor people. That is why I have come here to see its activity, how they work and what are its good sides and limitations. This is the issue on which I study. I need to talk to you. But it is not possible for me and my assistant to talk to all 265 group members of Islamic Relief in this village. For this, I will talk to some of you from each group individually just like testing one or two rice which you do every time in your rice cooking. I am not from Islamic Relief and rest assured I will not share your opinion with others in your name, you have right to see what I am writing and if you do not feel comfortable even after starting my conversation with you, you can withdraw yourself at any time.

Conducting Uninterrupted Survey and Interview

This research used a multi-method data collection procedure including face to face survey and in-depth interview. The total survey participants were 165 out of 265 registered beneficiaries of IR at Kalikagaon village. Out of this 165, 11 cases were selected for in-depth case interviews following some selection criteria such as successful, failure, most active, religion and indigenous category. This chapter discussed earlier that the researchers used different gateways to reach the target community and also explained how the study objectives were clarified using local examples. In this regard, the researchers must say that their staying in the village and taking time to build a trusting relationship greatly facilitated easy access to people's homes whenever they agreed to give their time for interviews.

However, while collecting data from the participants, the researcher faced some practical challenges such as misconception among the non-surveyed IR beneficiaries, respondents' reluctance to give written consent, recording socio-economic data and interviews after being granted permission and compensating the respondents for sacrificing their time. For example, we selected 165 out of 265 IR beneficiaries as survey participants. The researchers clarified study objectives several times in the group meetings. Despite this, some non-surveyed participants thought that this survey was mainly being conducted by IR and there must be some benefits for the surveyed participants in future. Not being considered as surveyed participants means that they thought they were going to be deprived of some benefits from IR. The researchers had to face this misconception of some non-surveyed IR beneficiaries at Bangali Para area. After being informed by the group leaders, the researcher again made a clarification. However, the researchers could not convince one IR group member. She was adamant she should be a survey participant. Finding no other alternative, the researchers, upon request of the group leader and another member had to take her opinion though this has not been included in the main findings.

Similarly, the researchers were ready to give some token money to compensate the participants for sacrificing their time despite the funding limitations of this PhD research. However, the group leaders and IR staff members gave their opinions that this would create a misunderstanding among the other group members who would not be interviewed and who ultimately would hold accountable the group leaders erroneously. With the consultation of the group leaders and IR staff, the researchers changed the decision and took some refreshment such as biscuit and traditional sweets (*Jilapi*) for each participant's family. The researcher found this was very effective for building a friendly relationship between the researcher and the participants. A large number of survey and case participants were housewives with small children, and many times the children started crying which interrupted the data collection process despite the willingness of the participants. When this occurred, the refreshments brought by the researcher were given to the children to keep them quiet and calm and eventually ensured the data collection proceeded very smoothly.

Another challenge of data collection was to get written consent from the participants. In the rural area of Bangladesh, people are always reluctant to provide anything in written form fearing that it might cause a problem for them. Even some key informants were reluctant to give any written consent. The researchers discovered this reluctance while conducting the pre-test, and in the final survey and interview verbal consent was taken after guaranteeing participants' right to withdrawal from the interview at any time as well as checks about the data to be collected.

However, the researchers did not administer the questionnaire in one setting. To make the respondents acquainted with questions, the researcher followed two stages. First, data regarding the socio-demographic and economic conditions were collected, and then the questions related to empowerment domains were asked. At the end, the researchers debriefed and thanked the respondents and gave an opportunity to add or discuss about the issues which they considered important. However, the researchers immediately evaluated whether they had got accurate answers provided by the respondent, decided if further enquiry was needed and met the respondents again. This multi-stage administration of the questionnaire ensured the validation of the gathered information. This technique also eliminated fear, distrust, and nervousness which almost all respondents showed at the initial stages of interaction. Through this, it was also possible to discover new and unanticipated information about their livelihoods.

For an in-depth interview, this study considered the recording of participants very significant to avoid missing any valid data. According to our ethical guidelines, respondents' permission was obligatory prior to taking interviews. However, the researchers' experience reveals that asking permission for recording conversation prior to interview became difficult for the participants. Rather than informing them officially that the interview is being recorded, the researchers kept the recorder visible in front of them. It was found that when they did this, the following kind of conversation generally occurred:

Participant: Brother, are you recording my words?
Researcher: Yes, because what you are telling is very important to me and I do not want to miss any word. Is it okay?
Participant: No problem, it does not mean that you are taking me belongings. Does it (laughing)?

Those who are very strict about following the ethical guidelines may question the ethics of following such a technique. In this case the researchers' argument is that this study was not conducted on any sensitive issue and the researchers were committed to maintain confidentiality and ensure data accuracy. If the data collection in such a way does not harm the respondents and ensures their spontaneous participation and the issue of conversation is not very sensitive, it may be argued that the researcher does not need to receive formal permission for recording.

Another challenge was in conducting individual interviews in village. It is very common that neighbours join in and start answering the questions. The disadvantage of this is that the interview may be interrupted, or the respondents may be influenced. However, it is also found that this has a different dimension. When two people come together and interact with one another, the researcher may understand the accuracy of data by observing their faces. This is very important to get socio-economic data and to understand the dynamics of local contexts.

Arrangement of FGDs: Local Leaders Want to be Contacted Several Times

Regarding the arrangement of five FGDs, the researchers did not face any problem while arranging FGDs with the husbands, group leaders and the members of the Apex body. The study arranged FGDs between the last week of April and the second week of May 2018 while people were found not busy with their agricultural works due to no harvest season. FGDs with the Apex body were arranged at the local Union Parishad office where the monthly Apex body meeting is held in the first week of every month. FGDs with the husbands and the group leaders were arranged at Kalikagaon community clinic, Bamonpara. An initially FGD with husbands was arranged at D-Hat school room at 8 p.m. but had to postpone it due to bad weather. The following day at 10 a.m., it was arranged in Kalikagaon Community Health Clinic. The researchers provided the participants some financial incentives as compensation for sacrificing time and there were some food refreshments to keep the discussion lively.

However, the researchers faced challenges to arrange an FGD with the community leaders. This FGD was arranged almost at the end of data collection. The researchers' four months' stay in the village, regular attendance at local markets, the Union Parishad office, and offering prayer at mosques had helped to establish a relationship with the community leaders including public representatives, school teachers, community health leaders, head of school, and mosque and temple management committee. However, due to their busy engagement with other community activities, getting them together was found very difficult. For example, they agreed to join in FGD at D-Hat School at 4 p.m. but later only two could keep their commitment. Others said they had forgotten. The researchers then realized that the community leaders should have been phoned at least three times: at night before the date of FGD, in the morning of the FGD date and one hour before the starting of the FGD. Following this strategy, the researchers managed to arrange the FGD with the community leaders.

The Research Assistant (RA) who had a Master's in social work conducted the FGDs. The researcher selected him as he was a resident of this region and lived for seven years at the first author's hometown while studying at the Department of Social Work in Shahajalal University of Science & Technology Sylhet, Bangladesh. It was an advantage for the study that he understood the local language, culture and other issues of the Thakurgaon area and the local language of the researcher as well. His presence also helped the FGD participants feel comfortable about sharing their views. However, he did not actively participate in the discussion. Rather, he kept the notes, observed group interactions and ensured that recording was done properly (Boeije, 2010).

Understanding of Local Dialect and Culture

Though two of the authors of this chapter and the study community live in the same country, there is a difference in terms of language and cultural practice. For example, the Bengali word *Shala* (wife's younger brother) is also used to

Table 8.2 *Local dialects*

Land and agriculture related dialect		Common conversation related dialect		Common dialect used by the community people	
Local Dialect	English meaning	Local Dialect	English meaning	Local Dialect	English meaning
Kandor	Agricultural land	*Tui/Mui shala*	You/I	*Demand*	Dowry
kaught	Mortgage	*Uma*	We	*Dewnia*	Community leaders
Kotar gor	House made of mud	*Mui kohechu*	I said	*Tamdari*	Arranged after death of Muslim
Mulia	Contract	*Mui koba parona*	I cannot say	*Beti becha*	Daughters' marriage
Hewti season	Paddy production season (July–Nov.)	*Ala*	At present	*Biye atok*	Stopping marriage
China season	Paddy production season (Feb.–May)	*Agoth*	Previously	*Changra kal/ halka boyos*	Juvenile
Kamla	Daily labour	*Oschi*	Coming	*Julum*	Hardship
Jora	Adding money	*Konte jachit*	Where are you going?	*Pala palir bochor*	Year of liberation war
Adi	Shared production or animal rearing	*Jam nai*	I will not go	*Kecal*	Conflict
Ujgar	Income	*Fom nai*	Cannot remember	*Basha khoroch*	Household expenditure

Source: Authors.

scold someone, whereas the people in the study area use this word to address someone irrespective of father, mother, younger or older. For instance, the local people use *Tui shala* which means you and *Mui shala* which means I. Initially, the researchers felt embarrassed while talking with the people and hearing this type of word. The researcher was in a dilemma whether people's reaction was positive or negative. Another Bengali word *Julum* means injustice, but in the study area it means hardship. Considering the difference of local dialect, this study took the first 15 days to interact with community people more and to understand some commonly used words (Table 8.2).

Moreover, as an outsider, it was a big challenge to talk to a woman alone in a rural area of Bangladesh as this is a sensitive situation. Mindful of this reality, the study considered some IR staffs and village people as gatekeepers to reach the research participants. One IR staff is a former woman village motivator who is also a resident of Kalikagaon village and still has connection with one IR group at Bogra and Hotat para of Kalikagaon village. Another one was IR staff who was in charge of this village for group formation and mobilization under the APRIL project and was working in another project titled 'Promoting Women Empowerment, Rights and Economic Development' (POWERED) in the Horipur area during the study period. The study used him as one of the gatekeepers as well as a key informant because at the initial introduction to the IR group member this study heard a lot of praiseworthy comments about this IR staff member named Arif Bhai. The group members were expressing their satisfaction with his behaviour and his way of dealing with them. They also wished to see him again. Upon the request of the researcher, Mr Arif came to this area and met IR group leaders and the members with the researcher which was found very effective to get full cooperation from the participants without any fear and hesitation. Moreover, the researcher was accompanied by some local people including two college students, and some persons closely related to the respondents who were either paid or unpaid. The researcher selected them considering their availability, interest, and attachment to the respondent. Despite this, there are several contextual and cultural perspectives in the study areas that the researchers could not understand even after four months' stay in the study area. Even in the middle of fieldwork, the use of one sentence without understanding the local culture had made participants uneasy and feeling shy to interact with us. However, we were fortunate that such misunderstanding was noticed by one of the gatekeepers and we were able to correct ourselves immediately. The first author's experience is hereby mentioned as an example of cultural gap:

> Although interview with a female respondent by a male researcher is a challenging task in rural Bangladesh, I was able to remove this barrier while taking help from IR staff, local gatekeeper and attending the group meeting, staying in the village and interacting frequently with my respondents. However, use of one sentence while collecting data from East Shahapara area at Kalikagaon Village had created a barrier of data collection. In my hometown, we generally approach anyone to discuss using a Bengali sentence *Cholen apnar gore giye alap kori* (let us go to your house and discuss), no matter whether the person is a male or a female. It is a very common approach. I did not know that approach to a female respondent in Kalikagaon Village in this way is an expression of bad motive. To begin with, I saw the respondents from the Milon Group at East Shahpara area were very spontaneous during my introduction with them and talking in group meeting. I was happy when I read the respondents' names from the sampling list and it seemed they were more interested. However, on another day when I went to this area for data collection and approached them using the previously mentioned sentence (*Cholen apnar gore giye alap kori*), it seemed to me that some of the respondents were not spontaneous as they were the previous day. I was surprised and tried to figure out if there was any misunderstanding or anything problematic happened between them and me. While returning from the field, the local gatekeeper told me 'brother, do not approach like this. It means you are proposing something sexually misconduct or illegal. Rather than using the sentence *Cholen apnar gore giye alap kori*, please say *Cholen apnar barite jai (Let us go to your home).*' I realized then the mistake on my part and I apologized in the

> following weekly meeting explaining the meaning of this sentence in my hometown. I was fortunate that they accepted my explanation giving a reply with a smiling face: 'honestly speaking, we had felt embarrassed when you approached like this, but we also understood you did not mean it.' This specific occurrence made me more careful about choosing words and phrases for my later data collection period in the light of the local cultural context.

This kind of experience of the rural cultural practice has a theoretical linkage with the theory of mechanical solidarity which is based on collective conscience (Durkheim, 2013). The idea of mechanical solidarity in the rural setting entails that the rural inhabitants are obliged to follow the established norms and values by ignoring any type of individual interest. Therefore, the people's mind-set stands against individual will which is disempowered by the role of collective cultural practice. This study found the style of approaching is a collective cultural practice which a researcher needs to be aware of while collecting the data.

Maintaining Researchers' Commitment and Devotion to Data Collection

Collecting data from respondents in a poverty-stricken rural area in Bangladesh is not an easy task. People in such a community are fully engaged in their everyday survival and they are not very keen to sacrifice time for a researcher for which there is no immediate return of benefit. Moreover, it was also an exhausting task to ask the same questions repeatedly to the survey participants, though initially it ignites interest. Maintaining commitment and devotion to data collection was also a big challenge as there was no reliable internet access, no uninterrupted supply of electricity, and no improved transportation system in the studied community. The researchers followed some strategies to keep themselves vibrant, like recalling positive memories from their childhood. For example, due to urbanization, the researchers' hometown has lost its traditional agriculture-based rural community and social practice. What they observe at Kalikagaon such as community bonding, children's school going, local market, religious education, traditional sports activities of boys and girls – all were the part of life during the childhood at their own hometown. Recalling such memories was pleasant for the researchers and encouraged them to interact with community people, including spending time at the local market in the evening, accepting invitations, playing cricket with the boys and moving from one place to another with a bicycle. Moreover, the researchers helped community people to raise funds for their local mosque reconstruction through posting the ongoing construction work of the mosque on social media like Facebook. The researchers also drew the attention of the government's social service department through social media to issue an allowance card for a Hindu family (not the IR beneficiary) living with three disabled members. Though these activities are not directly related to the PhD data collection and one may raise questions whether the researchers had diverted themselves from the study objectives, the justification is that the study objective was to investigate the nature of community empowerment and if researchers find that responding to community demand using their social networks without harming anybody will provide a better impression and more acceptance by the community people, why should they refrain from advocacy in the interest of community people? The researcher found that involvement with such activities not only alleviated the tedious repetition which data collection involves but also helped build a friendlier relationship with community people particularly in arranging FGDs with community leaders.

REFERENCES

APRIL Project Proposal (2015–2018). Islamic Relief Bangladesh (Unpublished documents).

Bangladesh Population Survey (2011). http://sukhanpukhariup.thakurgaon.gov.bd/.

Boeije, H. (2010). *Analysis in Qualitative Research*. London: Sage.

Durkheim, E. (2013). *Durkheim: The Division of Labor in Society*, ed. S. Lukes. Basingstoke: Palgrave Macmillan.

Islamic Relief Worldwide (2018). 2017 Annual reports and financial statements. https://www.islamic-relief.org/annual-reports/.

Islamic Relief Worldwide (2019). 2018 Annual reports and financial statements. https://www.islamic-relief.org/annual-reports/.

The Daily Observer (2015, 18 February). BADC growers in Thakurgaon produce quality potato seeds. https://www.observerbd.com/2015/02/18/73207.php.

The Daily Star (2014, 1 December). Early variety potato growers in Thakurgaon reap benefit. https://www.thedailystar.net/early-variety-potato-growers-in-thakurgaon-reap-benefit-52810.

The Daily Star (2017, 6 March). Bumper potato yield. https://www.thedailystar.net/country/bumper-potato-yield-1371556.

9. The challenges and strategies of accessing hard to reach locations during fieldwork data collection: the case of northeast Nigeria

Nasa'i Muhammad Gwadabe and Adekunle Daoud Balogun

THE SOCIO-CULTURAL CONTEXT OF THE STUDY

The researchers conducted the study in the northeastern region of Nigeria. It was part and centre of the Kanem–Borno Empire. At its height, the Empire covered most of the present-day Republic of Chad, northeast Nigeria, northern Cameroon, and some parts of the Republic of Niger and Libya. The Kanem–Borno Empire flourished from the eighth century CE to the British occupation of northern Nigeria in the 1900s. This region is occupied predominantly by Muslims. However, there is a population of a few Christians. The Boko Haram insurgent groups are from this region, and they have overwhelmingly strengthened in terms of population and military might. A researcher who is not a Muslim may not be successful in a fieldwork study even with special approval of the government for free accessibility of the terrain and the public institutions because Boko Haram's mission is to administer the country with Sharia law. At the same time, they believe that Nigeria should be Islamised (Pierri and Barkindo, 2016). Hence, they arrest, humiliate, kidnap and sometimes kill non-Muslims who cannot recite any required chapter of the holy Quran.

MAJOR CHALLENGES ENCOUNTERED DURING FIELDWORK

The authors identified several data collection challenges for a full research study. While the authors of this chapter conducted mixed methods, quantitative and qualitative studies, the challenges we present focus on what is relevant for qualitative studies. Munyoro (2018) explained that:

> Challenges of data collection in developing countries include lack of appreciation of the importance of data collection as an activity, mixed with a general cultural ethos of not sharing personal information with outsiders; remote and thinly populated areas, posing logistical as well as technical problems, e.g., for application of area sampling; infrastructural deficiencies, including poor transport networks, roads, and telecommunication networks; and lack of political and administrative support for autonomous research.

The data collection challenges reported here include location and accessibility, insecurity, culture and religion, duration of data collection, researchers' fatigue, sensitive information and low amount of data collection budget.

Location and Accessibility

Location is an essential component in the process of data gathering (Gill and Baillie, 2018). In the two studies evaluated in this chapter, it was evident that the location impacted information gathering. The first study involved interviewing internally displaced persons (IDPs) in their camps and outside the camps. Also, it involved conducting interviews with humanitarian actors from national and international organizations. Considering the remote nature of the area being affected by Boko Haram and the security challenges, accessing the IDPs and the humanitarian workers to participate in the interviews proved very challenging (Rimando et al., 2015). Again, concerning location, another challenge encountered during the data collection was the difficulty of establishing contact with the sampled humanitarian stakeholders for the interview. The study identified most selected humanitarian workers to be interviewed in specific locations. However, there was no way to engage some of them for a long time during the interview session due to the demands of their work. As such, arranging meetings for face-to-face interviews was a tremendous challenge.

Insecurity

Nigeria, the main location of the fieldwork, is highly prone to insecurity as a result of the activities of the insurgents. Insurgencies are present across the country both in the southeast, south-south and the northeast where the violent activities of Boko Haram groups have led to the creation of the IDP camps for the affected victims of their attacks (Adamu and Rasheed, 2016). Kidnapping by the terrorist groups poses a danger, although in the southeast and south-south the crime of kidnapping has decreased in recent times. This is due to the amnesty policy introduced by the government to rehabilitate and train the militants. However, research access to locations in the northeast was much disturbed until the government security forces made a concerted effort to prevent the terrorists from carrying out these lucrative crimes across the region (the family of kidnapped victims paid a ransom while many who could not pay lost their lives). Government troops suffered a series of losses in their attempts to eradicate Boko Haram's criminal activities, but their effort was rewarded as peace returned to the region intermittently (Onuoha and Okolie-Osemene, 2019).

Culture and Religion

The social-cultural tradition of the region posed a challenge to the research because the most vulnerable are women and children. In this situation, the researcher needed to give absolute respect to the tradition as to how the interview was conducted with, for instance, a woman whose husband may have either been slain, shot or forced to join the army of the terrorist groups. In such cases, the aftermath of trauma suffered by the family members of such victims required particular consideration, although even where there is no such trauma special care has to be exercised in interviewing female subjects in the northern areas. In this predominantly Muslim area, a male researcher cannot interview women alone, and if the husband or in-laws are not available, a female research partner is required (Briggs et al., 2019).

In the IDP camps, the emotional state of many of the women, coupled with the shortage of food and other items, facilitated access by the researcher who was able to provide monetary assistance to the participants in exchange for their cooperation. As a result, the researcher observed a positive change in their mood and appreciation during the interviews. They expressed their gratitude for this generosity, and it helped them to temporarily forget their past ordeals during the terrorist attacks by Boko Haram (Oakley, 2016). The male participants, although still very resentful over their experiences, maintained responsibility as the heads of their families and were willing to talk with the researcher in a comprehensive fashion. They revealed how some of their relatives or friends had been victims of violent attacks by the terrorists and the circumstances surrounding the death of some of these people. They became very emotional and shed bitter tears over the fact that the security forces had not been on hand to help them and reduce the risk they faced at the hands of Boko Haram. During these interviews, the researcher shared their ordeal, and the interview process required a longer time than scheduled.

Duration of Data Collection

The researcher had scheduled adequate time for the fieldwork, but some unforeseen circumstances were responsible for delays. Some of the factors were:

- Occasional media reports of attacks on IDP camps by Boko Haram meant that Nigerian army troops frequently checked on the IDP camps which delayed the research interview process. On one occasion, the Nigerian air force carried out an aerial attack on an IDP camp, wrongly identified as a Boko Haram settlement. This led to the suspension of interviews in the camp for many days until the situation returned to normal after the repair of the houses in the camp (Sherman, 2018). Nigeria's air force admitted that the bombing was the result of a mistake (VOA, 2017).
- Absence of participants was another problem, and this occurred for various reasons. Some had to look after other people's children when the parents needed to go to hospital for treatment of an ailment which the IDP camp clinic could not handle. Excessive heat also had an adverse effect on the interview process; a heatwave meant that interviews could not be conducted even under the canopy of the camps' tents.

Infrastructural Deficiencies

In the process of data collection, the researcher arranged interviews with several participants, one immediately after the other. This was possible because as IDPs, participants' schedules were not routinized. Some people may be heading to the market to make their daily trading activities while others may accompany their children to the playground; hence the researchers carried out interviews while they (participants) happened to be available. One problem was that often the battery of the recording device ran low. Because of the intermittent and unreliable power supply in the camp while an alternative power source was under refurbishment, the researcher could not always charge the recording device when it was needed. As a result, the researcher sometimes had to pause an interview until power was restored.

Infrastructural amenities play a vital role in data collection in developing countries, particularly in Nigeria, where power supply is still a significant concern. Access to good roads is available in Abuja, the capital city, but the situation is not the same in some IDP camps located in remote areas (Eme et al., 2018). Therefore, the researcher must prepare for an uncomfortable journey sometimes, and it may be expensive when there is no public transportation to the research site.

Researchers' Fatigue

There is no doubt that interviewing many traumatized people is fatiguing. An aggravating factor was that the limited physical space for conducting interviews, either with the IDP management team or with individual IDPs, meant that the logistics of visiting the IDP camps required strict adherence to formality (Sherman, 2018). This also induced fatigue in the researchers, in addition to the long distances they had to travel to access some of the camps.

Sensitive Information

The research uncovered quite a lot of sensitive information that the researcher could not share with individuals outside the study. In respect to reports of corruption in IDP camps, there were some questions in the research which addressed this phenomenon. The refugees based their responses on what they saw and heard, and some acknowledged the inadequacy of the supply of some of the goods they needed for daily life, but they did not seem to link this problem with corruption within the camp and most of the IDPs were unaware of this issue in relation to their personal well-being. However, there is research that links reported corruption cases in the mainstream media with the reports of inadequacy in the resources and the amount of money earmarked for the procurement of essential and necessary materials for the IDP groups (Adeloye et al., 2020). The civil servants who are in charge of the management of the IDP camps such as those deployed from the Nigeria Emergency Management Agency (NEMA) and the National Commission for Refugees, Migrants and Internally Displaced Persons (NCFRMI), shared their knowledge of the accusation and what went wrong. In such cases, all the sensitive information that the participants shared was treated with the utmost confidentiality. This is in fulfilment of the ethical standards contained in the letter of invitation to the respective participants. The researcher treated them personally and the information they provided according to the required ethical standards.

Low Amount of Data Collection Budget

Finding a solution to reach a location where fieldwork research will be carried out is not the only obstacle facing the researcher. Obtaining the funds to facilitate movement and procure materials and logistics support are persistent challenges confronting researchers. It is important to note that a qualitative scientific investigation about a phenomenon or disease in research may not be carried out thoroughly where consistently adequate funding is not provided. Governments of some countries or organizations in developing countries do not put a premium on the importance and contribution of research. However, some universities are world leading research-based universities with massive funding from the US government and other sources (Baro et al., 2017). The Best College Reviews (BCR) (2019) uses the following criteria in ranking the top US research universities:

- The university has at least one research centre or institute that functions under the jurisdiction of the university but as a separate entity.
- There are opportunities for undergraduates to participate directly in research.
- The university receives federal research funds.

Some of the American research-based institutions which occupy the highest positions in the research ranking include the Massachusetts Institute of Technology (MIT) founded in 1861, a private research university located in Cambridge, Massachusetts and home to one of the most powerful university-based nuclear reactors in the United States. The University of California at Los Angeles (UCLA) has averaged $1 billion in research funding with over 350 research labs, centres, and institutes; 290 of these are medical centres, and over 1,800 inventions have been achieved. Johns Hopkins University was founded in 1876 as the United States' first research university. Texas Agricultural Experiment Station, which is now Texas A&M AgriLife Research, is a source for much-needed research into agricultural issues of the day. European Union universities are well funded for research as well, and the West therefore leads on research funding for inventions (Best College Reviews, 2019).

STRATEGIES TO OVERCOME THE CHALLENGES

There were tentative solutions to various challenges encountered during the fieldwork of this study. The strategies listed here may need to be applied differently in different circumstances. There is no magic formula for the success of inventions in scientific and technological research and this applies also in qualitative study fieldwork. It requires sufficient commitment from academics and the student concerned, and institutional support for the necessary funding, resources, and monitoring. The following are the strategies adopted to overcome the challenges encountered during the fieldwork of the study under consideration.

Application for a Cover Letter

It became imperative to apply for a cover letter written on the official letterhead paper of the agency in charge of the IDPs which spelled out the researcher's status and objectives in the IDP camps. This document reduced the researcher's problem of having to explain verbally on each mission to the IDP camp. Every researcher should submit a request and receive a response in the form of documentary evidence of permission to conduct the interview (Bengtsson, 2016). Even with such documentation, however, in this study most of the junior workers were not comfortable with the researcher's presence and perhaps perceived him as a whistle-blower. As corruption remains a matter of concern in Nigeria, it seems every civil servant is a bit wary of any strange individual present in the lobby of public institutions.

Gifts and Presents

Distribution of presents and candies to the children of the participants was an initiative to motivate their parents who were selected as participants for the interview. It also helped to prevent children disturbing their parents by demanding food or some other thing in the middle of the interview (Denzin and Giardina, 2016). The researcher realized that the presence of children could have a negative impact on the quality of the recorded information, perhaps in the form of background noise in the audio-recording. Children's demands for attention from their mothers (participants) may tempt the researcher to skip some critical questions to save time and thus miss out on recording valuable data.

Written Notes

Note-taking or jotting down of valuable information was imperative when a noisy situation became intrusive during interviews such as when construction works of cabins or tents in the IDP camps were in progress for new arrivals among the refugees. This was causing noise pollution on the content of the tape-recorded interview (Oltmann, 2016) and sometimes constituted a nuisance. Hence, the researcher resorted to note-taking even while recording was in progress.

Security

The state of insecurity in Nigeria was of great concern. However, the researcher dealt with the problem by remaining in one location long enough for an assessment of assignment to high-risk areas to be completed. Unfortunately, this was a significant financial commitment as a huge budget was required for lodging in a reasonably comfortable hotel for almost two weeks. Although this strategy helped to overcome the fear of security threats and to achieve the objectives and goals of the study (Pearce et al., 2016), the problem of security will remain until the Nigerian government secures a successful strategy against insurgent criminality. For a country that is aggressively pursuing a sustainable economic strategy, but which is likely to continue to experience a low level of foreign direct investment (FDI), it is unlikely that the security problem will be overcome in the very near future.

Financial Commitment

The Sultan Zainal Abidin University Terengganu has no research grants for data collection for postgraduate students. This was a challenging situation for the researcher. The fact that the study was a local based research meant it was incumbent on the researcher to travel by air from Malaysia to his country, Nigeria. Internal travel within Nigeria on long-distance journeys to IDP camps was not only stressful but also required financial resources to evade the criminal activities of kidnappers. Since kidnapping is a frequent and lucrative crime, the only solution the researcher could adopt was to either travel by rail or by air to a few destinations within Nigeria.

REFERENCES

Adamu, A. and Rasheed, Z. H. (2016). Effects of insecurity on the internally displaced persons (IDPs) in Northern Nigeria: Prognosis and diagnosis. *Global Journal of Human-Social Science*, 16(1), 10–21.

Adeloye, D., Carr, N., and Insch, A. (2020). Conducting qualitative interviews on sensitive topics in sensitive places: The case of terrorism and tourism in Nigeria. *Tourism Recreation Research*, 45(1), 69–79.

Baro, E. E., Bosah, G. E., and Obi, I. C. (2017). Research funding opportunities and challenges: A survey of academic staff members in Nigerian tertiary institutions. *The Bottom Line*, 30(1), 47–64.

Bengtsson, M. (2016). How to plan and perform a qualitative study using content analysis. *NursingPlus Open*, 2, 8–14.

Best College Reviews (BCR) (2019). 25 best online colleges 2019. https://www.bestcollegereviews.org/top/online-colleges/.

Briggs, L., Trautmann, N., and Phillips, T. (2019). Exploring challenges and lessons learned in cross-cultural environmental education research. *Evaluation and Program Planning*, 73, 156–162.

Denzin, N. K. and Giardina, M. D. (2016). Introduction: Ethical futures in qualitative research. In N. K. Denzin and M. D. Giardina (eds.), *Ethical Futures in Qualitative Research: Decolonizing the Politics of Knowledge* (pp. 9–44). New York: Routledge.

Eme, O. I., Azuakor, P. O., and Mba, C. C. (2018). Boko Haram and population displacement in Nigeria. *Practicum Psychologia*, 8(1), 76–98.

Gill, P. and Baillie, J. (2018). Interviews and focus groups in qualitative research: An update for the digital age. *British Dental Journal*, 225(7), 668–672.

Munyoro, I. (2018). Research data collection in challenging environments: Barriers to studying the performance of Zimbabwe's parliamentary constituency information centres (PCICs). *African Journal of Information and Communication*, 21, 81–95.

Oakley, A. (2016). Interviewing women again: Power, time and the gift. *Sociology*, 50(1), 195–213.

Oltmann, S. M. (2016). Qualitative interviews: A methodological discussion of the interviewer and respondent contexts. *Forum: Qualitative Social Research*, 17, article 15.

Onuoha, F. C. and Okolie-Osemene, J. (2019). The evolving threat of kidnapping for ransom in Nigeria. In O. O. Oshita, I. M. Alumona, and F. C. Onuoha (eds.), *Internal Security Management in Nigeria: Perspectives, Challenges and Lessons* (pp. 233–258). Singapore: Springer.

Pearce, J., Raleigh, C., Harris, C., Hume, M., Lee, U. R., and Cavatorta, E. (2016). Data collection in zones of violence and conflict [Online video]. https://www.youtube.com/watch?v=VHX-UAfzzbI.

Pierri, Z. and Barkindo, A. (2016). Muslims in northern Nigeria: Between challenge and opportunity. In R. Mason (ed.), *Muslim Minority-State Relations* (pp. 133–153). Basingstoke: Palgrave Macmillan.

Rimando, M., Brace, A. M., Namageyo-Funa, A., Parr, T. L., Sealy, D.-A., Davis, T. L., Martinez, L. M., and Christiana, R. W. (2015). Data collection challenges and recommendations for early career researchers. *The Qualitative Report*, 20(12), 2025–2036.

Sherman, P. (2018). *True Teen Stories from Nigeria: Surviving Boko Haram*. New York: Cavendish Square Publishing.

VOA (2017, 24 January). Death toll in Nigeria IDP camp bombing climbs to 236. https://www.voanews.com/africa/death-toll-nigeria-idp-camp-bombing-climbs-236.

10. Data collection on 'smartphone addiction and social capital effects' among the university students of Bangladesh: challenges and strategies for the way out

Ashek Mahmud, M. Rezaul Islam and Hamedi M. Adnan

RESEARCH CONTEXT

Bangladesh, a South Asian country, with an area of 147,570 km^2 and 161 million people (Etzold and Mallick, 2015), emerged on the world map as a sovereign state on 26 March 1971, after fighting a nine-month war of liberation, which was followed by many years of political turmoil and military coups (Interactions, n.d.). Over the years, the breakthrough of digitalization has become a great concern in this independent country. Through digital applications such as video chatting, email, photo sharing and messaging, social networking websites like Facebook, Twitter, Blog, Skype, Google and YouTube are being used in Bangladesh for teaching and learning (Mahmuda, 2016).

The advent of high-speed internet access and its availability on recently evolved smartphones has opened several new avenues. Recent data released by BTRC (2017) show that around 80 million people in Bangladesh access the internet and 73.8 million people access the World Wide Web by mobile phones, making up 93 per cent of the total users (bdnews24, 2017), expecting to extend to 75 per cent of the population by the end of 2025 (GSMA, 2018). Recently, in 2018, the mobile operators of Bangladesh launched the much-awaited 4G service with the provision of the 4G handset and 4G SIM card bearing the highest internet speed (10 Mbps) in Dhaka and some other major cities in Bangladesh (Hasan, 2018). This type of speed revolution and availability of smartphones with internet access has transformed the culture of communication into a speed culture of mind-blowing entertainment and connectivity targeting mostly the young generation of Bangladesh.

A report published in the *Financial Express* of India reports the shocking evidence that a majority of students are becoming highly addicted to smartphones: most university students engage in smartphone use for 5 hours a day, accounting for 22 per cent of the whole day (Rokonuzzaman, 2018). Another report shows that 62 per cent of Bangladesh's youngsters use mobile internet; among them, 75 per cent of educated users are bachelor and master degree students, and 65 per cent are between 15 and 25 years old (Nekmahmud et al., 2017). These data suggested a research study involving data collection with the objective of measuring smartphone addiction proneness and its impacts on social relationships, with private and public university students the chosen respondents for data collection (Aljomaa et al., 2016; Arefin et al. 2017).

Considering those facts and relevance, the university students of Bangladesh were the target group for this research. Here, both public and private university students of Dhaka city in Bangladesh were chosen for data collection. The reason for that is that among a total of 45 public universities of Bangladesh, Dhaka city is home to 9 public universities, and 48 private universities are located in Dhaka city among a total of 103 private universities (Jasim and Siddiqui, 2019). Among the public universities, the renowned University of Dhaka and Jagannath University and six private universities (North-South University, Northern University, East-West University, UIU, DIU, and IUBAT) of Dhaka city were identified as fields for data collection. Only the University of Dhaka has student halls with residential and internet facilities. Other public and private university students have to live in private shared rooms, and few of them live in their parental homes.

In this situation, university students have more opportunity to use a smartphone for different purposes, whether fruitful or injurious. Both hall life and private sharing room life make it easier for students to be addicted to a smartphone since they are not under parental supervision. While university students of Dhaka city were regarded as valuable targets for research of this kind, collecting data in both quantitative and qualitative ways is problematic in a number of respects. It is challenging to collect data from university students within these socio-cultural contexts. Therefore, overcoming the challenges with proper strategies and ethical safeguards was a critical task for the researchers.

CHALLENGES IN THE FIELD AND STRATEGIES OF OVERCOMING THE CHALLENGES

Among the various challenges experienced in the areas of translation, instrumentation, and data collection (Halder et al., 2016), accurate data collection is an important issue. Data collection, for social science researchers, is not only a fundamental aspect of research but more importantly, it is immensely challenging to ensure data are collected according to pre-planned guidelines and prepared questionnaires. Here, reflexivity is crucial to enhancing research accuracy and acknowledging challenges at each stage of the process of data collection (Ryan et al., 2014). Therefore, it is necessary for social researchers to critically reflect on how different kinds of data are collected regarding temporality and dynamism within research projects (Ryan and D'Angelo, 2018). In this context, the first task is to find out the specific challenges during data collection to have more reliable and authentic data as a precondition for research transparency.

Since university students of both public and private institutions in Dhaka city were the chosen field for data collection, it was no easy task to select the right respondents, and to ensure accurate and reliable data. The challenges are complex, comprehensive, sensitive, and multi-faceted. Regarding the reality and experiences from the field, the challenges are classified into two major themes; one is a substantive challenge, and another is an instrumental challenge. The substantive challenge includes methodological and structural issues (Table 10.1); on the other hand, environmental, motivational, and cultural aspects are instrumental problems (Table 10.2).

SUBSTANTIVE CHALLENGE AND WAY-OUT STRATEGIES

Methodological Challenges and Way-Out Strategies

Sampling difficulty is the central methodological problem in the data collection process. Though the sample size was scientifically selected for both survey and in-depth interview, choosing appropriate sampling techniques became a significant concern. First of all, simple random sampling was identified as the core sampling technique for survey research. Drawbacks of this sampling method include lower reliability of the findings, risk of inaccurate data, lack of standardized information, lower probability of confidential data, higher possibility of missing information from diverse sections of students and less researcher control upon the data collection process.

Moreover, the study results may produce suspect data because of a biased sample, which ultimately leads to generating inherently biased results (internal validity) and lack of generalizability (external validity) to the target population (Ngwakongnwi, 2017). Furthermore, it has been challenging to construct a sampling frame due to the possibility of having lower precision; simple random sampling cannot be representative of the total population (Malhotra and Birks, 2006). During data collection, stratified random sampling and purposive sampling generate a few difficulties. Though relevant stratified variables were selected, it was not possible to have an equal proportion of those

Table 10.1 *Substantive challenges in data collection and strategies for solutions*

Key points	Challenges	Strategies for solutions
Methodological	**Sampling difficulties:**	**Settling sampling techniques:**
	For the survey, a simple random sampling suffers from a lack of reliable, accurate, standardized, and confidential data	For the survey, stratified random sampling is more valuable, potentially covering different strata of academic levels
	Limited time and field-setting procedure created difficulties in equal stratified sampling	Unequal stratified sampling was finalized
	Convenience sampling was chosen for an in-depth interview, but deep information could not be produced	For in-depth interview, purposive sampling was adopted on the basis of addiction criteria
	It was complex to maintain sequential data collection like survey cum in-depth interview	Mixed-method of data collection was non-sequentially arranged, but KII was taken following the findings from data
Structural	**Problematic validity in the questionnaire:**	**Checking content, criterion and construct validity:**
	The questionnaire was complex and difficult to fill out	Complexity was minimized by translating into native language making it easy and simple
	A few showed reluctance after looking at the contents of the questionnaire	Content validity was checked by forming the questionnaire into a semi-structured one
	Respondents say that the open-ended questions were ambiguous, unclear, confusing and time-consuming, which affected construct validity	Open-ended questions were replaced by closed-ended questions including one option for open-ended answers for flexibility
	Difficulties in memorizing and predicting suitable answers to the questions created limited criterion validity	Criterion validity was managed by giving enough time for memorizing, and students were allowed to raise any question
	Construct validity was challenged by the unclear and confusing assessment of psychological issues and past experiences	Researcher delivered a briefing about the complex terms of the questions, and about the coding system

Source: Prepared by authors.

variables. Maintaining an equal proportion required colossal time, a higher rate of expense, an organized setting of consent and a broad range of research resources. However, the implementation of those preconditions was not possible because of many limitations. The random sampling technique itself made a bridge in forming an equal proportion.

For conducting an in-depth interview, convenience sampling was chosen primarily due to easy availability and accessibility of the respondents (Taherdoost, 2016) and it was less expensive (Ackoff, 1953). After realizing that in-depth information cannot be produced from convenience sampling, we changed the decision. On the other hand, during an in-depth interview, the purposive sampling throws up a few limitations. Although it helped us saving time and money, and provided information with a low margin of error while collecting data (Regoli, 2019), another problematic aspect of purposive sampling is that the selection criteria of respondents were ambiguous. For example, three respondents regarded themselves as previously addicted to the smartphone, but at present, they regard themselves as normal users. In this situation, qualitative data findings became more comprehensive for data analysis.

The most crucial drawback of this qualitative finding is that only six in-depth interviews have been cross-matched with 384-sample size of quantitative data. In this case, this study uses NVivo for triangulation. Finally, the study applies the sequential data analysis technique so that the qualitative data can be judged with the quantitative data. In this way, both the quantitative and qualitative data are maintained sequentially.

After identifying the shortcomings of simple random sampling through a pilot study, this technique was replaced by stratified random sampling seeing that the standard errors of estimators can be high (Ghauri and Grønhaug, 2005). Our observation shows that stratified random sampling is a powerful tool as it can cover different strata like age, gender, university level, study level (undergraduate and graduate), and residential diversity. The main reason for choosing this sampling technique is that every stratum is adequately represented (Ackoff, 1953). Finally, we decide to use stratified random sampling for the questionnaire survey. Limited time and field-setting procedure make difficulties for regular stratified sampling. Therefore, unequal stratified random sampling contributes to data collection for quantitative research.

Then we accepted purposive sampling instead of convenience sampling; particular settings, persons or events are selected deliberately to provide valuable information (Maxwell, 1996). For an in-depth interview, half of the respondents were selected based on smartphone addiction, while the rest of them were based on typical users, and in this case purposive sampling was more effective. The quantitative and qualitative data collection was arranged with the use of triangulation regarding the available opportunity of getting suitable respondents. In this context, the gap of quantitative data is not minimized by an in-depth interview. Nevertheless, we see many questions arise from the findings of both survey and in-depth interview. For example, several students answered 'no comment' to questions regarding romantic relations. We thought that we should find out why they were reluctant to answer such questions. This gap is minimized by taking a few key informant interviews (KII).

Structural Challenges and Way-Out Strategies

Researchers usually prioritize principled conduct, collection of accurate, reliable, and on-topic data concisely and objectively, while participants' priorities for the research encounter include subjective tools like relationship pattern, a chance to socialize, payment, or an opportunity to speak on a topic of importance to them (Holden et al., 2015). The dialectics between subjective and objective view affect data collection and data management. The structure of the questionnaire and checklist itself creates difficulties in conducting data collection, and so the contextual frame of the questionnaire fell into the risk area of accurate data collection.

Though the questionnaire survey is consistent with objectivity in reality, impartial, and free of the influence both researcher and the subject (Bielefield, 2006; Johnson and Onwuegbuzie, 2004), the gradual decrease in reaction to surveys poses the most prominent challenge scholars have regularly encountered (Schmeets, 2010). With field observation, we see that the rising apathy in the response of the questionnaire was mainly caused by the topic, structure and context of the questionnaire. During the pilot study, we found the questionnaire overly complex and problematic to fill out. When we tried to select respondents randomly, first of all, many of them were wary of the unfamiliar researcher; secondly, students struggle to understand the topic and context of the questionnaire by which data can be gathered. Many showed their reluctance to respond to some contents of the questionnaire with open-ended questions as a result of which generating factual data became problematic.

For example, Parts D and E of the questionnaire at first consisted of 20-item questions on social bonding and bridging capital. Each question was to be answered by agreeing or not, and also every question sought an open-ended answer such as 'if yes, why?' and 'if no, why not?' The problem arises during on-test data collection. The respondents take so much time and become annoyed while responding to such open-ended questions. During on-test data collection, we see that the answers to open-ended questions are ambiguous, unclear, and confusing. This kind of hazard affects content, criterion, and construct validity of the questionnaire (Onwuegbuzie and Johnson, 2006). Secondly, the fulfilment of the criterion validity of the questionnaire that comprises concurrent validity (compatibility of items) and predictive validity (Onwuegbuzie and Johnson, 2006) was difficult. At the time of data collection, we saw that respondents faced difficulties in memorizing and predicting suitable answers to the questions that are about the time and cost of using a smartphone for various smartphone applications, for multiple purposes and with various people in the past and present. That ultimately limits the criterion validity of the survey questionnaire.

Furthermore, the construct validity has been a prime concern in terms of the quantity of assessment mistakes in questionnaires (O'Leary-Kelly and Vokurka, 1998) as well as the correctness of the elements and their accuracy (Burton and Mazerolle, 2011; Parasuraman et al., 1988). We saw that respondents were confused about how to fill out the table of detailed demographics data with the use of coding format; which affects the reliability of their information. Even in the 37-item Part F section of the questionnaire, more than 18 per cent of the respondents seemed to be reluctant to give a response on the issue of romantic relations. Therefore, they answered 'no comment'. This type of attitude affects the accurate assessment of those questions. Moreover, in the 15-item Part C section, many students found difficulties in answering questions about psychological issues, such as 'Is it true that you tried to reduce the time for smartphone use but failed?' Many respondents became confused about the right answer, and whether it should be 'somewhat agree' or 'somewhat disagree'. Thus, we find complexity and uncertainty assessing the answers to a number of questions that creates a challenge to the construct validity of the survey questionnaire.

During data collection from the in-depth interview, the quality of the data depends on the quality of the unstructured questions, and also on the quality of the responses to those questions. The main challenges here concern the quality of the respondents' understanding of the terminology and ideas, their ability to respond meaningfully and the openness of their response. Some of the students from middle-range private universities failed to comprehend terms like 'smartphone addiction', 'social capital' and 'effects of addiction on social capital' compared with students in upper-tier private universities and public university students.

The content validity required reviewing the questions to make sure they were suitably worded to gather relevant facts from the targeted group of people (Collins, 2003). In this respect, ensuring content validity was a big concern, and formulating a reliable and valuable questionnaire was a challenging and laborious task. To make clear the contents of the questionnaire, firstly the English format of the questionnaire was translated into the native language (Bengali), and every sentence was carefully rearranged into the correct form. Secondly, all of the open-ended questions were changed to closed-ended ones, including the option of 'if all options are incorrect, please write the correct one'. This flexibility for the respondents helped to ensure the content validity of the questionnaire. Thirdly, to ease the difficulties, the demographic section, and the section about using smartphone apps were arranged using a coding system. Finally, the questionnaire was formed into semi-structured one.

Then, we gave further attention to validity after recognizing the many challenges this poses. Kim et al.'s (2014) addiction measurement scale items and Williams' (2006) social capital items were used in the questionnaire maintaining scientific procedure. This procedure is not simple. Every item in connection with measurement was reshaped into a conceivable and straightforward sentence to prompt a clear assessment from the respondents. Respondents were given face-to-face guidance, and the construct validity was maintained by personal supervision from the researcher and research assistants. Respondents learned how to fill out the questionnaire using the coding system, and also they received a brief lesson on the meaning of complex terms like smartphone addiction, social capital, bonding/bridging social capital, somewhat agree, strongly disagree, and they were briefed about how to answer the questions on a Likert scale.

INSTRUMENTAL CHALLENGES AND OVERCOMING STRATEGIES

Environmental Challenges and Way-Out Strategies

The inferences we make are highly influenced by our cultural background, which influences how we think, perceive, and react to situations around us (Cunningham et al., 1995; Dake, 1991). The cultural background, socialization process, and urban mind-set are external factors affecting whether students are interested in participating in research. During data collection, the researcher's task is to ensure the complete understanding of the participants, explaining to them the research objectives and the possible risks involved in the research (Drew et al., 2008). After that, confirmation of informed consent with direct involvement is a crucial element of legal data collection. From a legal stance, informed consent involves three elements: capacity, information, and voluntariness, all of which must be present for consent to be valid (Drew et al., 2008). From a practical point of view, we saw that obtaining informed consent was challenging because of the size of the questionnaire and the time needed to fill it out (Table 10.2). While higher-grade university students are usually competent to understand the language and terms of the questions, and their capacity and ability to respond are apparent, the students from lower-grade private universities usually have a lower level of understanding, and we faced difficulties in getting them to understand the contents of a few questions.

In some cases, during data collection, students were not very motivated in responding to the survey questionnaire due to their low level of interest, lack of instant reward, and feelings of boredom. Where this is the case, researchers may be in doubt about the correctness of the responses. A few of the semi-structured questions about the 'why' behind positive or negative

Table 10.2 Instrumental challenges in data collection and strategies for solutions

Key points	Challenges	Strategies for solutions
Environmental	**Difficulties in consent management:**	**Consent management strategy:**
	Took more time to get direct consent when faced with a large questionnaire	Many were selected by course teachers which helped to obtain consent more easily
	Less understanding capacity for the students of lower-grade private universities	Consulting with them to minimize the understanding gap
	Lack of instant reward and interest, and feeling of boredom limited the voluntariness of consent	Networking was built by searching for links between researcher and student; students experienced the link as a reward
Contextual	**Concerning privacy and failing to complete survey questionnaire:**	**Protecting contextual issues:**
	Demotivation to answer questions about private issues	Using a self-disclosure strategy to protect privacy
	Incomplete questionnaires	New interviews were taken instead of using incomplete questionnaires
Motivational	**Exterior and interior motivation crisis:**	**Motivational supports:**
	Faced fear of refusal without material reward	Students were given calm and quiet environmental support and food was provided during data collection
	Lack of trust, lack of experience, lack of awareness created complexity	Sincere consultation minimized lack of trust and overcame lack of experience
	Difficulties found in taking interview from key persons	Strong referencing helped more

Source: Prepared by authors.

responses were unclear to many students. Therefore, the accuracy of their responses was called into question. This also affected the voluntariness of their consent. Although a number of tutors preselected some of these respondents, their voluntary consent was still difficult to obtain.

The participants of the in-depth interview were selected mostly through voluntary agreement. Eight university students were identified as ideal candidates for interview considering not only their level of smartphone addiction but also their willing interest in participating in interviews. However, this study required a larger number of students interested in participating in the survey. Several course teachers selected students, and some interviews were organized with the help of the university students' hall management authority with political influence or social capital. Such network building or networking was a valuable tool in consent management. This networking was carried out by searching for or establishing links between the students and the researcher or data collector. Students often feel a hidden reward from such links, as they think they will benefit materially or non-materially from cooperating. In addition, private university students received more help and consultation where their lack of understanding might have been a problem.

Contextual Challenges and Way-Out Strategies

Another core drawback of ensuring confidential data is more or less contextual. In both quantitative and qualitative research, protecting privacy and encouraging self-disclosure are the necessary prerequisites of maintaining research ethics. During in-depth interviews, students are then willing to express their feelings and experiences. As mentioned earlier, however, despite these ethical guidelines being followed, some students were unwilling to answer questions about romantic relationships. Some of them were reluctant to answer, either because of fears about privacy, or because they felt shame in front of the data collectors. At the elementary stage of the data collection, the researchers posed questions to the respondents using a Likert scale. We observed that some of them were ashamed to give a verbal answer in front of us. While filling out the questionnaire, a few of the respondents failed to complete it, citing an urgent phone call to make or some other unavoidable issue.

Contextual challenges are managed carefully following a self-disclosure strategy. The strategy of self-disclosure is the means by which people are encouraged to discuss their feelings, attitudes, and experiences. As was said before, the researcher has the responsibility to fully inform participants about the nature of the activities in the process of obtaining consent (Drew et al., 2008). So, contextually, we used the self-disclosure strategy to protect respondents' privacy and to give them the opportunity of leaving the interview at any time. Their concerns over privacy or confusion were managed by providing the option of 'no comment' in a few of the questions. We also overcame reluctance to answering verbally by encouraging self-disclosure.

Motivational Challenges and Way-Out Strategies

The communication challenge has been regarded as a prime motivational challenge in data collection. Before starting each in-depth interview, a minimum of ten minutes was spent helping respondents understand the purpose, motives, and areas of the study. Nevertheless, completing the questionnaire survey individually is not only complicated but can also be a demotivating experience. Moreover, our observation shows that without reward, students often become demotivated to spend more than 40 minutes filling out the questionnaire. Besides this exterior motivation crisis, the crisis of internal motivation was also a concerning issue. Many students at the private universities have no experience of participating in such interviews, and they are uncertain about their capacity to fill out the survey questionnaire. They were sometimes confused about using coding in the questionnaire. Some female students were unwilling to provide their mobile numbers and their names, as they were scared of releasing such private information. Moreover, lack of trust, lack of experience, lack of awareness, and introvert attitude are factors in interior motivational crisis during data collection. We faced considerable challenges in the field setting for KII from renowned personages such as university professors, psychiatric doctors, and journalists. We sometimes could not reach them even through mobile phone calls.

In this study, all of the in-depth interviews and the questionnaire survey were conducted within the university campus and in classrooms for respondents' convenience, thus providing a calm, quiet and supportive environment. The surveyed students were also provided with food as a motivational factor. External factors regarding motivation were taken into consideration by assessing each participant's broad cognitive processing skills, communication ability, and general mood (Beuscher and Grando, 2009). Respondents were guided by the consultation to gain their trust and overcome any gap in experience. The course teachers of the students were sources that we used to identify motivated students who would be willing to participate in a 40-minute survey and up to two hours for an in-depth interview. To overcome the problem of anonymity, and to avoid refusal of participation in survey data collection, the course teachers of the private university students were approached with the help of networking and referencing. For the field setting, thorough referencing was a valuable tool in qualitative data collection, mostly for the key informant interviews.

REFERENCES

Ackoff, R. (1953). *The Design of Social Research*. Chicago, IL: University of Chicago Press.

Aljomaa, S. S., Al Qudah, M. F., Albursan, I. S., Bakhiet, S. F., and Abduljabbar, A. S. (2016). Smartphone addiction among university students in the light of some variables. *Computers in Human Behavior*, 61, 155–163.
Arefin, S., Islam, R., Mustafi, M. A. A., Afrin, S., and Islam, N. (2017). Impact of smartphone addiction on academic performance of business students: A case study. *Independent Journal of Management and Production*, 8(3), 955–975.
bdnews24 (2017). Mobile phone users in Bangladesh top 140 million. bdnews24.com, 14 November. https://bdnews24.com/business/2017/11/14/mobile-phone-users-in-bangladesh-top-140-million.
Beuscher, L. and Grando, V. T. (2009). Challenges in conducting qualitative research with individuals with dementia. *Research in Gerontological Nursing*, 2(1), 6–11.
Bielefeld, W. (2006). Quantitative research for nonprofit management. *Nonprofit Management & Leadership*, 16(4), 395–409.
Burton, L. and Mazerolle, S. M. (2011). Survey instrument validity part I: Principles of survey instrument development and validation in athletic training education research. *Athletic Training Education Journal*, 6(1), 27–35.
Collins, D. (2003). Pretesting survey instruments: An overview of cognitive methods. *Quality of Life Research*, 12(3), 229–238.
Cunningham, M. R., Roberts, A. R., Barbee, A. P., Druen, P. B., and Wu, C. (1995). Their ideas of beauty are, on the whole, the same as ours: Consistency and variability in the cross-cultural perception of female physical attractiveness. *Journal of Personality and Social Psychology*, 68(2), 261–279.
Dake, K. (1991). Orienting dispositions in the perception of risk analysis of contemporary worldviews and cultural biases. *Journal of Cross-Cultural Psychology*, 22(1), 61–82.
Drew, C. J., Hardman, M. L., and Hosp, J. L. (2008). Ethical issues in conducting research. In C. J. Drew, M. L. Hardman, and J. L. Hosp, *Designing and Conducting Research in Education* (pp. 55–80). Thousand Oaks, CA: Sage.
Etzold, B. and Mallick, B. (2015). Bangladesh: Country profile. https://www.researchgate.net/publication/285371220_Bangladesh_Country_Profile.
Ghauri, P. N. and Grønhaug, K. (2005). *Research Methods in Business Studies: A Practical Guide* (3rd edn.). Harlow: Pearson Education.
GSMA (2018). Country overview: Bangladesh mobile industry driving growth and enabling digital inclusion. https://www.gsma.com/mobilefordevelopment/resources/bangladesh-mobile-industry-driving-growth-and-enabling-digital-inclusion/.
Halder, M., Binder, J., Stiller, J., and Gregson, M. (2016). An overview of the challenges faced during cross-cultural research. *Enquire*, 8, 1–18.
Hasan, M. (2018). 4G: How and why? *The Daily Star*, 20 February.
Holden, R. J., Scott, A. M. M., Hoonakker, P. L., Hundt, A. S., and Carayon, P. (2015). Data collection challenges in community settings: Insights from two field studies of patients with chronic disease. *Quality of Life Research*, 24(5), 1043–1055.
Interactions (n.d.). Social, economic, and political contexts in Bangladesh. http://interactions.eldis.org/node/135.
Jasim, M. M. and Siddiqui, K. (2019). A university in every 5.38 square kilometers. *The Business Standard*, 2 November. https://tbsnews.net/bangladesh/education/university-every-538-square-kilometres.
Johnson, R. B. and Onwuegbuzie, A. J. (2004). Mixed methods research: A research paradigm whose time has come. *Educational Researcher*, 33(7), 14–26.
Kim, D., Lee, Y., Lee, J., Nam, J., and Chung, Y. (2014). Development of Korean smartphone addiction proneness scale for youth. *PLoS ONE*, 9(5), e97920.

Mahmuda, M. (2016). Teaching and learning through technology in Bangladeshi higher education. *International Journal of Scientific & Engineering Research*, 7(4), 257–262.

Malhotra, N. K. and Birks, D. F. (2006). *Marketing Research: An Applied Approach.* Harlow: FT/Prentice Hall.

Maxwell, J. A. (1996). *Qualitative Research Design: An Interactive Approach.* London: Sage.

Nekmahmud, M., Rahman, F. M., Huq, S. M., and Rahman, S. (2017). Generation Y consumer's attitude toward the uses of smartphone in the northern area of Bangladesh. *Australian Academy of Business and Economics Review*, 3(4), 207–223.

Ngwakongnwi, E. (2017). Methodological challenges to collecting valid research data: Researching English language barrier populations in Canada. *Health Science Journal*, 11(3).

O'Leary-Kelly, S. W. and Vokurka, R. J. (1998). The empirical assessment of construct validity. *Journal of Operations Management*, 16(4), 387–405.

Onwuegbuzie, A. J. and Johnson, R. B. (2006). The validity issue in mixed research. *Research in the Schools*, 13(1), 48–63.

Parasuraman, A., Zeithaml, V., and Berry, L. (1988). SERVQUAL: A multiple-item scale for measuring consumer perceptions of service quality. *Journal of Retailing*, 64, 12–40.

Regoli, N. (2019). 18 advantages and disadvantages of purposive sampling. 2 April. https://connectusfund.org/6-advantages-and-disadvantages-of-purposive-sampling.

Rokonuzzaman, M. (2018). Smartphones: From necessity to addiction, *Financial Express*, 31 July. https://thefinancialexpress.com.bd/views/views/smart-phones-from-necessity-to-addiction-1516548688.

Ryan, L. and D'Angelo, A. (2018). Changing times: Migrants' social network analysis and the challenges of longitudinal research. *Social Networks*, 53, 148–158.

Ryan, T., Chester, A., Reece, J., and Xenos, S. (2014). The uses and abuses of Facebook: A review of Facebook addiction. *Journal of Behavioral Addictions*, 3(3), 133–148.

Schmeets, H. (2010). Increasing response rates and the consequences in the Dutch parliamentary election study 2006. *Field Methods*, 22(4), 391–412.

Schmied, E., Jackson, D., and Wilkes, L. (2011). Interviewing people about potentially sensitive topics. *Nurse Researcher*, 19(1), 12–16.

Taherdoost, H. (2016). Sampling methods in research methodology: How to choose a sampling technique for research. *International Journal of Academic Research in Management*, 5(2), 18–27.

Williams, D. (2006). On and off the 'net': Scales for social capital in an online era. *Journal of Computer-Mediated Communication*, 11, 593–628.

11. Undercover fieldwork: a queer experience of healthcare in Bangladesh

Kanamik Kani Khan

RESEARCH CONTEXT

Bangladesh is a South Asian nation and one of the most densely populated countries in the world. In this country, socially conservative values are most dominant in the socio-cultural system (Riaz and Rahman, 2016). Religious values and patriarchal beliefs pertaining to sexuality have created a conservative society where a same-sex relationship is mostly denied by the general public (Ferdoush, 2013). In addition, colonial values have influenced the attitude of the people generating stigma and marginalization for sexual and gender diverse communities in Bangladeshi society (Bondyopadhyay and Ahmed, 2011). Consequently, these communities are frequently deprived of their basic rights, and one of the most prominent of these rights is healthcare. My doctoral research investigates the healthcare experiences of queer communities in Bangladesh and uses healthcare as a lens through which to understand the oppression of sexual and gender diverse communities in a society that privileges men. Historically, sexual and gender diverse communities in Bangladesh have been repressed because of the patriarchal social structure that has existed since at least the Mughal Empire (sixteenth century CE). Further, patriarchy was reinforced by customs, religions, and later by the British regime. Providing equal rights (e.g. healthcare) to marginalized communities would create equality, which challenges the patriarchal system; thus it becomes a human rights issue.

Patriarchy, human rights, healthcare, and sexual and gender diverse communities are the major elements in my research into the socio-cultural structure of Bangladesh. Understanding these facets may help us to look for ways to make a more inclusive society for every group of marginalized people, which is my research aim. For this, I assume that healthcare can be considered as a human right. However, there is no denying that the concept of human rights is substantially criticized in many parts of the world (Brown, 1997). The nature and context of human rights may vary in different regions and contexts (Mutua, 2002; Preis, 1996). Nevertheless, according to the Universal Declaration of Human Rights (UDHR), every individual should have the right to proper health, medical healthcare, and well-being (Global Citizenship Commission, 2016). Therefore, I plan to analyse the data and reflect my discussion through a human rights-based framework in order to investigate the deeply rooted issues of patriarchy embedded in Bangladeshi society. To investigate this research issue, I was able to collect data throughout an engaging fieldwork journey. I have an amazing fieldwork journey to share, with issues that I faced and valuable strategies that I followed to deal with them.

FIELDWORK CHALLENGES

There were different kinds of challenges I experienced during my fieldwork. There were also issues that I faced while communicating and negotiating with the organizations who work with sexual and gender diverse populations in Bangladesh. All these fieldwork challenges and issues associated with my fieldwork are discussed below.

Fear of Violence

Sexual and gender diverse communities are frequently threatened with violence and assassination in Bangladesh (Human Rights Watch, 2017). In sensitive research like this, there are potential threats for both me as a researcher and the potential participants. The ethics committee of Massey University was mostly concerned about this safety issue. The reason for this is that two LGBT[1] activists (Xulhaz Mannan and Mahbub Rabbi) were killed in 2016, and a few academics and bloggers have been attacked and threatened due to their efforts working for the rights of these marginalized people (Human Rights Watch, 2017; Sanzum, 2017). The threat of violence is one of the major fears that has made these communities virtually invisible in Bangladeshi society. Hence, working with them invisibly made my fieldwork journey an undercover research experience. Additionally, when I went to Bangladesh and met Ostitto[2] in person, they suggested that spreading a flyer or leaflet publicly for participant recruitment could put us at great risk, even though there were no identifiable details given in the flyer. It was mostly anonymous and contained only an anonymous email account for contact purposes that was created solely for participant recruitment. Nonetheless, I ended up not using the flyer because of the safety issue and fear of violence.

Unplanned Situations

Working as a volunteer in qualitative research is not very conventional from a theoretical point of view. I therefore had to challenge the orthodoxy of qualitative research methods at every stage of the fieldwork. In other words, some of my data collection process was somewhat serendipitous rather than planned. I have to confess that sometimes I had to push the boundaries of safety plans. For example, I was planning to conduct all the interviews in the offices of Bijito[3] to ensure safety and confidentiality. Yet, for one key informant interview (KII), I was invited to the informant's office. Despite the office being located in an urban area, it was a quiet place and I was slightly concerned about getting there. This was not part of my plan and I was not completely ready to do this. Nevertheless, I had to return the trust that the participants showed in me; thus I went to places other than Bijito's offices to conduct interviews.

For another interview, I had to travel a long way to get to the participant's residence. Since I trusted my key informant who had referred me to this participant, I decided to go to her residence as she was not willing to meet anywhere else. The place where she lived was one of the most densely populated areas and she lived in a house that I could not even locate myself, although I lived in this city. It was very nice of her to meet me on the main road and walk me to her place. We had to walk very far in an area that was densely populated and did not seem very hygienic and clean. Eventually, everything went well. I was a little nervous at the beginning of the session because I was in a place where I did not feel very safe at first. This is because it was a very small room with no windows and not enough light. It was very warm and I was sweating, as I had had to walk far. It took me about 10–15 minutes to feel at ease and I admitted to her that I was a little bit nervous. At the end of this session, I could not find my way back and I got lost twice trying to find the route to the main road.

Epistemological Differences

Since I am a heterosexual man, my worldview was likely be different from that of the participants. The reason for this is that I belong to a patriarchal society that suppresses sexual and gender diverse populations, and I do not have to live with the fear that they experience every moment due to their sexual and gender orientation. Thus, it is undeniable that even though we share the same cultural background, there could be differences in how we look at life and how a patriarchal society treats us. This is also important because my research methodology is phenomenological and I wanted to try and understand how the participants perceive healthcare and human rights rather than how I perceive these issues. To do so, I had to try and understand their worldviews. I have frequently been asked the same question in proposal defence and other seminar presentations regarding how I would deal with such epistemological differences.

Difficulty in Recruiting Participants

I was struggling to recruit participants for interviews because many gender and sexually diverse people do not disclose their orientations to healthcare professionals (Singh and Durso, 2017), consequently they are less likely to experience any sort of adverse reaction. Even if there were some healthcare experiences that they would like to share, they were often reluctant to come forward and share their experiences with me. Therefore, finding potential participants who interacted with the healthcare system was not an easy task. Furthermore, I struggled to find a healthcare professional to talk to because many may have misunderstood that my research was going to defame healthcare professionals.

Lack of Communication

After an interview, I accidentally found out that one participant worked as a sex worker but she had not revealed that to me, and it was none of my business. Eventually, I realized why people were staring at me strangely when I was walking behind her to go to her residence to conduct the interview. Perhaps she had thought, at first, that I was a customer who had contacted her in a different way. However, once we had talked for a few minutes about my research, she realized I was actually there for data collection. I am stating this because her attitude was a little different at the beginning and it changed once we started to talk about my research. I might be wrong too, who knows! It seemed that no matter how much rapport I built with the participants, in some cases, there was still a slight lack of interaction or communication.

Confidential Documents

There was a concern about photocopying the information sheet, interview schedule, and consent form. I did try to make enough copies in New Zealand but I still needed some more. Hence, I had to make some photocopies of these documents at a printing shop in Bangladesh. I was concerned that if some of those confidential documents got memory-saved in the photocopy machine and were leaked, they might fall into the hands of people who could target me. It was perhaps an over-anxious thought but I could not help it or do much about it. In addition to that, there were spare documents or papers left after finishing my fieldwork. These documents were mostly information sheets and consent forms where my name was visible. As a result, I was worried about securing these confidential documents.

Interpersonal Challenges as a Researcher

As a researcher, I had to go through different emotional and psychological barriers throughout my data collection period. Firstly, I had never involved myself with gender and sexually diverse communities in Bangladesh before my fieldwork. Hence, I was a little anxious about how they would treat me, as I am not a sexually diverse person. However, once I met them in person, I did not feel any different at all because of their way of accepting me as a researcher or volunteer to learn about their life. Secondly, being empathetic as an interviewer was a challenging role because in one situation a participant started crying while sharing their experiences; I sometimes became wordless and could not say anything. As the interview went on, I expressed to them the empathy I felt. Another participant thought that they were a curse to their family, and they could not stop crying. Despite my attempts at consolation, I admit that at some point I was failing to maintain eye contact. It was just too much to take in. After this interview, I was depressed all day; I could not stop thinking about them and it was hard for me to get through. Regarding this, I was asked in one conference whether I received any post-fieldwork mental health services. Unfortunately, there are hardly any mental health measures available in Bangladesh. Moreover, while listening to the audio recording and transcribing the words of the same participant, I felt very emotional again. This might be defined as controlled emotion when a social worker or a service provider is sensitive to the client's feelings (Weilenmann et al., 2018). This was one of my experiences in understanding the meaning of what my interviewees go through in their lives. Having an appropriate and purposeful use of emotional response to the feelings of the participants was effective learning for me. I believe that my fieldwork was an emotional journey and it shaped me to become an emotionally competent researcher. There was also a personal limitation. It is fair to say that I was quite a new interviewer and I needed a lot of nerve to listen to the participants' experiences. In the very first interview, I felt a little nervous, but I just did not know why. I was constantly sweating and it was creating a bad impression.

Transportation Problems

I experienced transportation problems during my fieldwork; finding transportation to get to the interview location was an issue on several occasions. For instance, once I could not get transport while going to an interview session as it was raining heavily. Thus, I was delayed in arriving at the interview location and starting the session. Similarly, a focus group discussion (FGD) was scheduled on the day before the national election of Bangladesh. Consequently, the government had shut down internet services for security purposes which precluded the use of Uber and other internet-based transport services. As a result, I had to struggle to get to the FGD location. Moreover, another interview was scheduled on a public holiday, thus transportation was limited and most shops and restaurants were closed. I met the participant on the street and we had to walk for about 30 minutes to find a fast food shop that was open. I felt very sorry for making them walk because it was very hot and humid that day and I later found out that they had back pain issues. I felt terrible after learning that and I apologized to them.

Interview Location Problem

Conducting the interviews in a suitable location to ensure a private and confidential conversation was another challenge. The reason why I was unable to conduct most interviews at the participants' residence is that the families of the participants are often unaware of their sexual and gender orientation, thus it was better for them to talk in a place where they would feel safe. For one interview, Bijito was unable to provide me with a separate room. There was not much time for the participant and me to get to know each other, and we had to start the session immediately. We were sitting at an office desk with other people. It was not the best place because we needed the maximum degree of privacy, whereas we had none there. We did not have much space for rapport building because of the limitations of space and time as the Bijito office was about to close at 5 p.m. and I had to rush to conduct two interviews in a couple of hours. To clarify, I am not criticizing Bijito because what they did for me was voluntary. I am more than grateful to them for letting me use their offices and separate rooms for most of the interview sessions as this was extremely useful to deal with privacy and safety concerns.

Other Challenges

There were other barriers in terms of the actual conduct of the interview. Firstly, the selection of language or word choice was not very easy during the session. It was quite a challenging task to let them talk about an extremely sensitive subject (sexuality) with a person whom they had met just once. Secondly, I was unable to identify an authority to provide ethical approval from Bangladesh because there is no such institutional body who provides ethical approval for academic studies in Bangladesh (Islam and Hajar, 2013). Thirdly, to dispose of spare confidential documents, I first decided to throw them in the rubbish bin but I thought it was better to destroy them permanently.

I took all the spare documents to the rooftop of my building and burned them. Lastly, there was an anonymity issue that I experienced during my fieldwork. As a volunteer of Ostitto, I was anonymously writing articles or essays on their blogs for awareness-building. Therefore, I had to log in to their blog website from my laptop and my home IP address.[4] Since I was determined to ensure a maximum level of safety measures in my fieldwork, I was slightly worried that someone might try to trace me as the author of this blog by tracing my IP address.

STRATEGIES TO OVERCOME THE CHALLENGES

The strategies to deal with fieldwork challenges were multifarious. Some of the strategies were planned and some were spontaneous. The assistance and guidance from my supervisors, Ostitto, and Bijito were extremely helpful to implement these strategies. Moreover, in a few cases, the participants helped me to overcome the challenges that I faced during interview sessions.

Fieldwork Preparations: Rapport Building and Gaining Trust

I started my communication and negotiation with Ostitto from the very beginning of my PhD, which was a part of my fieldwork preparation. I knew that my fieldwork was going to be challenging, and my communication had started five months before I started my actual fieldwork. I contacted two organizations (Ostitto and Bijito) who work with these communities in Bangladesh. I contacted them online by using email communication. I assumed that they would not trust me at first. As expected, Ostitto felt cynical about me and kept on contacting me for a month or so. I told them my real name and my personal information thereby allowing them to look for my details in Bangladesh and verify that I was a real person. This was necessary for them because, interestingly enough, my name is unique and peculiar in the Bangladeshi context and I would have been a little surprised if anyone thought I had a fake name, or even wondered whether I was male or female. This confusion actually happened: when I sent a message to Ostitto's social media page, they apparently thought that my social media account was fake just because of my name and they did not reply for a week. Then, I had to explain in the email communication that it was not fake and my real name is a little unusual. Subsequently, once they verified my information in Bangladesh, they started to trust me. It took them about a month and, finally, they asked me to show my face on a video call as a sign of further proof. I was happy to show my face, as I knew that we were building trust patiently and strongly, although I was not able to see their faces, which was completely understandable. Then we started to talk over the phone and our trust and faith improved gradually. At that point, they also accepted my request to work as a volunteer for them when I went to Bangladesh for my fieldwork.

Safety Measures

The reason I title my fieldwork as undercover is that I was mostly working with sexual and gender minorities secretly. I was not allowed to talk about the events and seminars that I attended for community involvement and building networks because most of their activities were not exposed to either media or public. For instance, I was not allowed to take photos or upload photos of the event on social media, or check-in on social media about events. I approved of these kinds of security measures to ensure the safety of both myself and the participants. Additionally, as a part of Massey University's ethical approval and safety plan, I was asked by the ethics committee to file a general diary[5] with a trusted police officer in Bangladesh so that I could get help in case of an emergency. During my fieldwork, I discussed my project with a friend – one of the closest friends I have ever had – who happened to be a police officer. I discussed my research with him along with the safety issue, and the requirement of the ethics committee to file a general diary with a trusted police officer. This diary was a part of the safety plan, and a way of keeping the trusted police friend informed about the sensitivity of my research. This was a requirement because, in case of any emergency relating to my research, I could call my police friend for help. I also explained about the sensitivity and privacy of my general diary to him. He advised me not to be anxious and asked me to call him any time I needed assistance in case of any emergency. In this general diary, no organizational identity or participant details were given; it was assured that everything was anonymous.

Measures for Participant Recruitment

I took advantage of chain referrals by participants, which is often found to be a helpful way of accessing and recruiting hidden participants who are vulnerable and 'hard to reach' (Ellard-Gray et al., 2015). Due to this referral, one of the key informants of my fieldwork put me in touch with a few potential participants. While struggling to find a healthcare provider to talk to, a friend of mine set up a meeting for me with a physician. It was very difficult to arrange a time for this physician to talk with me as she was very busy. A referral from my trustworthy friend was useful in this case of participant recruitment. Furthermore, Ostitto and Bijito used word-of-mouth communication approaches amid their networks to help me recruit participants. Word-of-mouth communication is found to be an essential way to reach out to participants who are 'hard to reach' and mostly hidden in our society (e.g. Ellard-Gray et al., 2015).

Volunteering

Working as a volunteer for community involvement was arguably a step beyond the orthodoxy of qualitative research methods. This is because a researcher working as a volunteer is often more common in ethnographic studies (e.g. Garthwaite, 2016; O'Farrell, 2010). Although my research is not ethnographic, I was still willing to work as a volunteer. The reason for this is that the participants are highly stigmatized, threatened, and hidden. Therefore, I planned to get involved with these hidden communities by volunteering. Most qualitative and/or non-ethnographic researchers may not be required to work as a volunteer because participants might not be as hidden as the sexual and gender diverse population in Bangladesh. After I was accepted as a volunteer of Ostitto and had negotiated with them, it was relatively easier to become trusted and involved with the community. Volunteering with Ostitto also helped me to increase my networking and recruit participants. As a volunteer of Ostitto, I performed different tasks, such as assistant accountant, volunteer coordinator, arranging seminars and events, giving a part of the presentation for a fund-raising campaign, voice dubbing for awareness building video campaigns, and Bengali to English translation of flashcards for awareness-building purposes. The outcome of volunteering was effective in terms of network building and participant recruitment (e.g. O'Farrell, 2010). For example, I met an intersex[6] person while volunteering for an event for Ostitto who showed interest in talking with me. This was very important for my data collection because it was the first time I had met an intersex individual who was willing to talk about healthcare experiences. I stayed in touch with them for a couple of months, and finally, we did the interview.

Dealing with Epistemological Differences

There was another purpose of volunteering, which was knowledge transfer with these communities (Akingbola et al., 2013) while I was trying to learn about their worldviews by understanding their experiences, beliefs, and philosophies. Getting involved with sexual and gender diverse communities made me feel like I was no longer an outsider and I felt like I was one of them. Gradually, this helped me to deal with the epistemological differences between me and the participants. Articulating an incident of safety anxiety helps to clarify what I mean by dealing with epistemological differences. While returning after an interview, I felt that I was being followed by someone and I became scared that it might be a terrorist or extremist who had been following me for days to attack me. Reports I had read about the killings and attacks on people who were supportive of sexual and gender minorities (Human Rights Watch, 2017; Sanzum, 2017) made me anxious and nervous. Eventually, this person did nothing and we separated on another street. However, it was a 'cold feet' experience for me. Perhaps this experience had nothing to do with my research and its safety issues. However, I was very scared at that moment when I felt someone was following me. It was one of the days that I will never forget; I was being tested for my patience, courage, and above all, my determination.

The reason for sharing this incident is to explain that the kind of fear I experienced that day is the same fear the participants experienced every day of their lives. This was the moment I caught a glimpse of the fear that they had been living with throughout their lives. Thus, I working alongside them made me realize to some extent what it is like to be a sexual and gender diverse person in Bangladesh. I would like to believe that it partly, although not completely, helped me overcome the epistemological difference. Overall, I was not very open about my research topic with the people around me because I was not sure what others would think about it. Being discreet about my research was similar to the way the participants would hide their orientations from their family, friends, and society. This secretive stance was another aspect that I had in common with the participants, and it made me realize how invisible and hidden they have to be in every sphere of life. This understanding was an additional insight to bridge the gap between our epistemologies.

Safe Location and Audio Recording

As per Massey University's ethics committee, Bijito's offices were considered as safe locations to conduct the interviews. While I also let the participants choose the location they generally were happy to do the interviews at Bijito's offices. Most of the interviews were conducted in a separate room at Bijito's offices. However, I had to conduct one interview in the meeting room where other employees were gathering for an official meeting that was about to start. They were talking and our session was interrupted a little, but we managed to finish the interview successfully. To deal with this, I used a double audio recording; one with my audio recorder and another with my Android device. In fact, I did a double audio recording in all of my sessions so that I would always have backup audio in case something went wrong with one device.

Ensuring Anonymity

To ensure anonymity while writing blogs for sexual and gender diverse communities, I used TOR Browser[7] every time I had to log in to the blog website. This browser was supposed to prevent me from being traced because it allowed me to use a different IP address with a different location (mostly abroad). Some would argue about how ethical it was to use TOR Browser as it is mostly used by online hackers on the dark web. The only justification I can give is that I had to use TOR to make sure that my volunteering with Ostitto did not put me or the participants in danger.

Research Ethics

Despite being unable to get ethical approval from Bangladesh, I had full ethical approval from Massey University to conduct this research. Additionally, Islam and Banda (2011) suggest that perhaps there might not be any strict or universal ethical standards required when conducting research as the contexts of people's culture in certain places and time need to be taken into consideration while following ethical guidelines. Similarly, my PhD fieldwork was in keeping with the ethical standards committee of Massey University which particularly emphasized respecting the culture of my target population and their (sexual and gender diverse) communities.

Respect to the Participants

I was given training from my supervisor and Bijito about how to talk in interview sessions, and what language or terms to use so that respect to the participants could be ensured. It was also emphasized in my training to be meticulous in word selection to ensure that the participants did not feel segregated from society. For example, terms like 'people from our community' and 'sexually diverse individuals like us' were emphasized instead of using terms like 'people from your community', and 'sexually diverse individuals like you' respectively.

Strategies to Ensure Comfort Zone

It was my responsibility to make the participants feel comfortable, trusting, and friendly so that they could open up and share their experiences. The strategies I followed to achieve this could not be planned in advance because they were mostly accidental and I needed to assess the situation quickly and find ways to create the comfort zone. Creating a comfort zone may refer to an environment of emotional safety (Edmondson and Lei, 2014). I mention below some of my strategies or experiences as examples of how I tried to manage this issue.

- One session was probably the best interview I had because to create a comfort zone with the participant we engaged in intimate conversation. I let her ask questions first, and she tested how comfortable I was with her to share intimate information about myself. I was very much open to answering anything she asked and thus we had a great conversation at the end. While creating a comfort zone between us, sometimes I had to go beyond my comfort zone by sharing intimate information. Going beyond one's comfort zone is often essential for qualitative researchers to think and understand the research issue thoroughly (Cassell, 2018).

- I noticed a rubber bracelet on one participant's hand that had a logo of one of my favourite metal bands. I asked them whether they liked the band and, of course, they did, or else why would they have it on their hand! However, I asked this question to create a distraction with an off-topic conversation to subconsciously inform the participant that it was not a formal session. We talked more about this band and, subsequently, it broke the ice and we started to flow more easily toward a comfortable discussion. However, conducting an informal interview may imply unstructured interviews (Adhabi and Anozie, 2017), but I employed semi-structured interview guidelines in my fieldwork which shows another unconventional aspect of qualitative research methods. Despite using a semi-structured interview structure, I needed to ensure an informal session with the participants due to the nature and sensitivity of the research issue.
- In FGD, we had a one-dish lunch party. After having some food, we started the discussion and it was good from my point of view because food always connects people in my culture. Since I share the same cultural background as the participants, it is a privilege to have this cultural awareness, which tends to ensure effective fieldwork and data collection experience in research (Kaihlanen et al., 2019).
- One participant asked about my personal life and once they noticed I was willing to disclose things about myself, the trust started to build up. Sometimes, sharing personal information is helpful to build rapport leading to trust and a good relationship between researcher and participant (Bell et al., 2019). However, these personal conversations were off the record, mostly not audio-recorded, and even if they were, I later removed them from the transcripts.
- One participant had a nickname that is similar to what my mother used to call me when I was a child. I hardly ever share that information with others. However, I did not shy away from saying that to her and we started to call each other 'mita', which is a Bangla word referring to the person who has the same name as yours. Thus, we became friendlier and gradually we could create a comfort zone between us.
- In some cases, the participants also helped me. For instance, when I was nervous in the very first interview, the participant noticed it and helped me to relax. It was very kind of him. Then I took some long breaths, and everything started to become normal. On another occasion, the participant

noticed my anxiety and nervousness, and then she started to talk about personal life, study, and work-life, which helped us to build up a good conversation.

Self-Reflexivity and Feedback Strategy

Safety anxieties in my fieldwork made me realize that 'perfection' was a vague term in my fieldwork journey because I kept on learning throughout the process. The most important aspect was to be honest, and vulnerable to different situations in the fieldwork to obtain self-reflexivity that tends to shape transparency and credibility of the methodology (Tracy, 2010). Thus, I rejected the conventional approach to conducting interviews by improvising my skills. For instance, I was prepared to answer any questions that participants asked so that it could become a knowledge-sharing session where nobody took the lead in thc discussion. It was mostly participatory where nobody felt forced to speak; it was more like a free-flowing and open conversation that people would have in a coffee shop. Additionally, as a naive researcher, I acknowledged to the participants that I might have limitations. Because one does not always recognize one's limitations, I collected feedback from the participants after each interview. Usually, qualitative researchers collect feedback to perform member checks, such as reviewing the transcripts by the participants to enhance data credibility (Thomas, 2017). However, my approach to getting feedback was not member checks or reviewing transcripts in the way many other qualitative researchers do (e.g. Kornbluh, 2015; Lo, 2014) because I was trying to get feedback about the interview session to improve my interviewing skills. As planned, this feedback was supposed to identify my limitations and help me to improve my interviewing skills in the following session. The feedback was mixed; both negative and positive, and I will quote some of the responses:

- "I felt happy to talk about my life and sexual orientation because I hardly get people around who are willing to listen to me".
- "You may want to read some more sources about the origin of the sexual and gender diverse population".
- "I felt very comfortable talking; felt like a regular conversation rather than a boring formal interview. There was no hesitation in him while asking sensitive questions".
- "You were shy, local Bangla accent could be avoided to make your statement much clearer".
- "You were rushing; it would have been better if you had a list of questions. It is better to start with childhood experiences to understand a person better".

- "He was shy and nervous at first but it went away soon; he was successful to ensure the comfort zone to talk freely".

NOTES

1. LGBT: this term refers to queer communities such as lesbian, gay, bisexual, and transmen.
2. Ostitto: the organization that helped me in community involvement and participant recruitment. For safety precautions, the name is kept anonymous by using a pseudonym because their work is not publicly exposed. Ostitto is a Bangla word that means *existence.*
3. Bijito: another organization that helped me in participant recruitment. For safety precautions, the name is kept anonymous by using a pseudonym because their work is not publicly exposed. Bijito is a Bangla word that means *winner.*
4. IP address: a unique string of numbers separated by full stops that identifies each computer using the Internet Protocol to communicate over a network.
5. General diary (GD): an entry or a daily diary entry made when any kind of complaint or anticipated incident is reported and the police enter the details in their records.
6. Intersex: refers to a variety of situations in which an individual is born with a sexual or reproductive anatomy that does not fit the conventional orientation of male or female.
7. TOR Browser: a free and open-source software to enable anonymous communication.

REFERENCES

Adhabi, E. and Anozie, C. B. (2017). Literature review for the type of interview in qualitative research. *International Journal of Education*, 9(3), 86–97.

Akingbola, K., Duguid, F. and Viveros, M. (2013). Learning and knowledge transfer in volunteering: Exploring the experience of Red Cross volunteers. In F. Duguid, K. Mündel and D. Schugurensky (eds.), *Volunteer Work, Informal Learning and Social Action* (pp. 63–78). Rotterdam: Sense Publishers.

Bell, K., Fahmy, E. and Gordon, D. (2019). Quantitative conversations: The importance of developing rapport in standardised interviewing. *Quality & Quantity*, 50(1), 193–212.

Bondyopadhyay, A., and Ahmed, S. (2011). *Same-Sex Love in a Difficult Climate: A Study into the Life Situation of Sexual Minority (Lesbian, Gay, Bisexual, Kothi and Transgender) Persons in Bangladesh.* Dhaka, Bangladesh: Bandhu Social Welfare Society.

Brown, C. (1997). Universal human rights: A critique. *The International Journal of Human Rights*, 1(2), 41–65.

Cassell, C. (2018). "Pushed beyond my comfort zone": MBA student experiences of conducting qualitative research. *Academy of Management Learning & Education*, 17(2), 119–136.

Edmondson, A. C. and Lei, Z. (2014). Psychological safety: The history, renaissance, and future of an interpersonal construct. *Annual Review of Organizational Psychology and Organizational Behavior*, 1, 23–43.

Ellard-Gray, A., Jeffrey, N. K., Choubak, M. and Crann, S. E. (2015). Finding the hidden participant: Solutions for recruiting hidden, hard-to-reach, and vulnerable populations. *International Journal of Qualitative Methods*, 14(5), 1–10.

Ferdoush, M. A. (2013). Living with stigma and managing sexual identity: A case study on the Kotis in Dhaka. *Sociology Mind*, 3(4), 257–263.

Garthwaite, K. (2016). The perfect fit? Being both volunteer and ethnographer in a UK foodbank. *Journal of Organizational Ethnography*, 5(1), 60–71.

Global Citizenship Commission (2016). *The Universal Declaration of Human Rights in the 21st Century: A Living Document in a Changing World.* Cambridge: Open Book Publishers.

Human Rights Watch (2017). *Human Rights Watch Country Profiles: Sexual Orientation and Gender Identity.* https://www.hrw.org/news/2017/06/23/human-rights-watch-country-profiles-sexual-orientation-and-gender-identity.

Islam, M. R. and Banda, D. (2011). Cross-cultural social research with indigenous knowledge (IK): Some dilemmas and lessons. *Journal of Social Research and Policy*, 2(1), 67–82.

Islam, M. R. and Hajar, A. B. S. (2013). Methodological challenges on community safe motherhood: A case study on community level health monitoring and advocacy programme in Bangladesh. *Review of Research and Social Intervention*, 42, 101–119.

Kaihlanen, A. M., Hietapakka, L. and Heponiemi, T. (2019). Increasing cultural awareness: Qualitative study of nurses' perceptions about cultural competence training. *BMC Nursing*, 18(38), 1–9.

Kornbluh, M. (2015). Combatting challenges to establishing trustworthiness in qualitative research. *Qualitative Research in Psychology*, 12(4), 397–414.

Lo, C. O. (2014). Enhancing groundedness in realist grounded theory research. *Qualitative Psychology*, 1(1), 61–76.

Mutua, M. (2002). *Human Rights: A Political and Cultural Critique.* Philadelphia: University of Pennsylvania Press.

O'Farrell, J. (2010). The volunteering self: Ethnographic reflections on "the field". Master's thesis, University of Waterloo.

Preis, A. B. S. (1996). Human rights as cultural practice: An anthropological critique. *Human Rights Quarterly*, 18(2), 286–315.

Riaz, A. and Rahman, M. S. (eds.) (2016). *Routledge Handbook of Contemporary Bangladesh.* New York: Routledge.

Sanzum, T. (2017). A deliberate attempt to silence the LGBT community in Bangladesh. *Huffington Post*, 19 May. https://www.huffingtonpost.com/entry/a-deliberate-attempt-to-silence-the-lgbt-community-in-bangladesh_us_591f6b5ee4b094cdba542a3f.

Singh, S. and Durso, L. E. (2017). Widespread discrimination continues to shape LGBT people's lives in both subtle and significant ways. Center for American Progress, 2 May.

Thomas, D. R. (2017). Feedback from research participants: Are member checks useful in qualitative research? *Qualitative Research in Psychology*, 14(1), 23–41.

Tracy, S. J. (2010). Qualitative quality: Eight "big-tent" criteria for excellent qualitative research. *Qualitative Inquiry*, 16(10), 837–851.

Weilenmann, S., Schnyder, U., Parkinson, B., Corda, C., Von Kaenel, R. and Pfaltz, M. C. (2018). Emotion transfer, emotion regulation, and empathy-related processes in physician–patient interactions and their association with physician well-being: A theoretical model. *Frontiers in Psychiatry*, 9(389), 1–18.

12. Ethical issues, challenges and solutions during fieldwork with homeless elderly people of Malaysia and Pakistan

Aqsa Qandeel and Welyne J. Jehom

STUDY CONTEXT

The purpose of the study was to assess the applicability of Goffman's theory of the total institution (1961) in a real-life setting. Goffman claimed that the personality of individuals within a total institution (boundary walls with rules and regulations) changes through a process of resocialization after spending some time there. The process of data collection was conducted within institutions in Pakistan and Malaysia. The study found that resocialization happened through a process of depersonalization of a person's self and individual traits. The research involved a comparison between the residential patterns of old-aged people that are destitute, with and without boundary walls and institutional settings. In this sense, it is an extension as well as critical analysis of Goffman's theory. The fieldwork focused on the social setting of street life, where the individuals were living in an open environment under a no-restriction strategy. The nature of the social setting was also different for both countries, due to different state systems, geographical conditions, and political factors in the extent to which each country tries to rehabilitate and reform the destitute people. The comparative context made the study very challenging, involving a comparison of responses of destitute people, within total institutions and with non-institutional respondents, and checking the variations and differences. This chapter discusses the research challenges that were encountered during the field visits to collect data from older people from different backgrounds who are destitute. Figure 12.1 shows the challenges encountered during fieldwork in Malaysia and Pakistan. These challenges are further described in the next section.

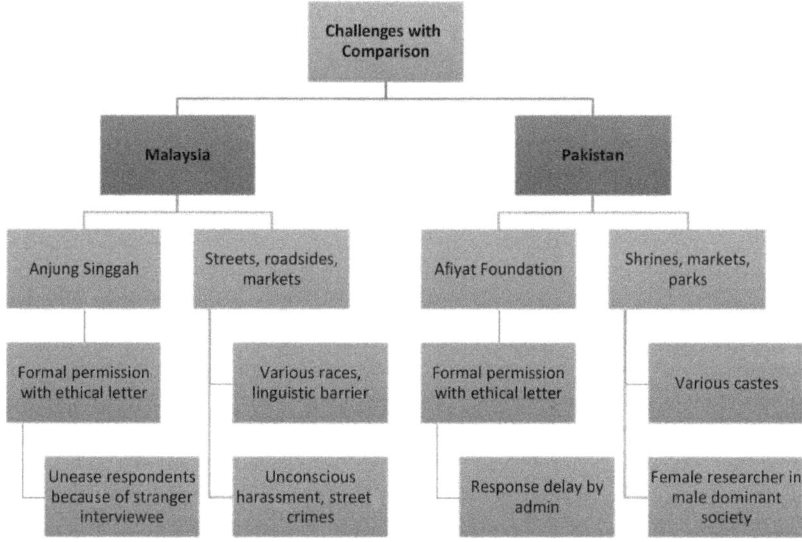

Figure 12.1 Challenges encountered in comparative fieldwork

CHALLENGES DURING FIELD VISITS

Ethical Approval

At the very first stage, getting ethical permission to pursue the research was itself a challenge, in terms of clarification and justification of the questions being asked in the application form. As a new researcher at a new institution, it was a challenge to understand the actual requirements of the institution. The ethical form with required documents were submitted to get the permission for data collection. Initially, this did not meet some of the required criteria of the university above satisfactory level. As a result, it took a long time to clarify the process of data collection for the university's ethical committee to gain approval. With the assistance of the professional administrative staff of the committee, I finally received the research ethics letter to pursue fieldwork through interviews at the institutions for old-aged people specified in the research proposal.

Ethical Letter and Permission Issue in an Institutional Setting

Formal ethical letter issuance was the first step to get into the field, to follow further steps of data collection. Firstly, I went back to Pakistan to collect data, because it was easier to interview local people than those overseas, owing to my familiarity with the local culture and psyche of elderly people there. Moreover, it is better to proceed from easier to more difficult situations, like following bottom-up approaches to collect data. This strategy helped to build my confidence to conduct the study in a different culture (Malaysia). I first approached the old-aged institution in Multan, Pakistan, that supports homeless old-aged people who have no family to look after them. The first challenge was to meet the head of the institution, as the officers did not respond to the very first request, due to a busy schedule as well as to show authoritative behaviour. The meeting was fixed after waiting for over five or six hours. However, the head of the institution (HOI) did not let me interview the elderly, despite the clarification of my purpose and arriving from another city. She made the excuse of having to prepare the old-aged people for dinner with some political personality. As I left the HOI's office, her assistant informed me that I could visit the institution. I told him what the HOI had said about this not being possible at this moment. Surprisingly, the assistant said that I could start the interviews because there were helpers dealing with the elderly residents. However, I preferred to follow the instructions of the HOI to avoid any problems. So, I decided to check the other sites to find elderly people to interview.

The next day, as promised by the HOI of the care home, I reached the institution early morning, and my introduction to the elderly residents began well. There was a campaign about dengue fever awareness and precaution, and the assistant presented me as the chief guest of the event in the presence of all the older people of the institution. They all were looking happy and warmly welcomed me. Interestingly, one of them was a poet and read some pieces of poetry in honour of the chief guests. After the event, the senior citizens went back to their rooms, and the assistant helped me to visit the institutional building and services provided to the elderly people. After the completion of the visit, I started interviews with elderly citizens by accessing their rooms, one by one. Fourteen elderly persons were there to talk with, these included males and females. My husband assisted me in talking to elderly males, to help them feel more comfortable.

Tracing the Destitute Elderly in Pakistan and Malaysia

The tracing of homeless elderly living in public places was the first challenge. The first target area for interviewing older adults was Pakistan, and I had already visited the old-age institution. On the same day of visiting the institute for the homeless elderly, I went to the shrine of Saint Hazrat Bahaudinn Zakariya Multani (R.A.), where many people were residing after being made homeless, of varying age groups, as I had discovered by carrying out a survey a month before this visit. As I got there, there was not a single destitute person who had been living there for a long time. When I asked a security guard about the reason for such quietness at the shrine, he told me that the government had passed and implemented some legislation and acts for the rehabilitation and prevention of homelessness by establishing the temporary shelters at different places.

There was also a restriction on homeless people sleeping in public places to avoid crimes. In those days, the new government of Imran Khan was enacting reform schemes for the betterment of homeless people. So, it was challenging to track the destitute elderly at such places, but I did not lose hope and moved on to the next place. Here, the condition was the same as the first, and the policeman on duty told me that a lot of homeless and beggars come at the time of Langar (free food) distribution and then vanish again. The police and security did not allow them to place their luggage and mattress there, to reside permanently. Some local people of Multan told us about the living places of such elderly destitute. Some of them mentioned Madani Park, Shah Shamas Park and Shah Shamas Shrine, and some marketplaces. By following these suggestions, I went in search of vagrant elderly people but could not trace them. There was a probability of their availability at night, as during the day they might be busy at some labour work or begging.

I visited Multan during the daytime, and the probability of finding the road-side homeless elderly was only high at night. Then I decided to find a target population at my hometown, Vehari, and surrounding areas, where there were chances of finding homeless people. With the help and discussion with family, a team of four members tried to trace the targeted population in the neighbourhood areas of the city. I also visited nearby villages and small shrines, where temporary residences of nomads were common. At one place, there were just two relevant respondents, and then I needed to move to the next destination. Some visited places did not contain any vagrant elderly, and at some places where they were present, the elderly persons started telling their life stories; while these were not related to the study, from an ethical standpoint I still felt I had to listen to them. Then I visited three small shrines, where I expected to meet destitute people, but unfortunately, I did not find any relevant case. At some places, I discovered many people that seemed to be destitute, but they were out of their minds because of drug addiction. Since I was the only female with the team, the rest of the team members did not consider these places were safe, even for observation. I therefore left these areas. The next day, with my cousin and husband, I then decided to go to the shrine of Haji Sher (R.A.) at a village 45 miles away from Vehari city. We reached there early in the morning, but it took time to trace homeless elderly. There were many older people around who had come to recover from various illnesses, especially psychological disorder, madness trauma, and medically incurable diseases.

Interestingly, the local people believe that, at the shrine of Haji Sher (R.A.), people with incurable diseases and those who are psychologically disturbed can be cured by being bound by chains at their hands, feet, and neck, at a specified place near the shrine. As the person recovers from disease, the chains automatically break down by the spiritual effect of Baba Haji Sher (R.A.). So, I saw various people bound with chains, waiting for their recovery, but it was more difficult to find homeless people relevant to my study.

The tracing of relevant respondents is always a challenge, but becomes more so when the area is not familiar to the researcher. My visit to Malaysia was my first ever experience of living in a foreign country. The values, lifestyle, places, and ethics were different from my hometown. Despite that, I decided to carry out research in Malaysia and I started searching the destitute for older adults in Kuala Lumpur, Malaysia, to compare the data with Pakistan. For this purpose, I needed two types of destitute old-aged people; the first type was homeless people living on streets or at marketplaces, and the second category was homeless people living in institutions for the elderly.

In Malaysia, I searched the institutions for old-aged people and found some names on the internet at Petaling Jaya. I visited this nursing home and talked to the owner about interviewing the old-aged people. The owner replied politely that such institutions were not to support the elderly destitute, but nursing homes where the old-aged people or their families were paying for their care and protection. By searching again in different areas of Kuala Lumpur, I found relevant institutes near Masjid Jamek and Titiwangsa, where these institutes were supporting the vagrant people under ministry or NGO establishment. Furthermore, there were many places where destitute older adults were living without any shelter, including Pasar Seni, Bukit Bintang, Ampang Jaya, around KLCC, Chowkit and Masjid India. There were different age categories of people living a life of destitution on streets and roadsides. The next step was to talk to these older people and get their consent for the interviews.

Variance in Living Situations and Circumstantial Differences within Two Countries

The field experience in two cultures is exciting as well as challenging. As a researcher, I have experience in dealing with elderly destitute in Pakistan, but did not know about the people of Malaysia. As I found destitute people in Malaysia, the first task was a thorough and deep observation of their lifestyle. In Pakistan, most of the homeless elderly were living at parks, roadsides, marketplaces, and especially near shrines. For food, they depended on the donated free food at shrines called Langar. They looked unclean, rough, and pitiable. Some of them were not mentally stable, and some were physically unfit and disabled. For sleeping, they used a thin piece of cloth, with a rough pillow to sleep on bare floor; some of them even had no pillow. Public toilets and bathing facilities were not readily available to them in Pakistan, so they were living in unhygienic conditions.

Nearly all of them lacked a National Identity Card, even when they were permanent residents of the state. Because they had no family members to support them, they did not have any family reference to show as proof of identity at the NADARA office (the institute issuing identity cards in Pakistan). That is why they were deprived of many facilities, including medical treatment, getting government aid for survival, the right to vote, and admission into care institutes.

In Kuala Lumpur, destitute people slept on the bare floor by spreading cardboard. They also carried bags with necessary items of life. Many of them wore joggers and boots, even the oldest people, to walk more easily and comfortably in the rain, which seems almost incessant in Malaysia. Among the multiracial people of Malaysia several problems stood in the way of carrying out interviews effectively, such as language barriers and the fact that many destitute people drink heavily and they are physically weak. Food was not an issue, as observed and confirmed by them on account of the free distribution of food at night by NGOs, including Soup & Kitchen and Kachara. Some families were also living lives of destitution at roadsides. In Pakistan, such people build temporary tents to stay there for a long time until someone forces them to move on. Sometimes they stay there so long that it feels they have always occupied the land. When they receive a government order to leave, it is very challenging for them to find another place to stay. In Malaysia, the destitute people I encountered belonged to different races, Malay, Chinese, and Tamils. Surprisingly, they were Malaysian citizens, but did not want to stay under any restrictions. All these circumstances were experienced by homeless and destitute people of Pakistan and Malaysia to varying degrees. However, the condition of old-aged people in institutions was quite similar in both countries as they were enjoying the necessities of life under a systematic pattern.

Interactional Hesitation with a Stranger

As I started interacting with older people, they were sometimes confused about the purpose of the interview. Some of them were unwilling to talk and displayed anger and disagreement while having a conversation with me. I respected their hesitation to talk and I did not force the issue. The elderly who knew the purpose of my interviews also displayed some hesitation in sharing their life events with a stranger. In Pakistan, as a fellow Asian, I was recognized quickly and I was asked why I wanted to collect information from them, as no one ever tried to help them to rehabilitate. Some of them considered me as a government official, who might get information about them and send them back to their homes. Often, the old-aged people thought that I would work for their rehabilitation for a better life, so they were ready and willing to talk. Although I had to explain that this was not possible, many were still willing to cooperate despite knowing the true purpose of the study.

In Malaysia, due to my Asian look, the destitute people easily recognized me as a foreigner. It was surprising to them that a foreign girl was trying to explore their life story and the reasons behind their destitution. Some of them reacted rudely about my presence in their country, as I could not rehabilitate them in return. So, it was complicated to make them understand the purpose of the interview. The solution was to leave the respondents that were proving stubborn and move to the next one. Although it was often a time-consuming process, some of them were very cooperative and shared the required information readily. Local Malay destitute elderly were more cooperative than the Chinese, who did not like either the interviewer or her purpose.

Issues of Gender

As a female, undertaking fieldwork among destitute people with different mental and health conditions and different age groups was itself a challenge. For my research, I needed to select the older adults, but young men also tried to interact and stared weirdly at me. They wanted me to talk to them, but I had to excuse myself by letting them know the nature of the study. Despite that, they sometimes used to stay around and participate in the conversation with elderly interviewees. Among old-aged people, many of them found it difficult to talk to a female, especially in Pakistan, due to the patriarchal system. It is a general view in Pakistan that to be safe, females should only appear in public with a male. A female walking alone around populated areas is not safe, especially the targeted places for the current study where the majority of people were male.

There were many males with different attitudes, who talked absurdly, used abusive language, were ill-tempered, and harassed females. Even some older people were of the opinion that I would not understand their conditions, being a female. During the conversation, I found multiple people standing around listening and watching what I was doing there. Mainly, it was astonishing for them that someone was sitting so close to older people and asking about their problems and life experiences. In Malaysia, the situation was particularly acute in this regard.

I encountered many situations where interacting with young males was difficult. Often they were drunk, and unable to stop themselves from touching me. I sometimes had to leave the place for security reasons. However, some old-aged homeless people were very comfortable talking to me and freely shared information, regardless of gender difference.

Linguistic Differentiation

Although I am a Pakistani, and it seems easier to interact with the local people, yet the language accents were different and not easy to understand in some areas. I was an Urdu and Punjabi speaking person, and in the area of data collection Saraiki was the dominant language. Saraiki is the local language of the Southern Punjab area, and the accent was not easy to understand for a nonlocal person. When I talked to older people, they replied in Saraiki, although I asked the question in Punjabi or Urdu. However, I noticed that, if I talked to them in Urdu, they tried to speak Urdu with some words of Saraiki for my comfort. I tried to talk in their local language, although I did not know much Saraiki; I was able to say some words in Saraiki to put them at ease. Likewise, my companion was an expert in Saraiki and helped me understand some terms that I was not familiar with.

In Malaysia, it was a unique experience to collect data in another language, Malay, and English. In Pakistan, it was easy to communicate in English as it is one of the official languages. In Kuala Lumpur, due to large numbers of tourists and multicultural people, most individuals are familiar with English. But the traditional or uneducated older people were not able to speak English. With the help of a local assistant therefore, I interviewed them in the local language, Malay. Often they were hesitant to talk as I was not able to understand their conversation, and some of them asked the assistant about my intentions, and whether I belonged to another country. The assistant told them the purpose of my presence and the data collection. In contrast, almost all the Chinese destitute people I interviewed could speak English, and they loved to speak it. Finding out about the life events of different language speaking people contributed to a richer variety of knowledge. I learned gradually to interview the people in their native languages to let them speak independently to achieve the research purpose with rich information.

Racial Difference

There were racial differences at research sites, including Malay, Chinese, Tamil in Malaysia and Saraiki, Punjabi, and Pakhton in Pakistan. As I was not of any of these races from Malaysia, it was problematic to interact successfully with them. Often they were sceptical about the purpose of sharing their living conditions with a stranger without any benefit in return. Some Malay elderly asked why I was researching in their country and suggested I should go back and do research in Pakistan. However, after some briefing, they agreed to dialogue.

Interestingly, in Pakistan, they asked about my background before they talked about themselves, and I had to brief them about my hometown, race, and association with institutions. Some of them were less talkative and reluctant to talk in front of a stranger. One older adult with a Pakhton background, known as very respectful and hardworking in Pakistan, was very straightforward and precise in answering the research questions. Intriguingly, the reason for his destitution was maltreatment and disrespect from his sons. He could not bear this insult. So, he left home and started living an independent life and never thought of going back home. Similarly, the attitude of the Chinese destitute elderly was also strict, and they were very conscious about their egos. This matter was also a challenge during field visits involving people with racial and cultural differences.

Mental Condition, Psychological Disturbance, and Mood Swings

In some cases, the older people whom I encountered were sensitive and childish in their attitudes. This was particularly difficult to deal with if they were suffering from a mental or physical disorder. In the case of destitute older adults, the situation was also sensitive as it involved asking personal questions about their lives. In recalling their previous lives, they often became sad. Sometimes they started crying because they missed their parents, siblings, and children. Some of the older people were not mentally stable and only talked about the most memorable events of their lives, even laughing when they disclosed the details of the circumstances that led to their state of deprivation. One old-aged person in the institute of Pakistan said with a laugh: "They [my relatives] snatched my house and land and kicked me out of the home. They gave me nothing and asked me to go and die."

Sometimes, during the interviews, elderly people grew silent and did not answer the questions. Occasionally they asked me to leave them alone and were unwilling to talk. In Pakistan, where the joint family system is ubiquitous, most of the senior destitute were facing isolation. They cried during the conversation because of maltreatment from their families. Some of the elderly homeless people could not bear to be a burden on their family and either entered a care institution or started working as a labourer and lived without shelter.

On the other hand, in Kuala Lumpur, Malaysia, the family bond is less strong than in Pakistan. It was less of an issue to live alone for many of the elderly respondents. They preferred to live alone to avoid their families facing difficulty although they still missed home. They respected the privacy and preferences of the family, when their families were not prepared to accept them and regarded them as idle, lazy, or drunk.

Unfavourable Response to the Interviewer

While some old-aged people were comfortable to share their life stories, there were quite a few who were suspicious of my motivation, thinking that I wanted to expose their families' pitilessness and make fun of their helplessness, while I was able to do nothing practical for them. Despite that, I tried to talk to them politely, but they were not prepared to welcome me around them. Some old-aged people looked down on me, asking who is this poor person, asking them to tell her about their stories of destitution. Unfortunately, such attitudes were prevalent in Malaysia.

Typical responses and questions were:

> Why are you doing this? What benefit will you get to talk to us? What will be our benefit to tell you our stories? You cannot understand what you ask of us, why should we expose our family secret in front of you? I will not share what my family did to me, that is still my family.

Even the respondents who shared their experiences sometimes left some questions unanswered and told me to ask something else. In some cases, it was important to keep them calm and help them relax as the questions were emotionally painful for them. In Malaysia, the non-Muslim respondents who used to drink sometimes tried to make physical contact by holding my hand or touching me; this may have been an unconscious action, or perhaps they were unable to see that this action might be irritating to me. It made me feel uneasy talking to them and sometimes I had to cut the conversation short. Other challenging respondents were those talkative older people who shared their life challenges but became visibly upset in describing their helplessness and lives of begging. While not always useful respondents in terms of the purpose of my study, from an ethical and humane standpoint I listened to them until they finished their stories and sometimes helped them with money.

Difference in Appearance of Interviewer and Respondents

The living conditions of the homeless were not satisfactory and hygienic. Even in the institutions, they had to live according to the instructions and rules because they had limited resources for self-care. On the other hand, the vagrant senior citizens at the public places were living in a contemptible situation by surviving hand to mouth. They did not have adequate clothing to cover them and look clean. Some of them were not conscious of the unhygienic conditions in which they lived. Sometimes, they did not take a bath for days, and because of the unavailability of public toilets in Pakistan they had to travel quite far to find any washing or toilet facilities. Due to their circumstances, they were not able to look neat and clean. The disparity between the appearance of the interviewer and the respondents created a clear difference which also made it difficult to put the old people at their ease. Sometimes their awareness of the difference in terms of appearance and status was apparent in their facial expressions and behaviour. Most of them kept their voice respectful and low as if an official was asking about their situations. Some of them highlighted the problems that they were facing, thinking that this would generate material resources to help them better their standard of living. Others were fearful of talking, thinking that I would complain about them, especially in Pakistan, because the government does not formally permit such people to live in public places. In Malaysia, some old-aged people were similarly worried that I would report their living conditions to the police or other authorities. Only after allaying these fears were they willing to talk.

This section has given a detailed account of the numerous challenges encountered during field visits and the ethical issues encountered by the researcher. These issues varied according to the comparative context of the two countries, Malaysia and Pakistan. Challenges were posed by institutional organizers, the respondents, the local people, and other people surrounding the targeted population. The challenges were overcome by following the ethical guidelines and training provided by the university administration and supervisor.

STRATEGIES TO OVERCOME CHALLENGES

Formal Permission Letter

I requested an ethics letter from the University of Malaya to collect data from different institutions. Having a formal ethical permission letter facilitated access to old-age institutions for data collection. I visited the institutions 'Afiyat' in Pakistan, and 'Anjung Sinngah' in Malaysia through the ethical approval letter. For the survey in the streets and public places to interview the elderly homeless, the permission letter was available to show the police on duty in case of any query. The police were likely to ask about the purpose of interviewing old-aged people in public places, as it was not a common phenomenon. The respondents were also informed about the permission letter, even though in many cases they were illiterate.

Promising Confidentiality

Confidentiality was a core ethical requirement, either in formal/written form or informally conveyed during the field visit, and the respondents were made to feel confident about the secrecy of their identity and data confidentiality. The older adults in public settings were more scared about the disclosure of their personal lives and identity. The assurance of confidentiality made it easier for the elderly in the institutions, because of the formal introduction earlier during a collective interview. The old-aged people trusted the staff and other supportive members of the institution. Moreover, they had prior experience of sharing their information with other students, who came to the institutions for their internship to attain their masters/bachelor degrees. It was surprising to find that some respondents were unconcerned about the disclosure of their lives and said that:

> There is no need for confidentiality when we have been made homeless because of the ruthless behaviour of our family members, or to hide or avoid telling you things. We want the new generation to know our story of destitution and learn to be polite with old members of the family.

Consent of Respondent to Interview

Before starting the formal conversation and questioning, the author asked for respondents' permission to interview, asking whether they were willing to talk and share their life experiences with me. When they expressed their interest in the conversation, I started interviewing them. Otherwise, I left them uninterrupted in whatever they were doing. When it was obvious that some of them were busy managing their small luggage, and their facial expressions showed that they were not interested in talking, I asked for permission to talk or to sit beside them. I found that people in the institutions were more comfortable in talking with me in both countries, Malaysia and Pakistan.

Snowball Sampling

Sometimes it was not easy to find suitably representative respondents during fieldwork, and in those cases I used snowball sampling to resolve this issue. An old person would tell me about another individual who was living in the same situation nearby. Nearly all of them knew about such people either at the same place or a little further away, because being homeless, they used to walk from one place to another. They were aware of the living areas of other old vagrant citizens. However, in the institutional setting, all the residents live in the same place and there was no difficulty in accessing suitable respondents for the study.

Assistance by Gatekeepers

Cultural differences prevail whether one is in one's home country or overseas, and I was not able to cope with all the challenges alone. I was not familiar with the places and that is why that in both places, I need a gatekeeper who knew about the culture, language, and psyche of such individuals, to get the required information accurately. Luckily, my husband assisted me as a gatekeeper as he had been living in Kuala Lumpur, Malaysia, for the past six years. He also knew the local language, Malay, well enough to help me in interviews with local people. So, he was not only able to guide me to the usual locations of homeless people (Majid Jamek, KLCC, Chokit, and Ampang), but also assisted in conducting some interviews in the local language, with those who did not understand English. In Pakistan, independent movement of females in society is not general practice, especially in public places. As this is a matter of cultural background, I could not disregard this factor. It was necessary to use a male gatekeeper in order to visit the field to access the targeted respondents. The gatekeeper was the front-man, who told the senior citizens about the purpose of the study. With his help I was accepted pleasantly, and some of the respondents welcomed me warmly and prayed a lot for both of us.

Moreover, in the old-age institutions, the majority of destitute persons were males, and they were more comfortable talking to a man than to a woman. At some points, when sharing some personal experiences, they whispered in my husband's ear and said that he could understand better since he was a man. So, his presence as gatekeeper assisted in gaining a deep insight into some hidden aspects of their lives. More surprisingly, the female respondents tended to consider him as their son (due to the patriarchal system in Pakistan, boys are regarded as more important as they support the family) and showed much affection with him. It created a loving environment for the context of research, which was very pleasant for both interviewer and interviewee.

Local Companion for Tracing Target Population

Although I got assistance from my spouse, I still needed to understand the mentality of the local people when seeking the location of destitute people in Kuala Lumpur. Some of my friends were initially unwilling to admit that there were homeless people in Malaysia. After some prompting, they started talking about the usual places such people stay. They also told me that the homeless people would not talk to me because I was a foreigner. However, I did not lose hope and joined a lot of Facebook groups involved in the rehabilitation of homeless people, and asked for assistance. Luckily, I got positive responses from some local Chinese and Malay social workers, including a female working for homeless people of all age groups. She invited me for a field survey at night, in

Masjid Jamek. By visiting the place, I found numerous destitute people, sleeping randomly on the floor. She told me to come at night because that was when they all gathered to get free food and sleep. These guidelines and observational analyses were beneficial for subsequent field visits.

Interlingual Communication

In Malaysia, I was able to communicate in English only. However, many vagrants did not know the English language or preferred to talk in Malay. The gatekeeper was able to communicate in both Malay and Chinese language and this interlingual communication assisted me in gaining access to more in-depth information about the vagrants and their lifestyle. In Pakistan, I used to speak Urdu, but among the targeted population Saraiki was the local language. Here, once again, the gatekeeper communicated in their local language. Although, I was not an expert in that language, I learned the basics for better communication and understanding of them. The old-aged people seemed happy when they found me talking in their language and empathizing with their pains.

Informal Intermingling with Respondents

It is generally easier to interview people by communicating with them in a natural and easy-going way, rather than displaying a formal attitude and status difference. The vagrant older people were living in miserable conditions. During my visits, I preferred to sit on the ground like them in order to make them feel more relaxed. Some of them hesitated and offered me a piece of cloth to sit on. However, I refused with affection and sat like them. Such small actions of care made them relax and feel comfortable and be more willing to speak to me. Sometimes, I used to tell them that I once lived in the same area, and this made them feel more at home with me. Through such 'we feelings', they started talking as they felt they were sharing their information with someone close to their hearts. It was also a way to win their trust not only to collect the data, but to rebuild their belief in humanity and love.

Respectful Behaviour with Elderly People

There is a common proverb that "Give nothing to others but respect, it is more important than wealth". I experienced this with older people, who became happy when I used to ask them to pray for me. Asking them to sit with me, or sitting down on the floor with them, while humbly requesting to know about their life story if they did not have any objection, were acts of respect and filled them with love and respect in return. They cooperated in providing the required information by experiencing a sense of recognition with me. This condition prevailed in both Pakistan and Malaysia, because respect influences people everywhere in the same way. Such actions in honour of them made them feel happy, even if for only a short period, during the meeting. Some of them still remember and pray for us if I contact them through the assistance of the institution. In Kuala Lumpur, some of the targeted elderly persons live outside near my home and meet with me whenever I go out. I always ask about their health and if they need anything. Their faces fill with joy and pleasure when they see me. Even when I do not know the language, such feelings need no words.

Provision of Compensation

Indeed, the provision of compensation (in the shape of money) was not an attractive element for some people. However, those older adults who were living in pitiable conditions accepted it happily. I observed that the provision of compensation at the end of every conversation was effective and considered respectful in most cases. Sometimes the old-aged people asked in advance what they would receive to share their stories. So, it was necessary to tell them about the provision of compensation in the form of money, food, and drink. Then they allowed me to ask the required questions and responded excitedly. In institutions, I presented some amount as a gift to the head of the institution, to buy whatever they needed for all of them. If the head of an institution considered it necessary to tell the elderly residents about it, he would do so, but I preferred not to tell them, as it might hurt them by making them feel degraded and in need.

Most of the old-aged people in the institutions belonged to well-known families, and when young they had enjoyed all the facilities of life. They did not expect compensation in form of money, but they valued time and affection. So, it was necessary to respond to their psychological needs for care, connection, and conversation. In Kuala Lumpur among the destitute the elderly happily accepted food and drinks as compensation as this was their primary need. Then, they shared the ups and downs of their lives from domestic settings to the condition of destitution. The elderly people who live near my home often ask me to provide food or money for food. I notice that they never ask anyone else to assist. This is a result of the bond of attachment that grew from our initial encounters when they expected me to provide something at every visit, and I also tried to provide them the necessities of life, as much as I could afford.

Freedom to Not Answer Unwelcome Questions and Emotional Stability

During the interviews, all respondents were free to dodge any question they did not want to answer. Some of them simply refused to answer some questions, but others started thinking about their past lives, and that was disturbing for them. In such cases I tried to make them feel like one of their daughters was with them and this helped them to relax through a caring attitude. Also, my husband and I used to hug them, depending on the gender of the respondent. I guided the conversation around the research questions, related to their surroundings or other people like them, or any interesting point they had already highlighted. In the institutions, I asked about their unique qualities, and the management told me about them before starting an interview with every older person.

Interestingly, many people forgot their pain and indicated interest in how I came to know about them and started telling stories smilingly. Other times, I used to divert their attention by asking about the designing or stitching of their clothes, any item of jewellery with them, even praising things placed around them in a quite excited way. This helped the respondent to relax and feel normal and they would instantly start talking about the highlighted item.

Freedom of Speaking Out of Context

It seemed unethical to interrupt the older people while talking, even if they were not telling me relevant information, and spoke about other events of life instead. This happened in the institution in Pakistan, when an old lady continued talking for one and a half hours about family, daughters, daughters' family, and so on. Respectfully, I did not interrupt her, even though she sometimes asked whether she was taking up too much of my time. I had to say that I was happy to listen, because such elderly people often do not have many people to talk to and find it difficult to keep their conversations brief in such situations.

Similarly, the people who were homeless, but not representative respondents for the study, also used to share their challenges of life and feelings of helplessness. I also listened to them politely and assisted them as much as I could. Patience is essential for successful fieldwork, and accumulation of representative information, like every good thing, requires perseverance and determination.

REFERENCES

Goffman, E. (1961). *Asylums: Essays on the Social Situation of Mental Patients and Other Inmates*. New York: Doubleday.

13. Field research in the conflict zone: an empirical study of the Chittagong Hill Tracts in Bangladesh

Md. Rafiqul Islam

STUDY CONTEXT

The aim of my PhD study was to explore the impacts of climate change events in migration decisions of the Bengali people who have settled in the Chittagong Hill Tracts (CHT) and the implication of migration and settlement in conflict and peacebuilding. The field of the study is the CHT, a conflict area in Bangladesh. From 1972 to 1997 the area witnessed a prolonged ethno-political conflict between the Bangladesh army and Shanti Bahini (the military wing of the tribal people). The root cause of the conflict is the denial of the constitutional recognition of the identity and right to self-determination of the tribal people in the CHT (Levene, 1999; Mohsin, 1997, 2003). Although a peace accord was signed between the Parbatya Chattagram Jana Samhati Samiti (PCJSS) and the Bangladesh government in 1997, there is still conflict in the region between the Bengali settlers and tribal people for the ownership of land, resources and social position (Mohsin, 2003; Panday and Jamil, 2009). Different sources confirm that 400,000–600,000 Bengali people have been settled in the CHT during 1977–1989, which contributed to the escalation of the CHT conflict (Reuveny, 2007; Suhrke, 1997; Ullah et al., 2014). With the widening of Bengali migration and social networks, even more Bengali people might have been settled in the CHT.

From a geographical point of view, Bangladesh is one of the most climate impacted countries in the world. People are adversely affected by multiple climate change events, e.g. floods, drought, sea-level rise and riverbank erosion. Bangladesh is also termed as a fragile state regarding demographic pressure, population displacement and the rule of law.[1] During the CHT conflict, the successive governments in different periods settled the poor and destitute people from the plain land to the hill areas of the CHT. Existing research has mentioned that a significant number of environment and climate change displaced people have been resettled in the CHT by the government which consequently contributed to the escalation of the CHT conflict (Hafiz and Islam, 1993; Homer-Dixon, 1994; Lee, 1997, 2001; Reuveny, 2007; Swain, 1996). However, there has been no empirical study to support the view that Bengali settlers in the CHT are climate change driven, and that they are contributing to the escalation of the conflict. The proposed research aims to investigate the complex relationship between climate change induced migration and conflict in the CHT using environmental security and conflict theories.

CHALLENGES IN THE FIELD

The fieldwork in the CHT was a challenging task which involved a number of concerns and issues as follows.

Permission Limbo

Seeking permission from the concerned authority[2] is one of the prerequisites for conducting field study which provides legitimacy for collecting data from the field. As per the ethical guidelines of my Doctoral studies, I sought permission from the CHT ministry to conduct interviews in the proposed field. In a conflict zone, permission from the authority is a legal as well as conceptual issue for carrying out a field study in a conflict and post-conflict society. In this study, I applied for permission from the CHT ministry for carrying out a study on 'climate change, migration and conflict in the CHT'. However, the authority refused to provide the permission letter on the grounds that the CHT conflict is not climate or environmentally induced; rather, it is merely a political problem. They argued that I had an evil intention to divert attention from the CHT people. I also faced the issue of breaching the confidentiality of the research question as the concerned government officials (one official of the CHT ministry and one of the foreign ministry) advised me to apply formally with the questionnaires and proposal of what objectives I aimed to achieve from the study. The questionnaire sharing seemed a risky idea as this process might hamper the research if the questionnaires were transferred to the law enforcing agencies.

Difficulties in Accessing the Field

In a conflict area like the CHT in Bangladesh, the study site is characterized as risky and conflicting between the adversaries. There is also the possibility of abduction and extortion. As a result, researchers face difficulties in reaching the study sites for collecting data from the appropriate respondents. I also faced challenges in reaching the different corners of the CHT to conduct a survey and qualitative interview. The CHT consists of three hill districts but located in separate places. The Chakma people dominate the Rangamati district, and the Khagrachari and Bandarban districts are dominated by the Tripura and Marama people respectively. Due to the long existing conflicts, Bengali and tribal people are living in the CHT but as a separate location in different districts. In some locations, Bengali and tribal people are also living side by side. From the location and demographic distribution, I noticed that the Bengali people own most of the business centres in the three hill districts and, thus, they are living in the core of the cities. On the other hand, tribal people are either job holders or mostly doing farming. As a result, they live either in the city centres or in the remote hill areas. This distinct character and present demographic location inhibit the researcher in collecting the data. Most importantly, it was almost impossible to reach the people who are living in the deep jungle and hill areas. Extortion is also a problem in reaching some places. Some organized groups kidnap people and demand ransoms. My research assistants and I were very scared to enter some locations and conduct the survey. Fortunately, no problem arose while conducting the survey in the CHT.

On the other hand, Bengali people (particularly the settlers) have built their dwellings close to the army camps or adjacent to the security forces' location and close to the urban centre. This arrangement is called the United Village (Ghusso Gram)[3], which is heavily supervised with surveillance by the security forces and intelligence agencies concerned with security. As a result, I faced difficulties accessing the Bengali respondents. One day, I was forced to stop the survey process and explain to the security forces "what I am doing in the CHT and why this research has targeted the Bengali people". Thereafter, I always tried to avoid the location of the army camp so that they would not notice me and my research assistants. In the army camp area, a stranger needs to justify their reason for visiting the CHT. In fact, the army as the security force of Bangladesh claims that they are the sole people to look after every matter in the CHT. Therefore, the army discourages sensitive research in the CHT on the grounds that this information sharing may increase the hostile relationship between the Bengali and tribal people. However, increasing numbers of graduate students in Bangladesh are conducting research in the CHT and managing the ethical and methodological difficulties.

Approaching the Respondents

Approaching the respondents at their place of residence is a difficult task. In the research design, I decided to knock on the door of every household for conducting the survey. I intended to interview any person of each household above 18 years of age who was willing to give an interview. In practical terms, I faced challenges to identify households and appropriate respondents. The dwelling system in the CHT is different from other parts of Bangladesh, particularly from the plain land. In the urban area of the CHT, most of the housing is sited closely together, but in the remote areas, housing areas are located at long distances from each other. I managed to conduct a field study in the urban areas smoothly as it was comparatively easy to reach the households. However, in the remote areas, I faced difficulties in reaching the households and identifying appropriate respondents. In most cases, the male resident was often absent from the house. In that case, I dared not enter the house. I asked for a suitable time to return, and was told to come the next day, morning or afternoon. When I arrived at the fixed date and time, the female householder or an under-aged girl/boy responded that their Ma and Baba (mother and father) were absent from the house. This situation often occurred when conducting the survey among the tribal people. As a result, I visited those places several times to gain access to the respondents, and therefore it consumed time and labour to complete the survey process. Transportation for accessing some places was also a major concern. There were some locations where at least a day is required to reach it, and there is no suitable accommodation facility for the outsider.

Trust-Building Issues

Every field study depends on building trust between the researcher and the respondents (Norman, 2009). Researchers first need to introduce themselves and their project to the respondents. After getting information, the respondents decide whether they want to participate in the research or not. I applied the same process for collecting data. However, I faced problems in developing trust with the respondents in some study sites. In some cases, respondents straightforwardly declined to participate in the research. They did so due to previous bad experiences with the research studies and activities of some local academics and NGO activists. For example, some researchers, academics and NGO activists blindly support either tribal people or settlement of Bengali people in the CHT. This practice has already created phobia and panic among the general people about research and surveys. Some people also showed their anger and anguish by uttering the name of some renowned academics and NGO workers of Bangladesh. Alimuddin, a 50-year-old Bengali settler in the CHT said that:

> Some Bengali people named 'X, Y. Z'[4] are the dalal [interest seekers] of the tribal people. They work against us. They want us to be repatriated from the CHT. However, we will not leave this place; this is our land now.

As a result, they (Bengali respondents) told me that they would not talk to me as they did not know me. I became puzzled in such a situation and took the time to reapproach them. I wholeheartedly tried to persuade them not to regard me as the same as other academics and NGO workers they had come across. In some cases, tribal people are very scared, and they live in a state of insecurity and anxiety. When I approached them and introduced myself as a researcher, they also refused to participate in the research. One respondent said that:

> We do not believe the outsider. All are selfish. People come for their interest. They are the paid agents of other organizations. People come and collect data, take photos and earn money. However, they do not do anything for us, and for our community. We are living in a miserable condition for a long time. Many people like you have come and talked to us, promised us to do something for our community. However, we have never seen them after their research.

It became a challenging task to continue the work under these conditions, in which people have already had bad experiences and hold stereotypes about researchers.

Silence of the Respondents

In research in conflict areas, the silence of the interviewees hampers the integrity and validity of the research. In the current research project, I faced the problem of silence and non-response of the interviewees from the Bengali and tribal people. Due to their experience of conflict and violence in the CHT, the respondents felt insecure and were afraid of sharing information with outsiders. This terrain of fear has created a culture of silence and non-response. Bengali people often displayed negative attitudes to participating in the survey process. A female respondent named Amina in the Longudu said:

> Why should I take part [in] the survey; this survey will not carry any good result for them. Many people come to us. However, our condition is remaining as same as it was.

Since the signing of the peace accord in 1997, there has been a transition period. Bengali people, particularly the settlers, are seriously scared of eviction, losing their land and houses. Rumour has already circulated in the CHT that settlers will be returned to the plain land and government will take away the land and redistribute it to the tribal people. This rumour seriously hampered the survey process among the Bengali people. Bengali settlers hardly ever wanted to share any information. Likewise, tribal people living with past trauma and psychological stress also showed negative responses to participating in the survey process. Most of the tribal respondents argued that "Silence is the best way to live peacefully. Otherwise, we might be a victim of extortion and persecution." In many cases, they (Bengali respondents) perceived me as a government agent who was working to identify the number of settlers.

Unwilling, Twisted and False Information

In conflict zones, respondents may provide false and twisted information. I asked the respondents about the causes and consequences of the CHT conflict situation. The respondents provided the answer in line with their political identity. The CHT is now a multicultural society where more than 30 ethnic groups including Bengali people are living. Currently, the tribal and Bengali community are divided in terms of their political, social and cultural causes. Particularly, the tribal and Bengali people are engaged in conflict to keep control over land, resources, social position and political power. As a result, both the parties blame each other for their condition in the CHT. The tribal people particularly perceive Bengali settlers as the main cause of their plight in the CHT. In the field study, I identified the presence of partisan views and hatred between two groups. While interviewing both communities, I noticed that both of them twisted information in order to make a trap for the other. When I interviewed the Bengali people, they replied that CHT is part and parcel of Bangladesh and tribal people are the primary cause of ongoing conflict in the CHT. Abdul Awal, a young shopkeeper of Khagrachari district, argued that:

> In the age of globalization, people are going everywhere and living as per their qualification and expectations. We as Bengali people have come here to live. We are happy to live here. It is the part of our country. We can come and settle here.

On the other hand, tribal people told me that they are the original people and have been living peacefully from historical times in the CHT. However, the settlement of the Bengali people has shattered the happiness and prosperity of the tribal people. In this situation, the researcher faces difficulty in identifying the exact meaning of the research findings. Even the professionals are partitioned according to party affiliation and ideological point of view. They see the CHT affairs through the prism of their party and ideological perspective. I observed this when interviewing professionals. Some of them have a preconceived idea about the CHT conflict and, therefore, they are unwilling to see the CHT conflict from a different angle. For example, one expert asked whether I have any prior knowledge about the CHT and why I had selected this topic for my study. Another expert argued that there is no connection between the environmental destruction and Bengali migration to the CHT. Rigid opinions such as these sometimes undermine the confidence of the researcher to carry out the study.

The Issue of Confidentiality and Anonymity

Maintaining confidentiality and anonymity is the key issue in conflict research. Researchers sometimes find themselves in situations that may breach the confidentiality of the research subject and objects. I also faced difficulties in maintaining the confidentiality of the researcher and research subjects. For example, sometimes outsiders came during the interview session and intervened with the respondent. In some cases, more than one person came and tried to take part in the interview. In several places, an outsider interfered during the interview. As the CHT is a conflict prone area, different people – e.g. law enforcement agency, intelligence agency, journalists – may have an interest in what is going on. In several places, I had to give a detailed description of the project, for example, the nature, purpose, for whom the study is carried out, and the involvement of the government and international agency. In this situation, I was not able to continue the interview for two reasons: one was an ethical issue of maintaining the confidentiality and anonymity of the research, and the second was that respondents were not willing to share their information in the presence of outsiders.

Personal Safety and Security

During the field study, I was concerned about the safety and security of myself and my research assistants. In a conflict situation, personal safety is the most important concern for the researcher. I faced two unwanted situations while conducting the field study. One day (in Longudu) a few tribal young people came and wanted to know what we were doing in the CHT. They asked where I had come from and for what purpose. Immediately, I showed the identity card, but they did not accept me as a researcher. They introduced themselves as members of the UPDF (United People's Democratic Front). My research assistant and I became rather scared. They took us to a place and examined the questionnaires and other papers. After an hour or more, they set us free to work. On that day, we did not continue our work but returned to our hotel.

Another incident arose with the Bengali people. We proceeded to interview a Bengali household. We introduced ourselves and sought permission from them to conduct the interview. Surprisingly, they misunderstood, shouted and called us agents of the government. They thought we were working for the government and making a list of the Bengali people. Some of them said that:

> We will die, but we will not leave the place. For the twenty years, we are living here in this land. There is no question to leave the land and our house. We will sacrifice our blood.

I became puzzled to hear such words from the Bengali people. I realized that there is frustration, anger and anguish among the Bengali people for their deprivation, and they fear losing their land and homes. A 55-year-old woman loudly said that:

> We want chal [rice], we do not understand what government is in power. We came here for chal and land. Now the government has stopped giving us chal. We will die. We will not be able to live.

I came to understand that the government has stopped the rationing system in that area which had operated since the Bengali settlement in the CHT. In such an environment, conducting a field study becomes a difficult task for the researcher.

Language Barrier and the Integrity of Research Assistants

Language is also a critical issue while conducting a field study in the CHT. More than 13 major ethnic communities are living in the CHT who have their distinct languages. Thus, researchers from outside the CHT face enormous difficulty in conducting a survey among all the communities in the CHT and may need to employ research assistants. Of course, there are some shortcomings in accepting help from local research assistants. They may influence the research through misguiding, providing misinformation and concealing appropriate respondents. They may also manipulate the response as the researcher may not know the language of the local people.

STRATEGIES TO OVERCOME THE CHALLENGES

The above challenges were practical and situational in nature. The long-standing conflict and current competition between the Bengali settlers and tribal people over resources and social positions have complicated the social, economic and political environment in the CHT. In such a situation, this study adopted practical measures as well as conventional ethical and methodological principles in order to overcome the challenges.

Informal Permission

As per the ethical guidelines of my Doctoral studies, I sought permission from the CHT ministry to conduct the interview in the proposed field. As mentioned above, in conflict zones, permission from the authorities involves legal as well as a conceptual issues, and questionnaire sharing seemed a risky thing to do if questionnaires might be transferred to law enforcement agencies. Therefore,

I avoided this process and proceeded to the CHT to conduct a questionnaire survey among the respondents. In doing so I relied on the specific permission and the consent of the community leaders of each of the study sites. In each study site, I sought permission from the respondents of the survey procedure. I verbally read out the major points of the consent form and assured them that their participation in this study is voluntary and they can withdraw at any time from the study. My observation is that formal permission from a higher authority for conducting research in a conflict zone is tough for an individual researcher. In some instances, a concerned person does not like to share the information in case they get in trouble or face difficulties in their professional life. The individual permission system from the respondent and verbal consultation with the community leaders helped to overcome this challenge and conduct the field study in the proposed study area.

Local Assistance to Reach Every Corner of the Field

Assistance at the local level – i.e. appointing research assistants and gatekeepers[5] – offers ample scope to reach every corner of the field to collect data and information. I appointed two research assistants from the tribal community who helped me to access some of the remote areas for conducting the survey. In some cases, however, the research assistants also felt insecure visiting some places where there is ongoing conflict among the tribal people regarding political affiliation and supporting the peace agreement. In this case, I accepted help from the gatekeepers who assisted me in entering study sites and approaching the respondents. I noticed that one gatekeeper had a good relationship with influential local people, such as the chairman of the union parishad and schoolteachers. For example, in Naniarchar and Longudu the local chairman helped us to go to study sites for the data collection. Moreover, I always tried to avoid the location of the army camp so that they would not notice me and my research assistants.

Considering all these aspects, I went to each study site and conducted the survey with great care. In this regard, I accepted help from the Bangladesh ANSAR[6] to discover more about the region, the possible challenges and the ways to overcome the challenges. As I have a previous connection with a few of the top officials of Bangladesh ANSAR in the CHT region, I sought help from them for knowledge about the situation in the region. I proposed that the study was being conducted for educational purposes. Accordingly, the ANSAR officials supported it in a number of ways, e.g. finding the appropriate location of the study site, getting access to remote areas, and ways of avoiding any unwanted circumstances. ANSAR staff even accompanied me in some places which they perceived as risky areas where I might have encountered problems. This assistance was vital in getting access to my targeted respondents for conducting the survey. ANSAR-VDP officials arranged every possible aspect, e.g. hiring a motorbike to reach the remote areas, identifying the settlement area, locating hostile zones in the CHT, finding a hotel and food sources. This information helped to conduct the study smoothly. In fact, some places (for example, Vuachori, Panchari, Diginala, Myney, Baghaisari, Manikchari) are situated in very remote areas in the CHT. Without motorbike or private car, it is quite impossible to visit and collect survey data. Fortunately, my prior knowledge in working in the CHT region also helped to identify possible challenges. In 2014, I worked as a researcher in a project funded by the UNDP and have been able to build up relationships with a few people working as peace activists in the CHT. I also sought help from them while conducting the study in the proposed study sites.

Several Visits for Reaching the Respondents

As mentioned earlier, gaining access to respondents in the remote areas is challenging as they are often busy working in their fields. One visit to the place may not be enough to catch the respondents. As a result, I visited those places several times for getting access to the respondents, which was time consuming and involved much work to complete the survey process. Where transportation problems arose, and where at least a day's travel was required to reach some destinations, I was lucky enough to be offered accommodation with a few local families.

Good Approach and Identity Card from a Foreign University

An appropriate demeanour and an identity card are very useful in helping a researcher break down the silence of respondents. The identity card from my university helped me to overcome the problem of silence in a number of cases. I also faced a similar problem when approaching the tribal people. As I noted earlier, the tribal people were often scared and anxious. When I approached them and introduced myself as a researcher, they initially refused to participate in the research. I softly explained about the project and that no community living in the CHT would be cheated. I confirmed that I had no relation with the government. Finally, they agreed to participate in the survey although they asked whether something could be done for them if this research were to have any impact on the policy of the government. I again confirmed that I had no power to change the government policy regarding the CHT. However, I believe that the research work may have some positive impacts on policy guidelines in the case of climate change and migration issues in Bangladesh in the future.

I managed to convince them that this work was solely for educational purposes. This explanation and my student identity card persuaded them to participate willingly in the interviews. During the interviews I remained calm and quiet, tried to break the silence by discussing general issues and their life in the CHT. Where the respondents could not read or write, I arranged for letters and consent forms to be translated and read out verbally in the local language by the research assistants. Through such measures, I managed to motivate them to participate in the survey.

Follow the Ethical and Methodological Guidelines

I followed the guidelines of the ethics application process and the principle of confidentiality so that confidentiality and anonymity were ensured. In the case of outside interference, temporarily stopping the interview and dealing with the interruption was the best way to ensure the confidentiality of the research. In this study when outsiders intervened, I stopped the interview and explained to them that this was a survey conducted for educational purposes and that their presence would hamper the survey process. In some cases it became necessary to show my identity card, mentioning the name of locally influential people who were assisting me as well as using my portfolio.[7] This technique sometimes worked. Some unwanted individuals who intended to interfere with the interview session left after seeing the identity card or hearing the name of influential people (e.g. headman karbari or local political leaders).

Flexible Approaches and Techniques

Flexible approaches and techniques enabled me to overcome the challenges in many respects. Before conducting the field study, I decided where I should go first and accordingly made a map for the entry point and ending point. I also collected phone numbers and addresses of police officials in case of emergency. I did not inform the law enforcing agency people about the study in the CHT. For safety and security, I communicated with some local development workers.

I initially appointed two research assistants from the tribal community to help me conduct the survey. However, those research assistants were not familiar with all the languages spoken in the CHT. Finally, I changed the design and hired a research assistant from each community in which I carried out interviews. This process helped to reach the people of different tribal communities and approach them to conduct the interview. Although this process was risky in some respects, I adopted it for the sake of completing the survey within the time frame. As a graduate student, I had a time constraint to finish the questionnaire process within a certain period. Therefore, I needed to complete the survey through all options at my disposal. Research assistance in this context played an important role in introducing me to the respondents.

In a conflict area like the CHT, a research assistant from the local people is very valuable in guiding the researcher as well as ensuring the security of the respondents. A training session was arranged for research assistants to explain the project and how to conduct the study. I accompanied them at all times while conducting the field study. My previous experience reminded me that research assistants or enumerators sometimes do not take a risk and conduct research thoroughly by going from door to door.

NOTES

1. Fragile state index, 2016, available at http://fundforpeace.org/fsi/.
2. Here, authority refers to a person with whom I talked and from whom I sought the permission. I sought permission from a joint secretary working in the CHT ministry and looking after CHT affairs.
3. The concept of the Ghusso Gram was formulated after the 1980s by the then government to protect the Bengali people in the CHT and avoid the communal violence between the Bengali and tribal people. Now there are around 86 Ghusso Gram in the CHT where the Bengali people are solely living.
4. I have intentionally mentioned the name 'X, Y, Z'. They mentioned some name of the renowned academics and NGO workers of Bangladesh. But I cannot mention their actual names in the report of my own research experience.
5. Gatekeeper refers to the person who helps the researcher to know the place, approach the respondents and collect data. Gatekeepers also help the researcher deal with fear and psychological stress in the conflict zone (Cohen and Arieli, 2011).
6. Bangladesh ANSAR is one of the largest security forces in Bangladesh along with the Bangladesh Army with the aim of ensuring peace, security and development. Bangladesh ANSAR has set up their camp in different places in the three hill districts.
7. I teach in a university in Bangladesh that enables me to approach people and motivate them to participate in the research project.

REFERENCES

Cohen, N. and Arieli, T. (2011). Field research in conflict environments: Methodological challenges and snowball sampling. *Journal of Peace Research*, 48(4), 423–435.

Hafiz, M. A. and Islam, N. (1993). *Environmental Degradation and Intra/Interstate Conflicts in Bangladesh*. Zurich: Swiss Peace Foundation.

Homer-Dixon, T. F. (1994). Environmental scarcities and violent conflict: Evidence from cases. *International Security*, 19(1), 5–40.

Lee, S.-W. (1997). Not a one-time event: Environmental change, ethnic rivalry, and violent conflict in the Third World. *The Journal of Environment & Development*, 6(4), 365–396.

Lee, S.-W. (2001). *Environment Matters: Conflicts, Refugees & International Relations*. Tokyo: World Human Development Institute Press.

Levene, M. (1999). The Chittagong Hill Tracts: A case study in the political economy of 'creeping' genocide. *Third World Quarterly*, 20(2), 339–369.

Mohsin, A. (1997). *The Politics of Nationalism: The Case of the Chittagong Hill Tracts*. Bangladesh: University Press Limited (UPL).
Mohsin, A. (2003). *The Chittagong Hill Tracts, Bangladesh: On the Difficult Road to Peace*. Boulder, CO: Lynne Rienner.
Norman, J. (2009). Got trust? The challenge of gaining access in conflict zones. In C. L. Sriram, J. C. King, J. A. Mertus, O. Martin-Ortega and J. Herman (eds.), *Surviving Field Research: Working in Violent and Difficult Situations* (pp. 71–91). New York: Routledge.
Panday, P. K. and Jamil, I. (2009). Conflict in the Chittagong Hill Tracts of Bangladesh: An unimplemented accord and continued violence. *Asian Survey*, 49(6), 1052–1070.
Reuveny, R. (2007). Climate change-induced migration and violent conflict. *Political Geography*, 26(6), 656–673.
Suhrke, A. (1997). Environmental degradation, migration, and the potential for violent conflict. In N. P. Gleditsch (ed.), *Conflict and the Environment* (pp. 255–272). Dordrecht: Springer.
Swain, A. (1996). Displacing the conflict: Environmental destruction in Bangladesh and ethnic conflict in India. *Journal of Peace Research*, 33(2), 189–204.
Ullah, M. S., Shamsuddoha, M. and Shahjahan, M. (2014). The viability of the Chittagong Hill Tracts as a destination for climate-displaced communities in Bangladesh. In S. Leckie (ed.), *Land Solutions for Climate Displacement* (pp. 215–247). Abingdon: Routledge.

14. Research with coastal people in Bangladesh: challenges and way forward

Taj Sultana, Firuza Begham Binti Mustafa, Jillian Ooi Lean Sim and M. Rezaul Islam

STUDY CONTEXT

Tidal inundation – the periodic flooding of land and infrastructure normally situated on dry land by abnormally high sea water – is a severe coastal disaster with adverse impacts on coastal communities. Up to 80 per cent of people live on the coast, 1.2 billion live within 100 km of the coast, and an estimated 500 million people live near or in deltas around the world (Islam, 2004; Nhan, 2016). These are communities whose lives and livelihoods are put at risk at every turn of the season that brings a flooding event. Increased tidal flooding is the direct result of sea-level change (Barth and Titus, 1984). Houghton et al. (2001), referencing an Intergovernmental Panel on Climate Change report, warned of the serious problems faced by coastal communities as a result of global warming. Research has provided evidence for where these impacts have been occurring, for example in the seasonal flooding of urban areas in the Mekong Delta of Vietnam (Takagi et al., 2015) and in the low-lying coastal areas of Indonesia (Marfai and King, 2008).

Due to its unique geophysical characteristics, the coast of Bangladesh is vulnerable to disasters such as cyclones, storm surges, erosion, and sea-level rise – all of which result in tidal inundation. This country has been identified as one of the 27 countries that are most vulnerable to incidents such as drainage congestion, freshwater abundance in the monsoon, freshwater scarcity in the dry season, inundation of land, unsteady morphological processes and extreme events (Komol, 2011; Mohal and Hossain, 2007). It has experienced increasing frequency and intensity of coastal floods, cyclones and tidal surges, and for this reason it has been identified by Garai (2017) as a critical zone for coastal disasters. Some reasons for the vulnerability of Bangladesh are (a) its location in the path of tropical cyclones, (b) its wide and shallow continental shelf, (c) its coasts comprise low-lying and poorly protected land, much of it in the delta of the Ganges and Brahmaputra rivers, and finally (d) its overpopulation by communities that rely heavily on coastal resources (Flather, 1994). This last point about its population is an important one – Dewan (2015) called attention to the fact that Bangladesh is highly vulnerable to coastal floods because of the effect of sea-level rise in its densely populated coastal zones. Such threats have induced the migration of the Char (island) people of Bangladesh to developed cities (Islam, 2018). Also, Hasan and Navera (2012) foresee that climate change-induced sea-level rise will continue to affect the Bangladesh coast through permanent inundation, drainage congestion, increased intensity, frequency of cyclonic storm surge, and salinity intrusion in low-lying areas. Should these come to pass, the 30 million-strong coastal population that depends on agriculture, fisheries, forestry and salt panning for its livelihood (Islam and Salehin, 2013) will lose access to those economic activities, as well as suffer losses to health, food security, and overall biodiversity (Alam et al., 2003).

The study area in this research is the Chattogram city corporation area, previously known as Chittagong. Coastal dwellers of Chattogram city in Bangladesh have been severely impacted by tidal inundation and dwellers have been struggling to cope. A combination of rapid urbanization and climate change is reportedly responsible for urban storm waterlogging here, resulting in 13 vulnerable areas (Akter et al., 2017). Chattogram city is located along the southeast coast of Bangladesh, bounded by the Karnaphuli River and its division the Halda River to the south and east, by the Bay of Bengal to the west and by a range of hills to the north (Hassan and Nazem, 2016). The city covers an area of 185 km^2 (BBS, 2011; CCC, 2018) and its administrative area consists of 41 wards in 12 Thana. A ward is the smallest administrative urban geographic unit; a Thana is a sub-district and unit of police administration. Data collection in this study was performed in the five most vulnerable wards of Chattogram city, i.e. ward 4 – Chandgaon, 17 – West Bakalia, 26 – North Halisahar, 27 – South Agrabad, and 36 – Gosaildanga. Among the five wards, wards 17, 26 and 27 are residential and commercial areas. Most local inhabitants are in wards 4 and 36. A significant number of slums are located in wards 17, 26 and 27.

CHALLENGES IN THE FIELD

The challenges faced by the researcher can be divided into three categories and five sub-categories.

Challenge 1: Site Accessibility

Inaccessibility due to tidal inundation: Because this study was about tidal inundation, it was inevitable that the researcher experienced some of its impacts when collecting data. Households were in low-lying areas that were periodically flooded by tidal water for 4–5 hours at a time. Although the initial strategy was to visit areas that were currently dry, there were occasions when the researcher found the roads submerged on the return journey. This happened, for instance, in ward 27 (South Agrabad), making it necessary to wait for the water level to recede (Figure 14.1). The timing of data collection had an effect on the research in two ways: (1) when surveys were run during flooding events, respondents were reluctant to be interviewed, making completion of the research work a challenge, and (2) the mobility of the researcher was hampered, resulting in restricted access to households in flooded areas. The intrusion of tidal floods made roads impassable for mechanized vehicles, and people were forced to walk or use rickshaws (Figure 14.1(d)). For this reason, many hours were lost in waiting out sudden floods in wards the researcher was surveying. The initial rationale was to collect primary data *during* flooding events so as to depict tidal inundation impacts on the population as accurately as possible. However, on the part of the researcher there was a lack of foresight about the extent of tidal intrusion in the study area and how time-limited one could get when working under such conditions. This proved to be a big challenge for the researcher and required a shift in the data collection strategy.

Challenge 2: Social Issues

Lack of personal security and trust: As a female, the lead researcher faced several types of social challenges. The first challenge was regarding personal security. Residents in the study area were curious about females, but especially so in ward 36 (Gosaildanga) where the researcher felt particularly insecure. People of this ward were more curious than elsewhere – they questioned her reasons for visiting, and followed her around to observe her activities. In wards 17 (West Bakalia) and 27 (South Agrabad), she was approached by a group of people who asked for her identity before demanding her to leave. Following this, the researcher moved her work to other wards, having conceded that some locations were simply not safe for solo female researchers.

A second problem was the lack of trust shown to the researcher when approaching household dwellers for the survey. Some residents were unwilling to answer queries and in many cases, barred the researcher from entering their homes or talking to them. This may have been related to the perceived role of males as household leaders. When males of the household were away from their homes, female respondents were unwilling to participate in the survey

a)Rising tidal water

b) Road inundated by tidal water

c) House affected by rising tidal water

d) Tidal water intruded into transportation routes

Source: Authors.

Figure 14.1 Inundated areas in study locations

in their absence (wards 4 and 36). Other wards, for example ward 26 (North Halisahar) and 27 (South Agrabad) were located in commercial areas where strict entrance rules were imposed by the housing society, making it difficult to gain access to houses or apartments within. The researcher had to rely on convincing security guards and gatekeepers to allow her entry by explaining the objectives of the research to them. In almost all cases, the researcher was still not allowed to enter residences. The learning point here is that trust is an important factor for a researcher to consider when working with respondents, and the relationship between them has the capacity to determine the reliability and validity of data collected (Islam et al., 2014). In this case, the language barrier may have contributed to the lack of trust between researcher and respondents – when the latter observed the researcher was not a native speaker, they showed less interest in answering questions. In most parts of Chattogram city, local people speak what is known as the 'Chittagonian Dialect', which is distinctly different from the official Bengali language known as 'Suddo Bangla Dialect' spoken elsewhere (Mia et al., 2015). Local people trust native language speakers and are more likely to share information easily amongst fellow native language speakers. Chattogram city was no exception in this regard.

Mismatch between official address and physical address: Finding the location of houses according to their holding number (official address) was a major challenge in this study. The researcher attempted to use simple random sampling to collect household information and to do so, created a sampling frame consisting of all household numbers. The house holding number is used to collect holding tax from the city corporation areas of Bangladesh and was used as the identifier when selecting samples in this study. Holding numbers were provided by the ward commissioner office, along with total household-related information. Locating houses according to their holding number, however, proved to be problematic because the physical location of houses did not match the official holding numbers, i.e. houses were not where they were supposed to be. In each ward, there were several houses outside the holding number given by the Chattogram City Corporation. When the researcher visited ward 36 (Gosaildanga), for example, the first sampled house was found to be located 600m to the south of its official address. Similarly, the second sample was located 1000m to the north of its official address. To further complicate the search, the location of houses was not sequential.

Challenge in arranging meetings: Focus group discussions (FGD) and key informant interviews (KII) were two of the methods employed in this study. FGD sessions involved getting collective input from community leaders such as schoolteachers, government officials, non-governmental organization workers, and community leaders. However, attempts to get participants into the FGD sessions were not always successful, mainly due to their perception that tidal inundation was the duty of the government to solve, and not theirs. One potential participant stated, "It is not our duty, how can we solve it. The government is taking steps to solve it" (Male/62 years/23 April 2019/10 am/ ward no.4).

On the other hand, KII sessions involved getting the viewpoints of government officials in positions that were relevant to the tidal inundation problem. Because of their rank in the administration system, however, getting an appointment in their schedule was extremely difficult and time consuming.

Challenge 3: Political Issues

Collecting data during a politically charged period: The primary data collection period was around the time of the eleventh national election (Bangladesh National Election 2018), resulting in the community being especially mistrustful of outsiders – including researchers. In ward 36 (Gosaildanga), for example, the researcher was collecting data from a respondent when all of a sudden, a crowd of people gathered around and started to ask questions such as "Why are you moving around here at this time?", "What is the need to report on the problems of the area at the moment?", and more disturbingly, "Are you here to damage our reputation with your report?"

The researcher's attempts to provide them with answers were not entirely successful. Their opinion was that: "This is not the right time to collect information related to tidal inundation, you came here to collect our election-related news" (Male/50 years/22 December 2018/3 pm/ward no.36).

It became apparent to the research team that this was a case of pre-election fear occurring in the community, resulting in heightened sensitivities. Dwellers did not believe that researchers were there for the purpose of an independent study but instead, were surreptitiously collecting election-related information. One dweller remarked: "Now is the time for the election, for these reasons they have come here. No one asked us any information about tidal inundation before the election" (Female/32 years/10 December 2018/11:05 am/ward no.27).

The local people's idea was that this research team was working for the opposition party. As a result, data collection was halted in these wards.

STRATEGIES TO OVERCOME CHALLENGES

Strategy 1: Site Accessibility

Implemented the use of local tide chart: Working efficiently in an area known for tidal inundation required prior knowledge about the timing of possible tidal floods. For this, we relied on the use of local tide charts for the Chattogram district (Figure 14.2). A tide chart represents the heights of tide and timing of the day and night throughout a year. Local residents were known to also use a web-based tide chart (Bangladesh Tides 4 Fishing, Tide chart from Bangladesh NAVY or other sources). Another strategy was the careful selection of the sampling season. Despite the initial desire to conduct sampling during events of tidal inundation, the challenges to mobility were far too great. The solution was to restrict sampling to the drier season, i.e. November 2018 to April 2019. During this time, rainfall is generally less in Bangladesh and the impact of tidal water is greatly reduced.

DAY			TIDES FOR CHITTAGONG					SOLUNAR ACTIVITY
			1st TIDE	2nd TIDE	3rd TIDE	4th TIDE	COEFFICIENT	
1 Sat	▲ 5:35 h	▼ 18:10 h	4:03 h ▲ 4.0 m	10:54 h ▼ 0.8 m	16:17 h ▲ 3.9 m	23:13 h ▼ 0.7 m	62 average	
2 Sun	▲ 5:36 h	▼ 18:09 h	4:45 h ▲ 3.8 m	11:38 h ▼ 0.8 m	17:01 h ▲ 3.7 m	23:59 h ▼ 0.8 m	53 average	
3 Mon	▲ 5:36 h	▼ 18:08 h	5:39 h ▲ 3.4 m	12:26 h ▼ 1.0 m	18:00 h ▲ 3.4 m		48 low	
4 Tue	▲ 5:36 h	▼ 18:07 h	1:02 h ▼ 0.9 m	6:57 h ▲ 3.4 m	14:01 h ▼ 1.1 m	19:33 h ▲ 3.2 m	51 average	
5 Wed	▲ 5:37 h	▼ 18:06 h	2:35 h ▼ 1.0 m	8:41 h ▲ 3.4 m	15:51 h ▼ 1.0 m	21:21 h ▲ 3.3 m	60 average	
6 Thu	▲ 5:37 h	▼ 18:05 h	4:20 h ▼ 0.9 m	10:08 h ▲ 3.7 m	17:19 h ▼ 0.9 m	22:38 h ▲ 3.6 m	74 high	
7 Fri	▲ 5:37 h	▼ 18:04 h	5:37 h ▼ 0.8 m	11:09 h ▲ 4.0 m	18:18 h ▼ 0.7 m	23:34 h ▲ 3.9 m	88 high	
8 Sat	▲ 5:38 h	▼ 18:03 h	6:33 h ▼ 0.6 m	11:58 h ▲ 4.2 m	19:05 h ▼ 0.5 m		100 very high	
9 Sun	▲ 5:38 h	▼ 18:02 h	0:21 h ▲ 4.3 m	7:19 h ▼ 0.5 m	12:42 h ▲ 4.5 m	19:47 h ▼ 0.4 m	107 very high	
10 Mon	▲ 5:38 h	▼ 18:01 h	1:03 h ▲ 4.4 m	8:01 h ▼ 0.4 m	13:22 h ▲ 4.6 m	20:25 h ▼ 0.3 m	109 very high	
11 Tue	▲ 5:38 h	▼ 18:00 h	1:43 h ▲ 4.6 m	8:40 h ▼ 0.4 m	14:00 h ▲ 4.6 m	21:01 h ▼ 0.3 m	104 very high	
12 Wed	▲ 5:39 h	▼ 17:59 h	2:21 h ▲ 4.6 m	9:17 h ▼ 0.4 m	14:37 h ▲ 4.6 m	21:36 h ▼ 0.4 m	95 very high	
13 Thu	▲ 5:39 h	▼ 17:58 h	2:58 h ▲ 4.4 m	9:52 h ▼ 0.5 m	15:13 h ▲ 4.3 m	22:09 h ▼ 0.5 m	82 high	
14 Fri	▲ 5:39 h	▼ 17:57 h	3:35 h ▲ 4.2 m	10:27 h ▼ 0.6 m	15:49 h ▲ 4.1 m	22:42 h ▼ 0.6 m	67 average	
15 Sat	▲ 5:39 h	▼ 17:56 h	4:12 h ▲ 4.0 m	11:03 h ▼ 0.8 m	16:26 h ▲ 3.8 m	23:17 h ▼ 0.8 m	53 average	
16 Sun	▲ 5:40 h	▼ 17:55 h	4:52 h ▲ 3.7 m	11:43 h ▼ 0.9 m	17:06 h ▲ 3.4 m	23:56 h ▼ 0.9 m	41 low	
17 Mon	▲ 5:40 h	▼ 17:54 h	5:42 h ▲ 3.4 m	12:34 h ▼ 1.1 m	18:02 h ▲ 3.1 m		34 low	
18 Tue	▲ 5:40 h	▼ 17:53 h	0:51 h ▼ 1.1 m	7:05 h ▲ 3.1 m	13:58 h ▼ 1.2 m	19:56 h ▲ 2.9 m	35 low	
19 Wed	▲ 5:41 h	▼ 17:52 h	2:25 h ▼ 1.1 m	9:07 h ▲ 3.1 m	16:17 h ▼ 1.1 m	21:51 h ▲ 3.0 m	42 low	
20 Thu	▲ 5:41 h	▼ 17:51 h	4:33 h ▼ 1.1 m	10:24 h ▲ 3.3 m	17:35 h ▼ 1.1 m	22:52 h ▲ 3.2 m	53 average	
21 Fri	▲ 5:41 h	▼ 17:50 h	5:40 h ▼ 1.0 m	11:12 h ▲ 3.6 m	18:15 h ▼ 0.9 m	23:33 h ▲ 3.4 m	63 average	
22 Sat	▲ 5:41 h	▼ 17:49 h	6:20 h ▼ 0.8 m	11:48 h ▲ 3.8 m	18:46 h ▼ 0.8 m		73 high	
23 Sun	▲ 5:42 h	▼ 17:49 h	0:05 h ▲ 3.7 m	6:53 h ▼ 0.7 m	12:19 h ▲ 3.9 m	19:14 h ▼ 0.7 m	82 high	
24 Mon	▲ 5:42 h	▼ 17:48 h	0:35 h ▲ 3.9 m	7:23 h ▼ 0.4 m	12:47 h ▲ 4.1 m	19:41 h ▼ 0.5 m	88 high	
25 Tue	▲ 5:42 h	▼ 17:47 h	1:03 h ▲ 4.1 m	7:52 h ▼ 0.5 m	13:15 h ▲ 4.2 m	20:09 h ▼ 0.5 m	92 very high	
26 Wed	▲ 5:43 h	▼ 17:46 h	1:31 h ▲ 4.2 m	8:22 h ▼ 0.5 m	13:43 h ▲ 4.3 m	20:36 h ▼ 0.5 m	93 very high	
27 Thu	▲ 5:43 h	▼ 17:45 h	2:00 h ▲ 4.3 m	8:52 h ▼ 0.5 m	14:12 h ▲ 4.3 m	21:05 h ▼ 0.5 m	90 very high	
28 Fri	▲ 5:43 h	▼ 17:44 h	2:31 h ▲ 4.4 m	9:23 h ▼ 0.5 m	14:43 h ▲ 4.2 m	21:36 h ▼ 0.5 m	84 high	
29 Sat	▲ 5:44 h	▼ 17:43 h	3:03 h ▲ 4.3 m	9:56 h ▼ 0.6 m	15:17 h ▲ 4.2 m	22:08 h ▼ 0.5 m	74 high	
30 Sun	▲ 5:44 h	▼ 17:42 h	3:40 h ▲ 4.2 m	10:33 h ▼ 0.7 m	15:55 h ▲ 3.9 m	22:46 h ▼ 0.7 m	63 average	

Source: https://tides4fishing.com/as/bangladesh/chittagong.

Figure 14.2 Tide table for Chattogram

Strategy 2: Social Issues

Working in a team instead of individually: The solution to the personal safety issue was to set up a four-member team for data collection, rather than having the lead researcher work alone. Having assistants who were proficient in the native language was an added advantage. Consequently, working in a larger team solved the dual problems of personal safety and communication.

Revising the sample collection design: To solve the problem of mismatching official and physical household numbers, the simple random sampling design was replaced with systematic random sampling, i.e. households were sampled every 20m (walking a distance of 30 steps). As a result, the complexity of holding numbers was eliminated.

Building rapport with local people: Rapport with local residents was built by engaging with them outside the scope of the study. Team members made a practice of eating at local fast food shops to mingle with local people. This technique worked well to get information about tidal inundation-related problems. Those who were approached in this setting were interested in giving information and some readily gave the research team access to their homes, and permission to take photographs.

Adopting a formal approach to FGD participants: To increase the participation rate in FGDs, the research team adopted a more formal, top-down approach; they selected a local influential person in a particular ward, whom they would convince about the goals and significance of the FGD. With his help, a government primary school in the area would be designated as a meeting place. A select few local leaders were then invited to the meeting via the ward commissioner's office. Phone calls were made a day before to remind the participants about the meeting. This proved to be a good solution because the turnout of participants at subsequent meetings was greatly improved.

Strategy 3: Political Issues

Obtaining permission from the local authority: To overcome the problem of collecting data during a time when local sensitivities were heightened by election fears, the research team made it a point to inform the ward commissioner's office about data collection efforts. Because this office has a good relationship with local community leaders and influential persons, this was seen to ease the way for the research team into wards during politically charged times. The research team also communicated closely with local political leaders, schoolteachers and other influential persons in the study area because they were respected within their communities. Hence, their acceptance of the researchers and the study led to acceptance by the wider community.

Table 14.1 Summary of data collection challenges and accrued strategies

Categories	Data collection challenges	Accrued strategies
Site accessibility	1. Inaccessibility due to tidal water	1. Implemented the use of local tide chart
Social issues	2. Lack of personal security and trust 3. Mismatch between official address and physical address 4. Challenge in arranging meetings	2. Working in a team instead of individually 3. Revising the sample collection design 4. Building rapport with local people 5. Adopting a formal approach to FGD participants
Political issues	5. Collecting data during a politically charged period	6. Obtaining permission from the local authority 7. Assuring respondents about research and affiliation

Assuring respondents about research and affiliation: Team members were diligent in explaining the research aim to local people, and in assuring respondents that their information would be kept confidential and in accordance with standard research ethics in data collection. People were also reassured that the research team would refrain from collecting data for the ongoing national election campaign.

The research team used identification cards to ensure their affiliation as researchers was made transparent. All members of the research team were briefed to answer questions about their identity and affiliations politely if anyone was curious. Table 14.1 summarizes the data collection challenges and accrued strategies discussed above.

FURTHER GUIDELINES FOR FEMALE RESEARCHERS

Female researchers often face unique challenges when working in the field. Here are five suggestions that may help in alleviating some of these challenges: (a) always work in a team, to provide 'safety in numbers'; (b) make sure to inform local authorities about your work and your daily location before the start of the study; (c) keep an identification card on you at all times; (d) build rapport with local people, especially females and elderly persons in the area, to ease getting access to their homes for interviews; (e) if possible, keep all your survey work in the field to daylight hours.

REFERENCES

Akter, A., Mohit, S. A. and Chowdhury, M. A. H. (2017). Predicting urban storm water-logging for Chittagong city in Bangladesh. *International Journal of Sustainable Built Environment*, 6(1), 238–249.

Alam, M. M., Hossain, M. A. and Shafee, S. (2003). Frequency of Bay of Bengal cyclonic storms and depressions crossing different coastal zones. *International Journal of Climatology: A Journal of the Royal Meteorological Society*, 23(9), 1119–1125.

Barth, M. C. and Titus, J. G. (eds.) (1984). *Greenhouse Effect and Sea Level Rise: A Challenge for This Generation*. New York: Van Nostrand Reinhold.

BBS (2011). *Statistical Yearbook of Bangladesh*. Bangladesh Bureau of Statistics (BBS) Statistical Division, Ministry of Finance and Planning, Government of Bangladesh, Dhaka.

Chittagong City Corporation (CCC) (2018). http://ccc.org.bd/welcome-chittagong-city-corporation.

Dewan, T. H. (2015). Societal impacts and vulnerability to floods in Bangladesh and Nepal. *Weather and Climate Extremes*, 7, 36–42.

Flather, R. A. (1994). A storm surge prediction model for the northern Bay of Bengal with application to the cyclone disaster in April 1991. *Journal of Physical Oceanography*, 24(1), 172–190.

Garai, J. (2017). Qualitative analysis of coping strategies of cyclone disaster in coastal area of Bangladesh. *Natural Hazards*, 85(1), 425–435.

Hasan, M. M. and Navera, U. K. (2012). Impact of climate change induced cyclonic surge on the coastal island: Kutubdia and Sandwip and proper adaptive measures. *The International Journal of Ocean and Climate Systems*, 3(4), 217–227.

Hassan, M. M. and Nazem, M. N. I. (2016). Examination of land use/land cover changes, urban growth dynamics, and environmental sustainability in Chittagong city, Bangladesh. *Environment, Development and Sustainability*, 18(3), 697–716.

Houghton, J. T., Ding, Y., Griggs, D. J., Noguer, M., Van der Linden, P. J., Dai, X., Maskell, K. and Johnson, C.A. (eds.) (2001). *Climate Change 2001: The Scientific Basis*. Cambridge: Cambridge University Press.

Islam, M. R. (2004). *Where Land Meets the Sea: A Profile of the Coastal Zone of Bangladesh*. Dhaka: University Press.

Islam, M. R. (2018). Climate change, natural disasters and socioeconomic livelihood vulnerabilities: Migration decision among the Char land people in Bangladesh. *Social Indicators Research*, 136(2), 575–593.

Islam, M. R., Cojocaru, S., Hajar, A. B. A. S., Wahab, H. A. and Sulaiman, S. (2014). Commune and procedural level challenges and limitations in conducting social research in Malaysia: A case of disabled people. *Revista de Cercetare si Interventie Sociala*, 46, 255–272.

Islam, M. S. and Salehin, F. (eds.) (2013). *Coastal Zone and Disaster Management in Bangladesh*. Dhaka: Coastal Research Unit (CRU).

Komol, K. U. (2011). Numerical simulation of tidal level at selected coastal area of Bangladesh. Unpublished master's thesis, Bangladesh University of Engineering and Technology, Dhaka, Bangladesh.

Marfai, M. A. and King, L. (2008). Coastal flood management in Semarang, Indonesia. *Environmental Geology*, 55(7), 1507–1518.

Mia, M. A., Nasrin, S., Zhang, M. and Rasiah, R. (2015). Chittagong, Bangladesh. *Cities*, 48, 31–41.

Mohal, N. and Hossain, M. (2007). *Investigating the Impact of Relative Sea Level Rise on Coastal Communities and Their Livelihoods in Bangladesh*. Draft Final Report. Dhaka: Institute of Water Modelling (IWM) and Centre for Environmental and Geographic Information Services (CEGIS). Submitted to UK Department for Environment Food and Rural Affairs in May.

Nhan, N. H. (2016). Tidal regime deformation by sea level rise along the coast of the Mekong Delta. *Estuarine, Coastal and Shelf Science*, 183, 382–391.

Takagi, H., Ty, T., Thao, N. D. and Esteban, M. (2015). Ocean tides and the influence of sea-level rise on floods in urban areas of the Mekong Delta. *Journal of Flood Risk Management*, 8(4), 292–300.

15. Data collection from the Santal community: a journey towards an unknown world in ascertaining the nexus between reality and dream

Munira Jahan Sumi, M. Rezaul Islam and Ramy Bulan

THE SOCIO-CULTURAL CONTEXT OF THE STUDY

In Bangladesh there are two categories of indigenous communities. The first category of indigenous groups belong to the Chittagong Hill Tracts area and other hilly areas of Bangladesh. The second category, like the Santal community of Bangladesh, mainly lives in the plain land area of the country. In Bangladesh, the Santal community lives in the 17 districts of the north-western part of the country. For the present study, the researcher visited some areas among those districts to collect data and experience these places. Figure 15.1 shows the locations where the researcher made several visits to collect field-level data.

Bangladesh is a democratic country with a pluralistic society and culture. Nevertheless, the state has failed on many occasions to recognize its diversity. For example, the Santal community of Bangladesh is one of the oldest peoples of the entire Indian subcontinent (Tobarak, 1984). They possess all the characteristics that an indigenous community needs to fulfil to achieve the status of 'indigenous people'. Even the British rulers did not deny this fact. In the undivided subcontinent, they used to respect their indigenous customs and traditions. However, successive governments over time, for political reasons, have tried to forcibly assimilate diverse communities like the Santals into the wider society. Long-practised indigenous traditions have been ignored and denied by the state governments.

On the other hand, the Santals themselves are gradually forgetting and sacrificing their traditions, cultures, and indigenous group identity to cope with the reality of the country. They are becoming assimilated with the mainstream

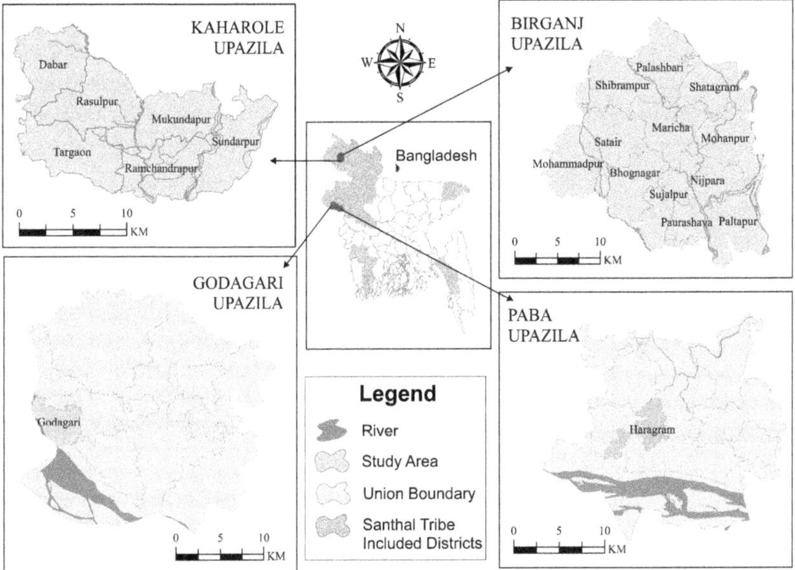

Figure 15.1 *The study context*

but not as equals. Mainstream society has always looked down on them and ignored the diversity and beauty of the indigenous society. The Santal community, like other indigenous communities of Bangladesh, are struggling to maintain their traditional customary practices.

Most of the researchers in this subcontinent have categorized the Santal community either as the Pre-Dravidian or Proto-Australoid group. According to some anthropologists, at the beginning of British rule in India, they used to live in Chotonagpur, especially in the districts of Hazaribagh, Palamau, and Singhbhum, and also in the neighbouring districts of Madinipur and Beerbhum (Murmu, 2004). In 1836, the British government granted them a permanent region for undisturbed habitation. Thereafter, the region was known as Santal Pargana, where they lived a happy and peaceful life. They used to cultivate crops in their land, which produced enough for them for the whole year (Toru, 2007).

Though there is confusion regarding the origin of the Santal community in the Indian subcontinent among researchers, they all agree that the Santals of Bangladesh are not the original inhabitants of this country and that they migrated mostly from the Santal Pargana of India (Debnath, 2010). According to Chaudhuri (2001), with time, due to the increase of population, deforestation and scarcity of wild animals and birds, they had to migrate to different places, mainly to the plain land area for their livelihood. They migrated from the Santal Pargana of India to the north-eastern part of Bangladesh after the great Santal Revolution in 1855. This incident caused them to flee and take shelter in distant lands and geographically isolated places. They moved to the hill and forest area of Bangladesh and started to clear the forest for their livelihood. Very soon, those lands came under the control of the local Zamindars who used to engage them in agricultural farming or day labouring.

Though the Santals have lived in Bangladesh for only a few hundred years, the numbers of Santals are very significant. They are the largest community in the plain land area of the country and the second most significant in the whole of Bangladesh (BBS, 1991). They are settled mostly in the north-western part of the country especially in the districts of Dinajpur, Rangpur, Panchagarh, Nator, Thakurgaon, Gaibandha, Kurigram, Lalmonirhat, Nilfamari, Naogaon, Nawabgong, Joypurhat, Bogra and Rajshahi. According to the census of 1881, a small number of Santals also lived in the districts of Khulna, Jessor, Pabna, Sylhet, and Chittagong (BBS, 1991).

Nowadays, a large number of Santals live alongside the mainstream Bangalee people in the plain land areas of the north-east region of the country. Here, the majority of peoples are Bangalees, and the Santal villages are distinct from the Bangalee villages. The Santals exclusively inhabit some villages, but at some places they have to live with the Bangalee people. Their traditional way of life and culture has come under threat through the influence of Bangalee Muslims, Hindus, and Christian culture. They are socially, politically, and economically oppressed by the local authority and influential people which means that they often move around within the territory of Bangladesh.

The development projects implemented by NGOs, who represent the West and the state, most of the time refuse to share the interests of the development projects with the community. Therefore, the community and their traditional way of life are the victims of modernization and civilization which compel the indigenous peoples to become separated from their roots and traditional practices. In the field research, it was found that one family of four participants (P2, P4, P6, and P9) had to change their residence within the territory and the whole family of one participant (P10) has had to leave the country because of oppression by local people and lack of protection by legal authority.

CHALLENGES AND STRATEGIES TO OVERCOME THE CHALLENGES

A significant part of the study builds on the current literature, including Bangladesh constitutions, national and international legal documents, and conventions. At the field level, the researchers arranged five focus group discussions (FGDs) (with the Santal community, the community leaders, and also with the key people such as NGO workers, legal practitioners mainly working for the legal rights of the indigenous people, development practitioners, human rights workers, journalists, and media people) and a face-to-face in-depth case study involving 12 people from the Santal community. Both approaches concentrated on how the Santals are facing problems in exercising their traditional land right practices and aimed to build a picture of the Santals' traditional way of life, culture, religion, and belonging in Bangladesh.

As mentioned earlier, first of all, the researchers read a great deal of literature to understand the indigenous land tenure practices in different countries. It helped the researchers in understanding the difference between general land rights practices and indigenous land rights practices and to prepare the field researcher to conduct field research. The researcher prepared a short but specific questionnaire as per the guideline of research supervisors which helped in collecting relevant data. The primary objective of this questionnaire is to generate data pertaining to Santal customary laws, the customary tenure/land practices of the Santals, the mainstream legal procedures for claiming land rights, and the formal legal structure of the Santal land rights practices. The ultimate aim is to elucidate the differences between the Santal land rights practices and mainstream land rights practices. Moreover, the study also investigates whether the present legal instruments are sufficient to support the Santals' land rights practice and if the answer is no, then why and how the laws are not being applied in a proper and equal manner. Finally, the study endeavours to analyse the law to identify the grounds on which to claim those laws as discriminatory. Before going to the research field, the researcher consulted with the research supervisors and some experts who have long years of experience in working with indigenous communities, especially with the Santals of Bangladesh. With their essential guideline, the researcher proceeded to field research.

A great deal of time was spent and efforts made to gain access to the Santal community living in the research site. During the field visit, the researcher accumulated field data and also collected some locally published books and other documents which were useful to understand the current situation of the Santal community in Bangladesh. While visiting the Santal community living in the rural northern districts of Bangladesh, the theoretical insights that were gathered earlier motivated the researcher to investigate in more depth the lives of these peoples, who are the victim of colonialism and its legacy. Thus, the researcher was relating the theoretical understanding to practical hands-on experience. For example, while analysing the existing literature, the researchers had to justify that the Santal community of Bangladesh fulfils the international requirements to claim themselves as an 'indigenous community'. With the support of field data, they were further able to provide a brief ethnography on the Santals of Bangladesh as per the requirements of the board of examiners at the proposal defence. The ethnography included the origin and settlement of Santals in Bangladesh, their unique lifestyles and cultures, traditional social and political organizations, distinct language, own script and religious belief, and traditional justice system showing that they are entirely separate from the mainstream society. Thus, the secondary data consisting of locally published books and documents on the Santal community of Bangladesh, together with the field data, collected through 12 in-depth interviews and five FGDs, combined to provide an overview on the Santal community of Bangladesh and to identify gaps in knowledge that the research was intended to fill.

Nevertheless, this journey was not as smooth as the researchers thought it would be. When the researcher went to the field, she found many things difficult and challenging. However, the researcher supervisors were always there to keep the researcher in touch with reality and encouraged her so that she could find ways to overcome the difficulties she encountered.

Challenge to Visit Different Places to Get Diverse Information

The researcher conducted the fieldwork among the Santals living in Dinajur and Rajshahi district. She visited different places of Dinajpur, including four villages from Birgong upazila, namely, Mission para, Somvugao, Chakbanarashi gram, Doriyapur gram, and Kollani gram. From Kaharol upazila, the researcher visited Pakortola Bazar and Bikrampur gram. On the other hand, in Rajshahi, she visited villages such as Ramnagor, Kakonhaat, and Shagrampur from Godagari union and Purbo bagan para from 2 No, Hargram union. The researcher went to different places so that she could collect diverse information regarding the Santals' actual land rights practices. Before going to the field, the researcher made sure that she could collect maximum data, and for this, she communicated with the local people who could help her.

Fortunately, before going to Dinajpur, the fellow researcher received a warm invitation from the parents and cousin of one of her colleagues and a well-wisher from her workplace. They have lived in Dinajpur from many generations, and they have a perfect understanding of some of the indigenous Santals living nearby. She also contacted the local authority and local leaders. Then, she entered the field where she conducted eight in-depth interviews and three FGDs. When she went there, it was winter, and the temperature in north Bengal was often below 5 degrees Celsius. During this time, daytime was short, and the foggy weather created a serious problem in travelling to different places.

Moreover, the indigenous areas were in the far distance. The researcher's field visit was made easier with the help of her colleague's cousin. She travelled to different places on his motorcycle, which not only saved time but also enabled her to collect maximum data. His family was a considerable support for the researcher not only in logistic terms, but also they narrated the history of the grievances of the Santals living in those areas.

The next destination was Rajshahi, and her visit was again made easier by friends who made all the necessary arrangements so that she could conduct the field research with full concentration. In both places, she was able to overcome the challenge of working in remote areas of Bangladesh in adverse weather and environment because she pre-planned the field visits. The researcher not only prepared the questionnaire, but also ensured necessary logistic arrangements were in place so that she could work peacefully without any other tension than research. The whole field research experience opened a new avenue in the researcher's mind and she started to think differently about the Santals than she had at the start. The researcher came to realize that they are more vulnerable and suffering from a massive identity crisis that was not apparent in previous research. Sometimes their vulnerability can only be felt, that is beyond expression in words.

Challenge to Cope with Different Individuals and Build Confidence in Different Social Context

After the researcher reached the field, she tried to build up relationships with the indigenous peoples living in the respective areas. The researcher had already built communication channels with the local political leaders and administrative authorities of the respective area. This acted as a safety net for the researcher as indigenous issues are very sensitive in Bangladesh. She knew very well that land is a crucial issue for both indigenous and non-indigenous people of the study areas. Therefore, the researcher took prudent steps so that her actions would not upset the local political and economically powerful people and at the same time the researcher's arrival would not generate suspicion and distrust among these indigenous peoples. She took every precaution so that the villagers did not suspect her as working against them or for the benefit of land grabbers.

For this reason, the researcher shared her aim and gave a proper introduction to the 'Manjhi', headman of the community, and then he introduced her to the others. Thus, she first cleared up any confusion they may have felt as to her visit. As mentioned earlier, there is very little research on the Santal community of Bangladesh, and most of it has been done on their social, economic, religious and cultural practices. When the researcher explained that she wanted to work on their land rights, she found this raised a number of expectations in their minds. As the researcher comes from a law background, besides collecting the field data she was able to give them some legal advice and tried to make them aware of their legal rights, especially of their land rights. The researcher came to understand their pain and their inseparable relation with the land. They used to refer to their land as their 'mother'.

Challenge to Adjust to the Lives of Indigenous Santals

The researcher spent a considerable time in Dinajpur and Rajshahi. Sometimes data gathering took a long time at Dinajpur because participants were very busy there during the day, as it was the cropping season, and at night they were tired. The researcher used to go to the agricultural fields where they worked. Whenever they were free, she talked with them. They always talked openly but used to be afraid when there was any question that related to locally influential people.

Also, there was another practical problem. The poor Santals do not have the money to enjoy the benefit of electricity in their daily life, and at night they live in the dark when it is not very easy to talk with them. Therefore, the researcher had to work very slowly as per their schedule. However, she completed the field research as per the plan of the research design.

Then, the researcher went to the Rajshahi district and communicated with some NGO workers, local writers, and researchers. She carried out four interviews and two FGDs there. The researcher held one FGD with some educated Santal young people who had converted to Christianity and now lived at Dhaka. They also enlightened her on how religious conversion creates differences among the Santal community, what is the reason for such changes and the impact of social and religious changes on their land rights.

Challenge to Settle the Question of Origin and Identity of the Santal Community as an Indigenous Community

The most vital challenge during the field research was to establish that the Santal community of Bangladesh fulfils the criteria of being an 'indigenous people'. Most of the time the state authority refuses the valid claim of indigenous communities like the Santals on the ground that they are not the indigenous people of this country and instead they recognize them as 'tribes, minor races, ethnic sects and communities' (Article 23A, 1972). Actually, from the beginning of their settlement in Bangladesh, the Santals have been experiencing an identity crisis as an indigenous community for various reasons. For example, the total number of indigenous communities and other information related to indigenous communities like the Santals in Bangladesh was last calculated in the 1991 census (BBS, 1991). Though, in 2011, another census was carried out by the government, no such separate information about indigenous communities was included there. Therefore, it is unfortunate that there is no exact record as regards the total numbers of the Santal community after the year 1991. The state is reluctant to work for the betterment of these communities. The Santals in turn find it hard to adapt to the rapid social and cultural change in the country. The main reason behind this difficulty is that the Santal community of Bangladesh, like other indigenous groups, are living scattered around the countryside.

Through the secondary documents, though it was repeatedly stated that the Santals are an indigenous community, it was only during the field visit that the researcher saw the whole picture. Almost all the participants, 11 out of 12, of the field research admitted that they are not the original inhabitants of this country. They have been living in Bangladesh for several generations but their ancestors migrated to Bangladesh from different parts of India such as Jharkhand, Mursidabad, Santal Pargana, Assam etc. One participant (P10) said that "though we are not the original inhabitants of this country, yet we are indigenous people of this area". He argued that when they first came here, the land consisted of forest and they cleared this forest and made it cultivable land. This statement was an encouragement for further study and to carry out ethnographic research so that a clear picture of their identity, social condition, their problems and the reasons for their problems could be produced. Therefore, the researcher collected the following data on the Santals to establish their indigenous identity.

Santal identity

People commonly say that the name 'Santal' is derived from the name of the area 'Santal Pargana', the place of their original residence in the Indian subcontinent (Sattar, 1975). The Santals inside their community address each other as 'Hor' meaning 'Man' and 'Horhopan' meaning 'Son of a Man' (Marandy, 2006). However, the participants of one FGD (5) vehemently claimed that the people of this community like to address themselves as 'Santals' rather than 'Saotals' as they are commonly addressed by the non-indigenous peoples of the country. They also said that "a person should be addressed by the name he/she prefers" and when they are addressed as 'Saotal' by the local people, they feel ignored, insulted and looked down upon.

Social institutions

Family and kinship: Family is the smallest unit of Santal society. There are three types of families in Santal society: the nuclear family, joint family and extended family. The Santal families are generally patriarchal and the father is the head of the family. Another old and significant aspect of the social life of Santals is kinship because this relationship defines both consanguine and affine roles in Santal society.

Clan: The Santal community of Bangladesh, like other indigenous communities, is divided into 12 clans: Besra, Chnorey or Core, Hasdak or Hansda,

Hembrom, Kisku, Marandi or Marnadi, Soren, Tudu, Murmu, Pauria or Paulia, Baskey, and Guasoren and Bedea (Fatema, 2007). Marriage is restricted between the same clan and a woman after her marriage adopts her husband's clan status and leaves her father's clan status.

Marriage system: Marriage is one of the most important and sacred events during the life-cycle of a Santal. In Santal society, marriage is known as 'Bapla'. The general customs that are followed by both Santals following Sanatan Dharma and Santals converted to Christianity are as follows:

1. Marriage between agnates or same group is prohibited.
2. Marriage between parallel cousins is prohibited.
3. Marriage is not possible if the bride and bridegroom are not in the same Christian group.

Divorce and dowry: Santal society allows both divorce and dowry. Women with bad character, commonly known as 'chhadwei' in Santali language, are usually divorced. Like widow remarriage, women are also allowed to marry a man who has been married before. In Santal marriage, as regards dowry, the parents of the bridegroom have to pay a bride price to the parents of the bride (Toru, 2007).

Cultural practices

The Santal community of Bangladesh have a long tradition of cultural heritage. Their religion is closely related to their culture. The participants of one FGD (4) said that "it is their cultural practices and religion that bring them together". This togetherness or social unity is one of their essential customary practices.

Language and education system: The Santals have their own language known as 'Santali' which falls under the Munda family of language, i.e. the Austro-Asiatic Munda language group (Toru, 2007). The Santali language does not have any script, but the language has been handed down from generation to generation through oral tradition and practice. In Bangladesh, most of the Santals are bilingual. The influence of Bangla is significant because they have to learn the Bengali language to communicate with the mainstream people and most importantly, to cope with the formal education system of the country. During the researcher's stay at different Santal villages to collect field data, it was quite clear that the people of the Santal community, both those who follow their traditional religion and those who converted to Christianity, recognize the importance of education. All the participants, converted as Christians, admitted that they renounced their religion and converted to Christianity because the mission provides suitable facilities for their children's education and better future careers.

Religious belief, religious myth and rituals: Religion is a vital element of culture for any group of people. However, nowadays, this culture has been rapidly changing because of education, poverty and conversion to Christianity. Education has a significant impact on their religious beliefs. During the field visit, almost all the participants confessed that it was the erroneous notion of their ancestors that "God creates land, therefore, the right ownership of land vests on God only". With the wrong conception, they rejected ownership documents, and did not pay any tax fixed by the administration of their times.

Traditional festivals, ceremonies and rituals: Festivals and ceremonies are the year-round rituals in the life of the Santals. The Santals performs festivals like Hindus (Sattar, 1975). Their year starts in Falgun (13 February) and ends at Magh (12 February). The Santals of Bangladesh used to perform about 12 festivals in the past, but at present, they only observe the Sohrai festival with the full festive mood, but others are observed partially (Ali, 1998).

Problem of Christianity among the Santals

In Bangladesh, the Catholic missionaries initiated Christianity among the Santals at the beginning of the twentieth century. The researcher covered the views of both groups of Santals, i.e. Christian (5 participants out 12) and Sanatan Dharma (7 participants out of 12) followers. According to the converted Santals, they have every right to be treated as indigenous Santals, despite being converted to Christianity. On the other hand, the followers of the Sanatan Dharma claimed that the persons who have converted to Christianity should not claim themselves as Santals because for them as an indigenous community religion is a cultural identity which has been disgraced by the so-called Christian Santals. They claimed that their social solidarity and unity has fallen due to those Santals. Conflict of interest, lack of faith and different religious views have broken their society into pieces. Moreover, they claimed that the Christian mission came to their country not only to spread their religion but also to grab their land in the name of development.

Economic conditions of the Santal community

Occupation: In the ancient period, the Santals were generally engaged in hunting wild animals and collecting fruits from the forest. As hunting and agricultural farming was their primary occupation, it was tough for them to engage in some new occupation. Moreover, due to lack of knowledge and skill, it was complicated for them to compete and adjust to the mainstream labour market. Therefore, most of the participants of the present study said that currently they are engaged either in agricultural farming or in day labouring. Their agricultural farming includes farming their land property or the land of another person as an agricultural tenant. Although in the past, all the farmers used to possess their land, at present, there are only a few farmers who work on their own land. Here, again they have to face wage discrimination due to Bangali nationalism. Bangali labourers are paid a higher amount of money than is paid to the Santal labourers. Sometimes they do not have work during the offseason. Then, as they do not have any work, they pass their time by fishing, hunting, and making handicrafts (Jalil, 1991). Due to lack of employment opportunities in rural areas, a good number of Santals, particularly the Christians, often migrate from the rural area to some urban places in search of non-agricultural employment opportunities and engage in small services and businesses (Tobarak, 2000).

Food and drink: Rice is the main food among the Santal community of Bangladesh but the poor Santals sometimes cannot afford rice three times a day. Santal men and women are very much addicted to alcoholic drinks. There is a very common proverb in Santali language, namely "give me alcohol, else death". During the field visit, all the participants admitted that their alcohol addiction is one of the main reasons for their backwardness and landlessness.

Land ownership: Land is said to be the mother milk of the Santals (Debnath, 2010). They possess a spiritual relationship with their land. The livelihood of the whole community depends on their land. Not only that, land is said to be a sacred resource for the Santals which determines their socio-economic condition (Islam, 2011). Most of the Santals of Bangladesh lost their ancestral land during the Liberation War of Bangladesh. After the independence of the country, this process of land alienation has not stopped and thus most of them have become marginalized and landless people. Most of the Santals do not possess even household property. They live either on the land of others or on that provided by the missionaries in return for conversion to Christianity. Some of them live in Khas lands (land that belongs to government) but this number is very limited.

Traditional justice system through socio-political organization

One of the basic customary practices of Santals is its traditional justice system through a socio-political organizational frame. Though there has been a huge change in their social, economic and political life, still the community has maintained the distinctive character of the traditional justice system. In every hamlet of a Santal village, there are specific political leadership and political structures. The main leader of a hamlet is called 'Manjhi Haram' or 'Para Manjhi' who has four assistants, i.e. Manjhi Haram, Paranik, Jog Manjhi, Jog Paranik and Godet to assist him. They control the hamlet as per their customary practices.

Depending on the nature and gravity of the disputes, different levels of courts were created under the traditional justice system, such as Gram Panchayat, Pargana Panchayat, Panchayat of the chiefs of Santal country and Law'beer or jungle grand assembly.

When there is a dispute between two individuals of the Santal community, they go to the Manjhi Haram. The Manjhi takes the initiative to solve the problem. He has to listen to the issue behind the problem from both sides. To hear each party's point of argument in the presence of both parties, the Manjhi Haram fixes a date for hearing. The Godet then takes necessary steps so that both parties to the dispute, the members of the Gram Panchayat and general villagers remain present at the hearing. After hearing both the parties, the members of the Gram Panchayat give their judgement. They consider the gravity and seriousness of the problem before giving the judgement. If one party is penalized with monetary compensation and the person is unable to pay the amount, as per customary practice, he is given extra time to pay the money later. At the same time the Manjhi has the jurisdiction to waive the penalty if the offence is not very serious or if the offender pleads his guilt and asks for forgiveness. All the money realized through compensation is collected and deposited as a fund by the headman for the development work of the village or to perform any religious ceremony in the village. However, if the dispute fails to be settled through the village Panchayat, the matter goes to the Pargana for final settlement. Again, if the dispute involves two villages, they would also be dealt with by the Pargana court.

From the field visit it was very clear that, of the traditional Santal justice system, the last two tiers are no longer functioning. All the participants except one of the in-depth interviews and FGD participants admitted that though the Gram Panchayat and Pargana Panchayat are still visible, the decisions of these courts are often ignored by the respective persons. Especially, the younger generation do not show interest in obeying the decisions of this socio-political structure as it is not legally binding upon its community people. Moreover, the huge number of Santals who have converted to Christianity tend to obey the orders and directions of the mission Fathers rather than the Manjhi. So, normally it is only the elderly Santals and those Santals still following the traditional religion, who still obey the decisions of the Manjhi. However, one participant (P1) said that in their village, they normally obey the decisions of the Manjhi Haram.

They try to solve the problem and also cooperate if they need to go anywhere else to solve the problem, e.g. if they need to go to the land office to solve a land related problem. Even if there is a problem for which they need to go to the court for legal protection, they have to sit together and it is their customary practice. They altogether decide what will be their further step and how they will handle the problem. They also arrange funds to bear the expense of the matter if the victim is not economically able to solve the problem.

On the other hand, most of the participants said that one of the most important reasons for the non-effectiveness of their traditional system is the formal governance system of the country. In an earlier period, when anyone wanted to grab the lands of a Santal, the Manjhi Haram ordered the whole community to protect the property of that person. Therefore, they used to fight with those non-Santal people with their traditional weapons, i.e. arrow and bow. Thus, under the leadership of the Manjhi Haram, they used to protect themselves but now if they do it, under the penal law of the country they will have to suffer imprisonment. When they go to prison, there is nobody to protect them inside the jail and their family in the outside world. So, they do not want to engage in these kinds of activities and the Manjhi does not have anything to do in this situation. Moreover, at present this situation seems to have changed once again because of the influence of the Christian mission within this region.

Thus, as time goes on, the Santals are becoming more and more marginalized. They are struggling with heart and soul for their survival but they do not have any proper direction to move forward or improve their living conditions. This is probably because there is a tension between the ritual-based traditional culture practised by the Santals and the forces of modern cultural transmission that compel them to change their socio-political and socio-economic conditions. The Santals often fail to reconcile their mythological past and its glorious traditions with the present and its untold misery and poverty. They are going through all these difficulties because of their ignorance, exploitation and oppression by their neighbours of other religions. The gap within the community on the question of Christianity has itself been exacerbating their problems.

Customary tenure or land rights practices

Indigenous peoples, like the Santals, all over the world share spiritual relationship and connectivity with nature. Their culture and identity are rooted in their land. The loss of their land follows the loss of traditional livelihood practices. So, for them, losing land means losing their identity (Gilbert, 2017). As regards the concept of ownership, one of the participants (P11) said that there was no question of class division among their ancestors. They had the belief that:

> God is the creator of everything on earth. Therefore, the ownership of land only vests in God. It is God who has gifted land to us. We should not care for anybody except God. All of us should live here and enjoy the food that comes from the land.

This belief generated several crises from the very beginning which made them landless and bound to move from one place to another. They followed this rule for land ownership and land management. Whatever they produced from the land was deposited with the Manjhi and everyone had rights over those foods. Each of them took as much as they needed and left the rest so that another person could also be provided for. They believed in unity and had no interest in preparing documents for their land and landed property.

This is the picture of most of the Santal families of the study area. In their customary land tenure system, they never thought of getting ownership documents. They used to transfer property among themselves. But due to their poor economic condition often they were unable to sell their land within the community. As a result, they have to sell their land to outsiders. But those outsiders were cunning persons and always took full advantage of their vulnerability and this is the common story of every landless Santal family. During the field visit, one of the participants said, "Our land is our mother. The way a mother gives milk to her child, land gives food to us. How can we sell our mother?" They sold their land only for survival and in most cases they were forced to leave their land by the mainstream society.

Right of inheritance

The Santal society is patriarchal and for this reason males possess a higher degree of position or status than females. Though a Santal female makes a huge contribution to her family, she cannot exercise the same right of ownership that a Santal male enjoys. In Santal society a son generally inherits the property of his father and a daughter get nothing but a cow if her father has cattle to distribute.

Dealing with Emotional Outbursts against the Discriminatory Policies of the State Authority

During the field visit very often this poor backward section of people became emotional while narrating the history of discrimination against them. The educated section of Santal people are very conscious about the reasons for the land alienation and landlessness of Santal community. They said that one of the fundamental flaws of the state legal system is the inadequacy of protection of indigenous lands through legal provision. Though some legal provisions regulate the rights of indigenous people living in the Chittagong Hill Tract area, the plain land indigenous people including the Santals are mostly excluded from the legal domain. The international indigenous laws and customary laws have no application in the national law of the country which is a clear violation of their human rights as per the Universal Declaration of Human Rights. Moreover, following the colonial legacy, the property rights established by the Bangladesh government have arisen from politics based on discrimination, domination and deprivation (Debnath, 2010). Therefore, this poor and vulnerable group of people have to follow the same procedure as the mainstream society.

In Bangladesh, there is only one provision regarding the restriction on transfer of indigenous land, namely section 97 of The State Acquisition and Tenancy Act, 1950. Though this is an operative provision regarding the Santal peoples' land rights, the Act is itself discriminatory. So, this provision has been often violated by the respective parties who made them landless and marginal agricultural farmers. A large number of Santals have only a piece of land for their household where they live with their family members and a huge number of Santals have no land property at all.

Land alienation is at the centre of other common problems encountered by the Santals of Bangladesh. This is one of the main reasons behind their poverty and other social problems. On the other hand, their land has also been subject to grabbing, either illegally (done in contravention to the law) or irregular (done through exploitation of loopholes in the law), because of the inconsistency between laws and customary tenure systems (Tobarak, 1984). Globally, indigenous peoples share communal land rights where ownership of those lands are not properly documented or officially recognized. But in Bangladesh, this concept of the communal form of ownership is not constitutionally recognized under Article 13 of the Constitution of Bangladesh. Again, due to their political and economic marginalization, the Santals have little control over their lands and the land policies are governed by the state.

In the case of Bangladesh, the actors behind the violation of their land rights are the influential and powerful mainstream community. A huge network has been developed in conjunction with local influential power holders, since the very beginning of the establishment of the Bangladesh nation state. The techniques that are being applied by them for grabbing and alienating lands of the indigenous peoples including the Santal community, are diverse. According to field information, land grabbing and land alienation are normally practised by opportunist groups to capture the indigenous Santal lands. Internal methods of land grabbing and land alienation include the following:

1. Fraudulent transfer of indigenous lands
2. Lack of education and knowledge about property rights
3. Language barrier
4. Lack of trust and unity among the Santals
5. Poverty and lack of empowerment
6. Division within the community and corruption by the village headman
7. Lack of strong political organization and leadership
8. Lack of seriousness.

External factors behind land grabbing and land alienation include the following:

1. Forged document of ownership
2. Coercion or intimidation
3. Violence and violation of human rights
4. Use of illegal and invalid land records
5. Distress sale of land under pressure and intimidation

6. Use of power through political influence
7. Lengthy court practice
8. Encirclement and harassment
9. Attack on culture
10. Harassment through false cases.

Other related factors behind land grabbing and land alienation include: government land taken by government officials; grabbing in the name of religion; and land alienation as an execution of a long-term blueprint of land grabbing.

REFERENCES

Ali, A. (1998). *The Santals of Bangladesh*. Dhaka: Institute of Social Research & Applied Anthropology.

Article 23A (1972). Constitution of the People's Republic of Bangladesh.

Bangladesh Bureau of Statistics (BBS) (1991). *Bangladesh Population Census, 1991: Analytical Report*. BBS, Statistics Division, Ministry of Planning. Government of the People's Republic of Bangladesh.

Chaudhuri, B. (2001). *A Bibliography on Tribal Studies in India*. Kolkata: Centre for Alternative Research in Development.

Debnath, M. K. (2010). *Living on the Edge: The Predicament of a Rural Indigenous Santal Community in Bangladesh*. Ontario: Institute for Studies in Education, University of Toronto.

Fatema, T. (2007). *Life and Living of Santal Women of Dinajpur*. Department of Anthropology, University of Dhaka.

Gilbert, J. (2017). Land grabbing, investments & indigenous peoples' rights to land and natural resources: Legal analysis and case studies from Tanzania, Kenya, India, Myanmar, Colombia, Chile and Russia. International Work Group for Indigenous Affairs (IWGIA) with financial support from the Danish Ministry of Foreign Affairs. Copenhagen, Denmark.

Islam, M. R. (2011). Changing patterns of economic life of Santals and Oraons in the Barind region of Bangladesh. *Social Science Review*. Dhaka University Studies.

Jalil, M. A. (1991). *Bangladesher Santal: Samaj o Shangshkriti*. Dhaka: Bangla Academy.

Marandy, J. (2006). Evangelization of the Santals in Bangladesh. *East Asian Pastoral Review*. Manila, Philippines.

Murmu, Fr. M. (2004). *The Santals: Their Traditions and Institutions in Bangladesh*. Santal Resource Page.

Sattar, A. (1975). *Tribal Culture in Bangladesh*. Dhaka: Muktadhara.

Tobarak, H. K. (1984). *The Santals of Rajshahi: A Study in Social and Cultural Change*. Tribal Culture in Bangladesh, Institute of Bangladesh Studies. Rajshahi University, Bangladesh.

Tobarak, H. K. (2000). The Santals of Bangladesh: An ethnic minority in transition. *Anthropology Bangladesh*.

Toru, M. I. (2007). 'Santals' in the edited book *Indigenous Communities*. Dhaka: Asiatic Society of Bangladesh.

16. Challenges in accessing rural area and managing sub-culture differences in Kuala Krai, Kelantan, Malaysia

Maria Binti Mohd Ismail and Raja Noriza Binti Raja Ariffin

RESEARCH CONTEXT

This chapter discusses villagers' transport needs in Kuala Krai, Kelantan, Malaysia by exploring the actual transport scenario in the study area. Villagers in Kuala Krai were interviewed to better understand their daily transport needs and behaviour. Comparatively, Batu Mengkebang is better developed and more accessible to nearby villagers than Olak Jeram and Dabong. As a result, the villagers of the latter two villages are facing more critical transport accessibility issues.

The hilly and mountainous geographical features of Kuala Krai have consequently resulted in quite a number of villagers being isolated from basic amenities such as schools, clinics and markets. In addition, poverty has further limited the mobility of some of the villagers due to them not owning any private modes of transport. The iron train of Kuala Krai, better known as the 'jungle train' that was first built by the British back in the 1920s, serves as the main transportation mode of the rural people. The cheap ticket and wide service network has made it the popular choice particularly for rural people. The train covers the remote areas where no other mode of public transportation has ever reached. The train in Kuala Krai's remote areas is not just like any other ordinary transportation; it is the villagers' lifeline especially for the school children. The train runs through the thick rainforest of Malaysia and serves the rural poor who are isolated from basic facilities enjoyed by other villagers. The train is popular among the school children due to poor alternative transport services and the distances of their commute to and from school.

Similar to many other developing countries, there are many weaknesses in the train service in the area. These problems were noticed during the data collection process. There is no integrated public transportation system. The absence of other forms of public transport or feeder services in connecting villagers or users directly to train stations has made accessibility the main problem for the villagers in the area. As a consequence, the villagers need to travel using their own transport or hitch a ride from neighbours to get to the available train stations. Most of the small stations in the remote areas are isolated and built far away from the nearby villages, which has further caused much hardship for the villagers. The number of train carriages was said to be insufficient during weekends and holiday festivals such as the Eid celebration as there are normally no more than three coaches available. Those who use their own transport to go to the train stations have difficulty in finding somewhere to park their vehicles due to the absence of parking spaces at the stations. Train stations were also designed without proper safety features, which has contributed to poor accessibility for passengers, especially for the elderly, children and women.

Findings from the interviews indicate that transport inaccessibility issues are more severe for those living across the river. Besides having to use boats as the transport mode for their daily social and economic activities, poor road networks in the villages had caused further inconvenience for the villagers. Consequently, this phenomenon has resulted in limited mobility, particularly for those who do not own private transportation. The basic infrastructure available such as jetty, boats and the pathway connecting villagers to the jetty and boats are also in poor condition. Water transportation facilities are insufficient and designed without safety features. Despite the existence of bus services, they are limited to only two types of services namely the express and shuttle bus with limited coverage. Although unregulated hired car services are available in Kuala Krai as an alternative to public transport, they operate at a cost that is very much unaffordable for the majority of the rural residents.

CHALLENGES IN THE FIELD DURING DATA COLLECTION

Unique Spoken Dialect

There were several challenges faced in capturing the villagers' insights on their transport needs. This chapter reports the three main challenges encountered during the data collection process. One of the most challenging undertakings was to understand and comprehend the Kelantanese dialect spoken by the villagers. Unlike the standard Malay language that is the national language, the Kelantanese dialect has its own unique slang and accent. Geographically, the Kelantanese dialect is only spoken in the east coast region of Peninsular Malaysia. Basically, it is mainly spoken in Kelantan, the region between Kelantan and Terengganu, the region between Kelantan and Pahang and some districts in South Thailand such as the area around Golok River, Narathiwat, Yala and Pattani (Mahmood, 1977).

The Kelantanese dialect differs from the standard Malay and the other local Malay dialects because of its historical relationship with Patani (Adi Yasran, 2005; Collins, 1986). Nik Safiah (1965) explains that there is a difference between the Kelantanese dialect speakers in the city and those from the villages. However, the unique Kelantanese dialect has made the whole data collection process in Kuala Krai an unforgettable experience. Despite the difficulties in understanding the dialect, the process presented an invaluable opportunity to indirectly learn the dialect among the native speakers. Some of the words used by the villagers like 'sokmo', which means 'always', and 'dok', which literally means 'no', were among the popular and easily remembered words uttered during the interviews. The villagers seemed comfortable with the standard Malay dialect used by the researcher during the interviews. This was shown by the way they diligently answered the questions.

Unique Socio-Cultural Background

Besides the language barrier, the different socio-cultural background in the study area made for another unforgettable experience during the data collection process. The rural folks were very polite and friendly in welcoming a visitor or an outsider. It is quite well known that the Kelantanese often refer to people from outside of the state as 'ore luar', which literally translates as 'outside people'. Regardless of the name calling, the remarkable hospitality is different from those situations that many may have experienced in the urban setting. Despite being poor and isolated from mainstream development and devoid of many basic necessities, the villagers welcomed the researcher warm heartedly. Light refreshments were always served during the house visits, which reflect their generosity amidst poverty.

According to Pawanteh and Kuake (2016) the Kelantanese are known for their fierce loyalty (taking pride in their home state of Kelantan), and close-knit, cliquish and clannish behaviour (among fellow Kelantanese). However, despite their cliquish and clannish behaviour, they seemed to immediately display their cordiality upon meeting a stranger. This is reflected by the way they address a stranger by calling them 'abang' or 'adik', which is literally translated as brother or sister. In this context, calling a person 'abang' or 'adik' signals the acceptance of that person within the community. Due largely to its historical background, Kelantan has always been a stronghold of traditional Malay culture and has steadfastly held on to Islamic teaching. Respecting the guest is one of the most important gestures in Islam, hence the warm ambience experienced by the researcher. Many aspects of traditional Malay values and beliefs are still considered as fundamental elements in Kelantan, whereas on the west coast these traditions have been eliminated by modernization and by contact with other cultures (Raybeck and Munck, 2010).

The politeness of the villagers in greeting outsiders signified the beauty of their culture, which is very much likely linked to the Islamic tradition of accepting guests. Similarly, the villagers who reside across the river were very hospitable and this was shown by them providing lunch for the researcher. It was made known that the cooked fishes were freshly caught by one of them. Basically, the majority of the villagers who live across the river are fishermen. Meanwhile, those with extra land area venture into small farming, planting fruits and vegetables. During one of the visits for data collection, a villager offered watermelons as a gift to be taken home. In fact, she also prepared fresh watermelon as light refreshment during the fieldwork. The behaviour and attitude of the villagers in treating the researcher with such courtesy and politeness allowed the data collection process to progress smoothly. In addition, the warm ambience created an effective mutual interaction between the villagers and the researcher.

Adventurous Geographical Landscape

The geographical landscape in the study area presented another challenge during the data collection process. Kuala Krai is a hilly and mountainous region with thick forest and some areas are separated by long, wide and deep rivers. There is limited infrastructure development in the area due to its remoteness and unique geographical features. The provision of roads, bridges and other basic facilities such as schools and healthcare facilities is met with severe difficulties as it involves high operation costs. As a consequence, reaching the remote areas to locate the villagers was a big challenge. The hilly terrain and thick forest contributed much to the difficulties in accessing the villagers. This situation is further worsened by the lack of a lighted road, which intensifies the somewhat eerie atmosphere at night.

Driving along the hilly slopes and uneven routes was rather difficult during fieldwork, particularly in the evening when it was pitch dark. As a result, the car had to be driven at a much-reduced speed in the attempt to put extra focus on the road. This often prevented the researcher reaching the destination at a more convenient earlier time. Taking a boat ride is another challenging experience. The boat ride is the main mode of transportation in accessing those who live across the river. The 20- to 40-minute boat ride crossing the Kelantan River was quite an adventure. Although a safety jacket was provided, seeing the width and depth of the river was an overwhelming experience. Upon reaching the village known as Kampung Bahagia, a four-wheel drive vehicle was used as the feeder service to reach the villagers' houses. Kampung Bahagia with a population of approximately 2,000 is extremely isolated due to the absence of a road network. Those villagers without private transport are more affected due to limited mobility, which restricts their access to many opportunities.

STRATEGIES TO OVERCOME CHALLENGES

Bilingual Speaker Assistance

To better understand and to interact with the villagers who speak the Kelantanese dialect, a bilingual speaker was needed to translate the dialect into a standard Malay language to facilitate the data collection process. A primary school clerk from the nearby village was solicited to assist in interviewing the villagers. His familiarity in preparing and reading school documentation that uses the standard Malay language made him invaluable during the interviews. Other than his ability to understand and converse in the standard Malay language and the Kelantanese dialect, he also has the advantage of being a well-known person in the area.

The clerk's familiarity with the study area charted an easier path in exploring the study area. To access and go deeper into the thick forest to reach the villagers was definitely an unforgettable and challenging experience. However, it was made easy by the help of the school clerk. He was responsible in leading and doing the introductions. The explaining and briefing of the study was again made easy with the help of someone who is familiar with the language as well as the area. Gaining the interviewees' confidence is fundamental in any data collection process and in this context the clerk made this possible. The seemingly initial reluctance of the villagers to participate in the interview was quickly dissipated by the presence of the clerk. This situation resulted in the villagers developing their trust and being willing to share their views of their transport needs and the current transport accessibility scenario in the study area.

Immersion in the Local Culture

Adapting to the local culture and behaviour is another challenge that needs to be mastered by any researcher, particularly for those who are utilizing a qualitative approach as the methodology. What followed after arriving in the villages was a process of immersion in the social atmosphere in an attempt to gain the villagers' trust to share information. Friendly acts were mutually met with a very positive and warm welcome. Food was always the medium to foster close relationships with one another. The culture of offering food to guests is at the heart of the Malay culture as in the Islamic teaching. A reciprocal approach in serving food was part of the effort to be accepted by the villagers. Maintaining respect and courtesy towards the villagers was also a fundamental requirement during the data collection process to maintain positive relationships with the villagers. In order to take their involvement to another level, the researcher stayed in the study area for about two weeks to better understand the villagers' lifestyles. The time spent was used to mingle with the villagers, asking about and observing their daily activities in the study area. This was done as a way to gauge the transport behaviour of the villagers in a more laidback and informal atmosphere.

Learning and immersing in the culture, values and behaviour of the villagers were made easier by their relaxed and sincere attitude. After gaining their trust, the data collection process became smooth and more vital pieces of information were shared, including some that are quite controversial. Some of the controversial information related to the local political culture. It was shared that the political culture has influenced the way money is being distributed, which has consequently affected development. During the interview session, some of the villagers shared their personal emotional distress about living in poverty due to the local poor economic environment. This is when some psychological skill is needed to defuse the highly charged situation. Silverman (2007) and Bunio (2008) acknowledge the existence of such dilemmas and stated that a researcher should always keep in mind personal motives for conducting the specific fieldwork. Nonetheless, the act of being an active listener eased the somewhat tense atmosphere amicably. Thus, maintaining some emotional distance may help create space for critical analysis and at the same time guards against converting the research interview into a therapeutic session.

Prepare a Well-Planned Schedule

A well-planned schedule is a must in conducting a fieldwork, particularly in areas devoid of many basic facilities. Among the strategies in facilitating the data collection process are getting people to guide by showing the routes and making sure that the car is roadworthy. Since the nearest petrol station is about 50 kilometres away and it took about 45 minutes to reach the destination by car, it became a routine procedure to ensure that the fuel was sufficient. This was done by estimating the distance and the fuel needed for each destination. Another critical challenge is due to the distance of the researcher's accommodation from the fieldwork area. The long travel time posed another issue for the time constraint in collecting the data. To solve this issue, data collection was done both during the day and at night. The barely lighted surrounding and the lack of a lighted path made the data collection an impossibility without the help of the assistant. Only the sounds of insects can be heard during the night travel to reach the destination. Despite the anxiety, the atmosphere was really quiet and peaceful.

The data collection process in Kuala Krai amid a challenging geographical landscape was made possible with the unconditional support and assistance from the villagers and the bilingual language assistant who voluntarily sacrificed his time in assisting the researcher throughout the data collection process. The data collection process in the rural setting was made easier by creating a mutual positive relationship. Understanding and acknowledging the participants' social and cultural background are fundamental traits in keeping a good rapport to further enhance the extraction of quality data.

REFERENCES

Adi Yasran, A. A. (2005). Inventori konsonan dialek Melayu Kelantan: Satu penilaian semula. *Jurnal Pengajian Melayu*, 16, 200–217.

Bunio, P. (2008). Friends or strangers? Relationship with an interviewee from interviewer's perspective. http://www.hanken.fi/qualitativeresearch2008/papers/paulina_bunio.pdf.

Collins, J. T. (1986). *Antologi kajian dialek Melayu*. Kuala Lumpur: Dewan Bahasa dan Pustaka.

Mahmood, A. H. (1977). Sintaksis dialek Kelantan. Masters dissertation, University of Malaya, Kuala Lumpur.

Nik Safiah, K. (1965). Loghat Melayu Kelantan. Tesis sarjana, University of Malaya, Kuala Lumpur.

Pawanteh, M. R. and Kuake, J. R. (2016). Orghe Kelantan: A preliminary study. *International Journal of Culture and History*, 2(4), 184–188.

Raybeck, D. and Munck, V. D. (2010). Values and change over a generation: Kelantan, Malaysia. *Cross-Cultural Research*, 44(2), 97–115.

Silverman, D. (2007). *Evaluating Qualitative Research*. Warsaw: PWN Lee.

17. Fieldwork experience: challenges and managing risks as a female researcher

Bushra Zaman, M. Rezaul Islam and Rosila Bee Mohd Hussain

THE CONTEXT OF THE RESEARCH SITE

This study was conducted in the Klang Valley area including its connecting cities and towns in the state of Kuala Lumpur and Selangor, which is situated in the greater Kuala Lumpur territory. The Klang Valley is geographically bounded by Titiwangsa mountains to the north and east and the Strait of Malacca to the west. The area also includes Rawang in the northwest, Semenyih in the southeast, and Klang and Port Klang in the southwest and the Klang river (Gin, 2018). This urban area is the core land of Malaysia's industry and commerce. The Klang Valley has become an important urban centre and home to almost 7.2 million people (Kuala Lumpur Population, 2020). These include not only many Malaysians, but also expat residents and a huge number of foreign workers. It is an area both economically thriving and culturally diverse. The population is supplied with an equally diverse variety of foods which forms an important part of Malaysian culture and economy.

Though Malaysia is one of the smaller countries in Southeast Asia, it has one of the largest proportions of migrants to total population in East Asia and the Pacific. In 2013, the fourth largest migrant stock was in Malaysia and it had the seventh highest (out of 19 countries) ratio of migrants to total population. According to the Malaysian Labour Force Survey, the proportion of immigrant workforce increased sharply between 1990 and the early 2000s from 3.5 per cent to around 9.5 per cent, which proves the demand for foreign labour in this country to keep up with the country's rapid economic growth (World Bank, 2015). Although there is still a shortage of labour in the domestic market, economic growth has driven the rise in numbers of migrant workers. Since hiring migrant workers is cheaper, labour costs are kept low in a number of sectors (Noor et al., 2011).

Migrant workers come to Malaysia from many countries in Asia, the majority of them from Indonesia. Other migrant workers are from Nepal, Bangladesh,

India, Pakistan, Vietnam, Cambodia, Thailand, and the Philippines. The migrant workers play a very important role in many sectors of the Malaysian economy, including manufacturing, plantation, agriculture, construction and services, and this is likely to continue for the foreseeable future (Robertson and Fair Labour Association, 2009). In 2019 the total number of migrant workers in Malaysia was 2,073,414 as reported by the latest statistics of the Ministry of Home Affairs in Malaysia. The number of migrant workers from Indonesia was 817,300, which amounts to 39.4 per cent. Both employers and government depend on migrant workers since they make up almost one third of the work-force in Malaysia. Low skilled migrant workers are often employed to carry out dirty, dangerous and difficult jobs (3D jobs). These migrant workers are not only inexpensive but also hardworking.

Indonesians constitute the highest proportion of migrant workers in Malaysia, and they have developed strong support networks of social capital (Zaman and Hussain, 2019). They share the benefits of networking among their own community and their cultural exclusivity has combined with their strong spirit of nationalism in caring for fellow migrants. In addition, they have very strong and positive support from their country authority and some agencies. For these reasons, the Indonesian migrant workers are able to use their social capital to cope with any situation in Malaysia. Moreover, the accessibility of social capital may also benefit development effort in the host country (Hasanah, 2015).

The government of Malaysia is aiming to achieve a target of USD15,000 or RM48,000 per capita income (as defined by the government and the World Bank) (Loh et al., 2019). To achieve this target, the government will continue to depend on migrant workers in the domestic labour market. Though migrant workers play a vital role, they face many difficulties and insecurities, such as wage manipulation, long working hours, verbal and physical abuse, no leave benefits and sometimes sexual harassment of female migrant workers (Amnesty International, 2010; Bormann et al., 2010). These problems and threats to labour security are exacerbated by legal and cultural issues. Migrant workers commonly face problems arising from differences between languages, cultures, ethnic groups, nation states and so on. Thus migration is not an easy option and it affects both the lives of the migrant workers and the society of the receiving country.

From this study, the researchers found that the migration perspective varies from country to country. For example, it is relatively easy for Indonesian workers to come to Malaysia and their cost of migration is not very high. But Bangladeshi workers have to spend a lot of money to come here as workers. Migrant workers are attracted to Malaysia for many reasons, such as higher income prospects, and to escape poverty and unemployment in their own country. According to the in-depth interviews, migrant workers struggled to earn 1000RM for the low skilled jobs in their home country, and this was an important factor in their decision to migrate to Malaysia for work. In this study it was reported that 58.1 per cent of workers came to Malaysia for a better income, 17.3 per cent due to poverty and 14.6 per cent because of unemployment.

When someone decides to come to Malaysia to work, their relatives help them to gather information about the country and its employment opportunities. Our study reveals that 47.3 per cent of the workers received information about jobs in Malaysia from their relatives. Job agencies were also a source of employment for 42.4 per cent of the migrant workers. Sometimes, the workers who are already in Malaysia convey information about job opportunities to their friends, relatives and neighbours in their home country. It was found that 27.6 per cent of the workers got jobs with the help of their friends and 21.4 per cent through relatives. When the workers arrive in Malaysia, 78.3 per cent share their living place with workers from their own country and 56.9 per cent live in apartments. They often share a house with nine or ten people where two to four persons live in the same room.

CHALLENGES IN THE FIELD

This section describes the challenges encountered during the research study. At the beginning, it was envisaged that data would be collected from representative samples from seven or eight labour sending countries to Malaysia. This posed a problem concerning language barriers as it is safe to assume the migrant workers were unlikely to understand English, and would only speak Bahasa Malaya or their native language. To overcome the language problem, researchers tried to get support from local students at the University of Malaya. Before commencing the fieldwork, English questionnaires were translated to Bahasa Malaya. But students had their own deadlines and examinations and they were not able to offer further help with the study.

Maintaining a proportionate sample size for each country became another challenge. As a result of these difficulties, the methodology was revised and Indonesia and Bangladesh were chosen to be the only two countries to be represented in data collection. In the following, the challenges with the workers from both countries will be discussed.

Gender Stereotyping

Socio-economic factors have a profound influence on migrants' attitudes and perceptions. In our study we observed that these migrant workers rarely displayed respect towards a female researcher. The respondents from both countries of the study treated researchers like any other foreign workers. Many of the male migrants who have worked in the country for a long time have female partners, whether legal or not, but this made very little difference in terms of respect shown towards women in general or the female researchers in particular.

Their attitude frequently made the fieldwork an uncomfortable experience. For example, they were very suspicious about our work, and expressed doubt as to whether I was really a PhD student or a socially excluded (sex worker) person or street walker. Despite much advancement in the society where females participate in almost every sector of work and sometimes perform better than males, gender stereotyping by men continues to prevail, as evident from the behaviour of the male migrant workers. As a female researcher, collecting data from these male respondents on foreign soil was very challenging. There are a lot of condominiums in the area where one of the researchers lived and many of the workers from Bangladesh were doing the 3D jobs there. When the researcher tried to contact them, one of them said "Do you think that these workers are your relatives, uncles and they have huge time to talk to you? It is not your country; it is a foreign country and you cannot work here according to your wish!"

Language Barrier

It has already been mentioned that the highest number of migrant workers are from Indonesia. So too, for this study the highest proportion of the sample consisted of Indonesian migrant workers. For the Indonesian workers, researchers faced a colossal challenge of language. To address this challenge, two Indonesian students were appointed to interview, and the questionnaires were translated into Indonesian language. But researchers identified that the quality and authentication of the collected data was not up to the mark. Back check and cross check of the data revealed that interviewers were not completely honest with the data collection and had been fabricating data. So, the researchers decided to continue the collection of data from Indonesian migrant workers for some days. By that time, the researchers had developed a good network with a few Bangladeshi migrant workers. After explaining this problem of data collection from Indonesian workers, four of these Bangladeshi migrant workers and one Bangladeshi international student at the University Malaya, who understand Bahasa Malaya, acted as interpreters during the data collection period.

Safety and Security of the Researchers

Poverty, unemployment, and the possibility of better income are not the only reasons why people come to work in Malaysia. There are also workers who come for political or other reasons. In any case, it is hard to predict their behaviour and the researchers may have to face different types of risks which can be detrimental to their physical or mental health (Islam and Banda, 2011). There was one respondent who was involved in a murder case. Somehow, the researchers knew this and decided to interview that person as an exceptional case. That person was working in a shopping mall and helped the researcher as much as he could. However, he made phone calls to the researcher late at night, having been given her phone number by his manager (also from his own country). He also interrupted her while she was conducting interviews with other persons from his workplace, asking irrelevant questions and harassing her with eyes and body language. This type of behaviour was not uncommon among respondents from both countries.

In such cases, the researcher's safety was a real concern. The researcher's respondents were usually males who lived in cohorts and it sometimes did not feel safe to visit their living place alone. Moreover, it did not always feel safe interviewing alone. Though the respondents did not seem to be involved in any criminal activities, they held stereotyped views about women which made for uncomfortable situations, as mentioned earlier. Some of the workers asked about the living place of the researchers and it was obvious from their language and behaviour that their intentions were not innocent.

Natural Reticence of Migrant Workers

The researchers discovered that there was frequently a 'natural reticence' among migrant workers to share information regarding their social capital and their livelihoods. This posed problems in building trust between researchers and respondents. For example, visa renewal is one of the major issues migrant workers face in Malaysia, which forces them to change workplace frequently, resulting in them becoming 'illegally legal'. Many migrants have a work permit, but what they are showing to get their visa is often different from the job they are in fact doing. Sometimes they receive a visa through agents after spending a huge amount of money. Very often the workers enter Malaysia with a student visa but come with the intention to work. The workers receive a very low salary which is often not sufficient to survive. They also face other costs such as for visa renewal, and the need to send money to their home country. Many of them come to Malaysia with existing debts which they need to repay. To meet their financial needs, some of the workers are involved in side-business which they do not wish to declare. For all these reasons, the workers were often anxious that if the researchers knew the real situation, they might face problems. And as mentioned earlier, those who came to Malaysia for political reasons or other motives were also reluctant to share their information with the researchers.

When the researchers went to collect data from the Indonesian respondents with the help of Bangladeshi migrants, it was very apparent that we were not trusted by the respondents. Some thought that we might be agents, or that we might do something with their information that may affect them negatively. There is an open secret in the migrants' community that many workers are not 'legal in the legal way'. For this reason, they are always anxious and struggle to trust others.

Even after explaining who we were, and what our purpose was, we were still regarded with suspicion and mistrust. Seeing us with papers in our hands (the questionnaire) made them think that we might be spies or agents of some kind. Questions about age were met with particular suspicion because most of the workers do not give their real age on their papers. Gaining trust and building rapport to get valid and reliable data was very difficult (Islam et al., 2014). Often respondents would refuse to answer questions or run away mid-interview. Problems with trust building were exacerbated by language barriers and the time constraints imposed by the respondents' working hours and desire for leisure or to be on their own. Often we felt that this study would be impossible to complete.

When we went to the field sites to collect data, we always showed our research permission letter to the authorities in all those places. Once again, however, this often was not sufficient to guarantee cooperation from the migrant workers from Indonesia. Sometimes, the officer in charge of these workers did not cooperate in this regard as well. Some of the Indonesian workers were known to the researchers by face as they were working in the living area of the researchers. After reaching out to them through the formal procedure, they were not willing to talk. This continued even after enlisting our Indonesian friends to make contact with the workers. When the workers' supervisor tried to convince them that it was nothing but an academic matter, they replied, "We are workers, not so educated, so we will not be able to answer your questions". The supervisor and the researchers had to talk to them and explain the purpose of the study repeatedly to persuade them, ultimately, to agree to be interviewed.

First Rejection from the Key Informants

First rejection was one of the most common challenges during the fieldwork, especially from manpower agents and concerned authorities. The researchers did some in-depth interviews with manpower agents, personnel from the high commissions of both Indonesia and Bangladesh, journalists, personnel from ministries of labour in Malaysia, and NGO workers. Not all of them were willing to provide information. The manpower agents, particularly, did not want to cooperate, nor did they allow us to record the interview. The same happened at the high commission of Bangladesh. After going through the proper channels to the high commission of Bangladesh, they did not give permission to conduct the interview with the personnel of the labour wing. Despite explaining the purpose of the interview was academic only, there was no cooperation. There are huge controversial issues regarding sending workers overseas from Bangladesh. After much effort on our behalf, other personnel from the high commission gave their consent to conduct an interview.

STRATEGIES TO OVERCOME THE CHALLENGES

In the end, by leveraging the power of networking, building relationships, developing acceptance, pursuing alternative avenues to address different challenges, persevering and being prepared, and utilizing the passion and purpose of a researcher helped us to minimize and manage the challenges described in the previous section.

Networking

Networking played the most important role here. Although some Bangladeshi workers did not show respect to the researcher, not all of them were like this. It was very normal that the researcher met a single respondent three or four times. During data collection, the researcher asked every respondent to tell their friends who were working there about the study and to mention others who might be willing to cooperate with the study, which proved to be a very effective method of reaching members of the target group. The power of networking is really great and it worked tremendously in this situation.

The researcher is very grateful to some of the Bangladeshi respondents who were very cooperative, and who properly understood the purpose of the research. As a result, they personally brought their friends and introduced us to other workers. Some of them used to go with the researcher during their days off to find respondents. It was a huge risk to go to the workers' living places, but those respondents helped us in this tough task also. Sometimes, when one of the researchers had to take her child with her during the fieldwork, some of the respondents who already knew her informed their work mates to come to the nearest place so that the researcher could meet them more easily. Maintaining interaction, networking and regular communication are very important in such research settings (Hussain, 2013).

To collect data from the Indonesian workers was almost impossible but some of the Bangladeshi respondents who know Bahasa Malaya well went with the researcher as interpreters during their days off. It was only with their help that the researcher was able to complete the data collection.

To give up after the first rejection is not wise. One of the worst things for a researcher is to hear 'no' from a respondent. But a researcher should have alternative ways to meet this type of problem. Moreover, the researcher must be prepared with some documents such as the consent from his/her academic institute, questionnaire and interview guidelines, abstracts etc. in case anyone asks about these. In addition, personal motivation is very important; being nervous on foreign soil is normal but the researcher must have determination, a positive attitude, personal commitment, and the courage to take on a challenge and overcome problems. The field may not be as the researcher imagines it, and such research may be very time consuming, but the researcher should have the mentality to enjoy the fieldwork. The experience of meeting different people, to know about their life is really interesting and every case is unique.

Formal Letter Provided by the Department

When we started the survey, a formal letter provided by the department of anthropology and sociology was given to the authority of different places where the migrant workers were working. The researchers submitted the letter to every place before starting the survey and took written and verbal consent before starting data collection. It was a very important formal procedure to get the help of the authority of a place because when they saw a letter from the university and knew the purpose of the researchers, they usually told their employees to cooperate.

Rapport

Building rapport with the respondents was a very important factor to complete data collection. Before collecting data from a worker, the researchers talked to them, fixed a time with them, then collected data according to the schedule. In this case, the researchers had to maintain a very respectful and friendly relationship with the respondents. After collecting data, the researchers maintained communication with them and as a result they helped to find other respondents. In addition, to build up rapport with the respondents, it was necessary to make them feel how important they were. When someone feels that he is an important person for a study, he will be more likely to cooperate. It was a key responsibility of the researchers to make the respondents understand that they were very important. They felt honoured by this and they tried to cooperate. Building a persuasive and prolific association was the means by which the workers were influenced and helped them to open up to the researchers.

Behaviour and gesture are important influences on people's attitudes. With due respect to all the workers we met, the respondents were from a lower income class, so the researcher maintained a very simple dress code while meeting them so that they did not feel a class difference. This researcher learnt from another researcher that the simpler you dress, the more friendliness you will receive. Moreover, very generous behaviour and gesture was important. There was a huge academic and socio-cultural gap between the researchers and the respondents and therefore very respectful behaviour was essential and helped to create a good relationship with the respondents for their cooperation and achieved acceptance from the workers to give of their time.

Acceptance

It is very important to have acceptance from both the researcher's side and the respondents' side. If the respondent feels that he is not accepted by the researcher, he will not cooperate with the researcher as well as he would if he felt accepted. To get proper information, it was an important strategy for the researcher to gain the respondents' acceptance by showing accepting attitude towards them. In addition, from the researchers' side, empathy to the respondents (who are workers) and courage helped to create the environment of acceptance. So, ultimately it was the relation and rapport between the researchers and respondents which helped to build a bridge between them.

REFERENCES

Amnesty International (2010). *Trapped: The Exploitation of Migrant Workers in Malaysia*. London: Amnesty International.

Bormann, S., Krishnan, P. and Neuner, M. E. (2010). *Migration in a Digital Age: Migrant Workers in the Malaysian Electronics Industry. Case Studies on Jabil Circuit and Flextronics*. Berlin: WEED – World Economy, Ecology and Development.

Gin, O. K. (2018). *Historical Dictionary of Malaysia*. Lanham, MD: Rowman & Littlefield.

Hasanah, T. (2015). Potential social capital of Indonesian immigrant in Malaysia: A preliminary research. *Procedia: Social and Behavioral Sciences*, 211, 383–389.

Hussain, R. B. M. (2013). Discourse analysis: A review in sociological fieldwork. *Man and Society*, 24, 97–115.

Islam, M. R. and Banda, D. (2011). Cross-cultural social research with indigenous knowledge (IK): Some dilemmas and lessons. *Journal of Social Research and Policy*, 2(1), 67–82.

Islam, M. R., Cojocaru, S., Hajar, A. B. A. S., Wahab, H. A. and Sulaiman, S. (2014). Commune and procedural level challenges and limitations in conducting social research in Malaysia: A case of disabled people. *Revista de Cercetare si Interventie Sociala*, 46, 255–272.

Kuala Lumpur Population (2020). https://worldpopulationreview.com/world-cities/kuala-lumpur-population.

Loh, W. S., Simler, K., Wei, K. T. and Yi, S. (2019). *Malaysia: Estimating the Number of Foreign Workers*. Washington, DC: The World Bank Group, Global Knowledge and Research Hub in Malaysia.

Noor, Z. M., Isa, N., Said, R. and Jalil, S. A. (2011). The impact of foreign workers on labour productivity in Malaysian manufacturing sector. *International Journal of Economics and Management*, 5, 169–178.
Robertson Jr, P. S. and Fair Labour Association (2009). Migrant workers in Malaysia: Issues, concerns and points for action. https://hdl.handle.net/1813/100839.
World Bank (2015). *Malaysia Economic Monitor, Immigrant Labour*. Washington, DC: World Bank.
Zaman, B. and Hussain, R. B. M. (2019). Usage of social capital among migrant workers for their livelihoods in Malaysia. In M. R. Islam (ed.), *Social Research Methodology and New Techniques in Analysis, Interpretation, and Writing* (pp. 160–189). Hershey, PA: IGI Global.

18. Data collection on acid attack survivor women: a PhD researcher's experience from Bangladesh

Tahmina Islam, M. Rezaul Islam and Siti Hajar Abu Bakar Ah

STUDY CONTEXT

Bangladesh, a rising economy in South Asia, was former East Pakistan and came into being in 1971, when the two parts of Pakistan split after a bloody war. The population stood at 164.7 million in 2017 and the land area is 143,998 km^2 (55,598 square miles). Islam is the major religion. It is a densely populated country and culturally male dominated. Bangladesh ranks quite high as compared to any other country in the world in case of acid violence. Rahman et al. (2014) and Mannan et al. (2004) report that Bangladesh accounts for 9 per cent of burn and acid injuries in the world. A statistic of the Dhaka Acid Survivor Foundation (ASF) showed that 3,303 cases of acid violence against women were recorded and 3,662 women had been subjected to acid attacks in Bangladesh from 1999 to 2015 (Dhaka Acid Survivor Foundation, 2015).

Even though the number of acid violence incidents is declining in Bangladesh at present, the fact remains that they still happen. The downward slope from 494 acid incidents in 2002 to 44 in 2016 (Siddika and Baruah, 2018) may seem like an achievement, but perhaps it is time to wonder what has become of the 3,000 plus acid attack survivors we have left behind. The government of Bangladesh has done a great job, implementing new laws that finally curbed acid violence to a great extent, but it has not been able to put a complete stop to it. So every year we see a number of new acid attack survivors. From available data regarding acid violence in Bangladesh, it may easily be seen that Bangladesh has a high number of survivors living a miserable life and therefore it seemed like an ideal location for conducting this study (Kalantry and Kestenbaum, 2011; Swanson, 2002).

The researcher selected ten cases from two divisions of Bangladesh: Dhaka and Sylhet. As acid attack survivors are scattered all over the country, it was not an easy job to bring them together. Therefore, the researcher decided to collect data from Dhaka and Sylhet divisions. Both the divisions represented similar socio-economic characteristics. Dhaka city, the capital of Bangladesh, is located in Dhaka division and most of the victims gathered here for medical facilities and education purposes. All of the respondents were listed beneficiaries of the ASF. Interviews of respondents from Dhaka division, five in number, were taken at the Dhaka ASF office.

Sylhet, an archaeologically rich region of South Asia, is situated in the northeast part of Bangladesh and has a diverse culture with people of different religions and ethnicity. The ASF divides the whole country into ten regions, where Sylhet and Habiganj districts, two districts of Sylhet division, topped the list of acid violence. Up to 2015, ASF recorded 72 cases of acid violence in this area. The researcher decided to pick five of the respondents from this division. In this case, interviews took place at the respondents' dwellings. It was easier for the researcher to get access to the respondents' houses as she also belonged to that community and spoke the Sylheti dialect. Selection criteria of respondents included age, year of incident, availability and willingness for participation in the study. The researcher followed a set of ethical guidelines during data collection.

CHALLENGES IN THE FIELD

According to Rimando et al. (2015, p. 2025), "Data collection is critical to the social research process. When implemented correctly, data collection enhances the quality of a social research study." It is very common for every doctoral researcher or early career investigator to face difficulties during data collection. Like others, the current study encountered different types of challenges at the data collection phase that had not been presumed at the outset. These challenges have been grouped into specific categories and are presented below.

Finding Potential Respondents

Finding potential respondents proved to be a big challenge in this research project. The Department of Social Services is the government office that deals with issues related to acid attack survivors, handling funds allocated by the government for them. But during a visit to its Sylhet office, while conducting key informant interviews (KIIs), it was found that this office had no record or information of survivors residing in their jurisdiction. They were only content with the fact that rate of acid related violence is very low at present and oblivious of the fact that there were more than 3,000 acid attack survivors in Bangladesh who needed rehabilitation and that funds allocated by the government for this purpose could be put to good use. Another visit to BRAC, the non-governmental organization (NGO) that works with violent crimes, produced similar results.

All the information about acid attack survivors was obtained with the help of the ASF. The researcher visited the ASF office in Dhaka on a regular basis during data collection. The first week at the office did not produce any result. Attending their office regularly from 9 a.m. to 5 p.m. did not help either. Most of the survivors that were found to frequent the office at that time were victims of recent incidents. The topic of the research is about rehabilitation of survivors. So in order to get relevant data, survivors from older incidents were required. Even though all the survivors that ever came in contact were listed in the ASF directory, the older ones were hard to locate as they often change their dwellings and contact numbers due to migration and other issues. So tracing potential respondents for the study was difficult at the initial stage and took a lot of time.

After finding potential respondents, getting them to talk also proved to be difficult. Even when they did talk, it was hard to obtain relevant information from them. Most of them had little time to spare, as they came to the venue of interview from faraway places and needed to go home early. While talking, the respondents spent a lot of time discussing their attacks rather than the needs and challenges facing them after the attack. On one occasion, a young girl did not answer any of the questions as she was with her mother, who was also an acid attack survivor. The researcher had to do a lot of work to persuade some of the survivors to talk and sometimes to no avail. Rima and Deepali (pseudonyms) did not cooperate at all and the researcher had to leave it at that.

Social and Physical Barriers

One of the physical barriers was that some of the respondents' dwelling places were in remote areas. The researcher had to travel long distances to conduct a number of interviews. Travelling to remote areas in Bangladesh is often difficult as the communication system is inadequate and most of the time there is no public transport. Roads in some of the areas are so narrow or broken or muddy that even private cars cannot pass through them. Being a woman, the researcher was conscious of the fact that travelling alone in remote areas of Bangladesh is not safe. Islam et al. (2014) and Islam and Hajar (2013) use the term 'cultural barrier' in their articles to illustrate some community level challenges and limitations, whereas the term 'social and physical barriers' is used in this chapter to represent similar challenges.

Jahanara (pseudonym), one of the respondents, lived in Jalalpur area, which is around 20 kilometres from Sylhet city. As no public transport was available, the researcher set out for that destination by taxi, which could go no further than half the distance due to road conditions, muddied by incessant rainfall. At that point, the researcher had to leave the taxi and walk to her destination in the rain and mud, accompanied by one of her students. On another occasion, even after arriving at Habiganj district, 100 km away from Sylhet city, the researcher could not reach the house of a respondent, as her house was situated at a place where no taxi could go. They had to meet at another place for the interview. Pierce and Scherra (2012) also faced similar types of challenges in conducting data collection in rural areas. They termed the challenges 'environmental barriers'. The authors also applied a 'locating appropriate participation' strategy to find appropriate respondents.

In some cases, family members of respondents remained present during the interviews and kept interjecting with pieces of information and in this way caused disruptions during data collection, which was sometimes exacerbated by the presence of children of survivors making a noise. Many people in Bangladesh are not familiar with the concept of research, and some of these family members hoped that they might receive some financial benefits from this research project, even though the researcher told the respondent the objectives of the study beforehand. In a country like Bangladesh where poverty is a major issue and most of the victims are from very poor backgrounds, they expected some form of financial help (Zafreen et al., 2010). After the acid assault, usually journalists and community leaders come to visit the survivors with promises. But a few days later they are forgotten. Sometimes, some of the survivors receive cash or in-kind benefits. One of the respondents refused to give an interview when she understood that no such benefits were forthcoming.

While conducting focus group discussion number 2 (FGD2), the participants who were members of civil society groups, got riled up over choices for a suitable venue, putting the researcher in an uncomfortable position. Although the researcher managed to fix a venue for the FGD, one of the participants, a reporter in *Prothom Alo*, a reputable daily newspaper, who exclusively worked on acid violence issues, refused to come. Because of this journalist's non-cooperation, the researcher failed to bring that particular media representative to the FGD session. Furthermore, most of the participants demonstrated some form of carelessness and negligence towards this issue as they made little effort to arrive punctually and seemed eager to get the FGD over with as soon as possible.

Identity Crisis

The disfigurement caused by acid attack makes the survivors ashamed of their existence and they tend to hide from the rest of the world. The common trend in Bangladesh society to stigmatize women who fall prey to gender-based violence like acid throwing aggravates this situation even more. As a result, the acid attack survivors find it hard to face society as a whole and suffer from identity crisis. All the women who were located with the help of the ASF were initially reluctant to speak.

Rumi (pseudonym), one of the survivors, said, "Everybody here knows that I was burnt from kerosene while cooking. They don't know that I am an acid survivor. If they come to know, they would hate me and consider me a bad person." Another survivor Rimu (pseudonym), a model, shared her experience saying, "Usually people cannot see my scars, but when I shared with the advertising agency about my incident they rejected me instantly even though I had been selected initially." When one woman, the friend of a survivor, was asked to accompany the researcher to that person's house, the woman declined saying, "No, no … I shall not go to there, be careful sister, she may be a prostitute in disguise." This 'friend' was an educated woman and yet her attitude towards the acid attack survivor was upsetting.

When the researcher approached a college principal with request for allocation of a seat at his college hostel for a student who was also an acid attack survivor, the principal granted the request immediately on the condition that this student would never disclose her identity as an acid attack survivor to other students. Another survivor agreed to become a respondent of this study only when she was assured that the interview would not take place at her home. All these situations were a constant reminder of the fact that women's identity as acid attack survivors is a serious issue in our society. The survivors have to hide it because of the way people, uneducated or educated, rich or poor, look at them, misjudge them and ostracize them.

Value Conflict

Talking with the survivors and hearing their stories was traumatic. People, born and bred in a privileged part of society, are sure to feel this pain when they are exposed to the harshness of reality that these survivors have had to endure. From the standpoint of any average person, living an average life, it is hard to bring oneself to believe and come to terms with the brutality that befell these survivors. So at different stages of data collection on a sensitive subject like acid violence against women, the issue of value conflict always lurked in the background as a stark reminder of the fact that there are some dark corners of society where you had never trod before and would never want to.

At the beginning, during a visit to the ASF in Dhaka, this reality struck the researcher at the sight of both old and newly burnt victims coming for treatments. Their distorted faces and disfigured bodies spoke volumes about the inhumanity of humankind. In the course of data collection, most of the survivors showed their pictures taken before the attack, showing how beautiful they once were and what these attacks had snatched away from them. This was only the beginning of the trauma for the researcher because the stories that followed were even more upsetting.

Among the respondents, five were married and had been burnt by their own husbands. Cuty (pseudonym) was always being beaten cruelly by her husband and in-laws. When she informed her mother-in-law about the indecent advances of her father-in-law, her mother-in-law again beat her and broke her arm. Rimu's husband, a driver, always wanted anal sex and would beat her up whenever she refused. Jhumi (pseudonym), a beautician, had to marry the man, a former lover, who had thrown acid on her, as she had nowhere else to go after the acid attack that destroyed her eyesight. That perpetrator only married her to avoid conviction and afterwards abandoned her anyway and now Jhumi lives with her aunt. Rumi's boyfriend had dumped her and after a few years, when she got involved with another person, the former boyfriend threw acid on her, making her blind from the attack.

Rehana (pseudonym) was six months' pregnant when an unknown person threw acid on her and eventually she lost her baby. Two unmarried acid attack survivors Tania and Happy (pseudonyms) wailed, "Sister, who will marry us now?" In Bangladesh society, staying single is taboo for women and for acid attack survivors it is like a curse. Jasmine (pseudonym), a divorcee and acid attack survivor, was regularly subjected to sexual harassment by her neighbour and did not get any remedy even after she had complained to a local leader. One survivor related how she was always being humiliated and undermined by her husband and in-laws because of her disfigurement and finally had to get a divorce. Another survivor told the story of how the police and public prosecutor put pressure on her to reach a settlement, in exchange for money, with the perpetrator who threw acid on her. The agony attached to these stories would affect anyone studying the survivors, even someone from a widely different socio-economic background. Being a female from the same community intensified this effect; the researcher became traumatized and had a difficult time coping with this situation.

STRATEGIES TO OVERCOME CHALLENGES

The challenges were overcome by application of intellectual and social networking skills and knowledge gained from counselling techniques as well as social work disciplines, which are described in the following sections.

Use of Alternative Channels of Communication

As the researcher could not find any direct way of accessing the acid attack survivors, she had to look for other channels of communication. The ASF arranged a training programme titled 'To learn to make pressure garments for acid victims' and a cultural programme on the Bengali New Year in their office. These two programmes created ample opportunities for the researcher to come in contact with a good number of acid attack survivors and find potential respondents among them. In the cultural programme, the survivors themselves performed and the researcher took part with them. This acted as an icebreaker for the researcher before the interview. Getting acquainted with the survivors through these two events enabled her to connect with them easily.

Taking Care of Respondents' Emotional Distress

The questionnaire was designed in such a way that the issue of acid throwing came first, thus giving the survivors enough time to talk about their grief at the beginning and give vent to their anguish. The researcher employed her ability to listen to the respondents intently and with empathy about whatever they wanted to say. Listening to their stories of pain and misery with sincerity helped build rapport with the respondents. While interviewing, the researcher made it a point to give each of the respondents a lot of time and never rushed them through a series of questions that was invariably going to bring back a flood of painful memories. She visited most of them multiple times. The first visit was spent merely on small talk, so as to give each of the respondents enough time and space to reflect on their situations, past and present.

Being a mental health worker in her country, the researcher was in an advantageous position regarding data collection due to her basic counselling skills. The experience gained from working in that capacity and application of the basic skills of social work like attending and empathy made the respondents feel comfortable and they easily opened up to her.

Making Use of Civil Society Engagement

On one occasion of holding interviews in remote areas, a local NGO and on another occasion a not-for-profit charitable organization was contacted to provide a suitable place for interview. As the researcher was familiar with these organizations, they complied with her request and the respondents also agreed as they too were familiar with those organizations and this strategy worked well. When stuck on the muddy road on a rainy day on her way to one of the respondents, the researcher reached her destination on foot. This determination facilitated the building of trust between her and the respondent. While travelling to remote areas, the researcher took one or two of her former students and on one occasion even took her younger brother to accompany her, to stay safe from the hazards that women face while travelling alone in Bangladesh.

In case of conducting FGD2 with the civil society groups, connections with Transparency International Bangladesh (TIB) Office, Sylhet saved the day. As the researcher is a member of the Committee of Concerned Citizens (CCC) of TIB, Sylhet, a number of journalists from other newspapers showed their interest in this study. Those journalists participated in the FGD and came up with fruitful responses. Communication, networking skills and goodwill of the researcher helped her navigate a number of social barriers.

Expression of Forbearance and Empathy

To avoid family gatherings, the researcher promised family members of the respondents that she would hear them after the interview was over and eventually she did. She also took some sweet treats and fruits as gifts for them. Gifts of sweet treats is a usual custom in these areas. Rimando et al. (2015) also applied the same technique called 'comfortable environment' while conducting data collection with women. Lending a sympathetic ear to these people and the show of love and respect through small gifts created a favourable environment for data collection.

No fund had been allocated for this study, let alone financial incentives for respondents who participated. But during data collection, seeing their hardships, the researcher paid for their transport. Most of the respondents living in Dhaka city were found to earn their livelihoods from giving tuition to children or some other small trades and were so hard up they couldn't even pay for their transport to the ASF office. On two occasions she gave small amounts of money to the respondents when needed for their children, and on another occasion bought token gifts. The researcher was shocked to hear the story of Lucky (pseudonym), an acid attack survivor and a college student who could barely manage one square meal a day as most of her money was spent on house rent. Seeing her sufferings, the researcher met with her college principal and persuaded him to allot a seat for Lucky at the hostel which would cost less. Later, the principal, a member of a UK based charitable organization, shared this story with the head of that organization, who assigned a monthly stipend to Lucky until she finished her Master's degree. Even though no fund was available for extending financial assistance to the respondents, the researcher made these contributions out of her own pocket. These small gestures of sympathy and fellow-feeling helped build trust in the respondents' mind and the researcher could easily connect with them. When dealing with sensitive issues like acid attacks, acting from a subjective viewpoint might prove to be beneficial for researchers.

Creating a Comfortable Environment for Interview

The respondents of the study were allowed to choose a suitable and comfortable place and time for the interview and the researcher went to meet them there, as some of them lived in slum areas and did not want to disclose their identity to others. Show of this empathy and respect towards the survivors helped them shake off the unease they usually feel about other people. This concept of 'comfortable environment' and a favourable location was followed by Rimando et al. (2015) during their data collection. Respondents living in Dhaka city were found to live in small, shared houses, where rooms were very congested and with little privacy. In those cases, the researcher persuaded them to come to the ASF office for interviews, as that office, a familiar establishment, would be a comfortable venue.

People living in rural areas of Bangladesh often display little common sense and go out of their way to inquire about personal matters of other people, asking questions that might make the acid attack survivors feel uncomfortable. So one of the strategies adopted during data collection was to avoid the presence of such people. Interviews were conducted in closed rooms where no outsiders were allowed. As a result, the respondents could express themselves with ease.

Assurance of Confidentiality

The researcher established a trustworthy relationship with respondents and assured them that all kinds of confidentiality would be maintained and no harm would befall them because of their participation in this study. Several phone calls were made to reach the respondents and make them understand the research objectives. In some cases, the researcher utilized the ASF hotline service to communicate with them, as it was decided that survivors who made contact with the ASF office once, would easily respond to their call.

Building Individualized Perspective

The trauma of investigating issues where subjects have been victims of brutal acts often generates a sense of value conflict in the researcher's mind and leads to depression. A non-judgemental attitude and individualized perspective may help researchers in the field of social work to remain objective in situations where value conflicts arise. Dearnley (2005) talked about facing ethical dilemmas while conducting her PhD thesis, which gave the researcher a new understanding of how to manage them. Advice from supervisors and finally professional help from counsellors at the ASF was sought in order to get over the depression resulting from trauma caused by data collection. Years of experience gained from providing counselling services and application of basic skills of social work also helped the researcher overcome emotional involvement with the respondents.

REFERENCES

Dearnley, C. (2005). A reflection on the use of semi-structured interviews. *Nurse Researcher*, 13(1), 19–28.

Dhaka Acid Survivor Foundation (2015). *Annual Report*. http://www.acidsurvivors.org/images/frontImages/Annual_Report_-_2015.pdf.

Islam, M. R., Cojocaru, S., Hajar, A. B. A. S., Wahab, H. A. and Sulaiman, S. (2014). Commune and procedural level challenges and limitations in conducting social research in Malaysia: A case of disabled people. *Revista de Cercetare si Interventie Sociala*, 46, 255–272.

Islam, M. R. and Hajar, A. B. S. (2013). Methodological challenges on community safe motherhood: A case study on community level health monitoring and advocacy programme in Bangladesh. *Revista de Cercetare si Interventie Sociala*, 42, 101–119.

Kalantry, S. and Kestenbaum, G. J. (2011). *Combating Acid Violence in Bangladesh, India, and Cambodia*. New York: Avon Global Center for Women and Justice, New York City Bar Association, Cornell Law School, Virtue Foundation.

Mannan, A., Ghani, S., Sen, S. L., Clarke, A. and Butler, P. E. M. (2004). The problem of acid violence in Bangladesh. *The Journal of Surgery*, 2(1), 39–43.

Pierce, C. S. and Scherra, E. (2012). The challenges of data collection in rural dwelling samples. *Online Journal of Rural Nursing and Health Care*, 4(2), 25–30.

Rahman, M., Bhuiyan, F. A. and Lovely, F. H. (2014). Acid violence: A burning impact on women of Bangladesh – case study. *International Journal of Advanced Research in Engineering and Applied Sciences*, 3(3), 40–57.

Rimando, M., Brace, A. M., Namageyo-Funa, A., Parr, T. L., Sealy, D.-A., Davis, T. L. and Christiana, R. W. (2015). Data collection challenges and recommendations for early career researchers. *The Qualitative Report*, 20(12), 2025–2036.

Siddika, A. and Baruah, B. (2018). Can understanding phenomenology and human capabilities help us address acid violence? *South Asia: Journal of South Asian Studies*, 41(1), 153–172.

Swanson, J. (2002). Acid attacks: Bangladesh effort to stop the violence. *Harvard Health Policy*, 3, 122–128.

Zafreen, F., Wahab, M., Islam, M. and Rahman, M. (2010). Socio-demographic characteristics of acid victims in Bangladesh. *Journal of Armed Forces Medical College, Bangladesh*, 6(1), 12–15.

19. Challenges, strategies, and way out techniques in conducting in-depth interviews among managers in Malaysian organizations

Nafisa Kasem, Shahreen Mat Nayan, Kumaran A/l Suberamanian and Sedigheh Moghavvemi

METHODOLOGY OF THE RESEARCH

The current study addresses social media's effect on customer relationship management, and its added-value, supported by the qualitative research method. Qualitative research is appropriate for this study to determine if actual business practices support literature claims. Literature consistently uses qualitative research while studying customer relationship management (CRM) (Chikweche and Fletcher, 2013; Elbeltagi et al., 2014; Mende et al., 2013; Parsons, 2013; Stelzner, 2012). For example, Elbeltagi et al. (2014) chose qualitative research to provide contextualized data in determining how CRM answers questions through a social media channel. In this regard, researchers often use a phenomenological design that is focused on description and interpretation of the lived human experiences of participants (Mayoh and Onwuegbuzie, 2015; Tuohy et al., 2013). Phenomenological researchers study phenomena by conducting in-depth interviews with people who at some point in their lives have experienced the phenomena (Marshall and Rossman, 2014). The phenomenological design was appropriate for this study, but as the objective of the study was not solely a focus on the lived experiences of the participants, the researcher needed to rely on both interviews and documentary evidence. Another point to be noted in this regard is that social CRM is a comparatively new tool for the business managers and one of the research objectives is to generate knowledge of their business strategies. In this scenario, in-depth interviews should be used, as the potential participants may not be included or may not be comfortable talking openly in a group. The primary advantage of in-depth interviews is that they provide much more detailed information than what is available through other data collection methods, such as questionnaire survey. They may also provide a more relaxed atmosphere in which information can be gathered in a setting where people may feel more comfortable having a conversation with the researcher (Boyce and Neale, 2006). So, this research chooses in-depth interview techniques to explain these phenomena in more detail.

The population of this study consisted of registered business organizations located in Klang Valley of Kuala Lumpur, Malaysia. These organizations have successfully implemented social media in their communication and customer management systems. From the study population, the researcher selected a person responsible for social media management (social media managers/communicational managers/corporate communication executives) to participate in the study. As the researchers progressed with the research design, it became apparent that the researcher would need to collect two sets of interviews, one set from the organizational managers who are implementing the social CRM and another set consisting of the agencies who are assisting and guiding Malaysian business organizations with the social CRM. While conducting initial secondary data collection regarding this phenomenon, the researcher observed that there was no proper database of Malaysian organizations that are using social CRM. So first, based on purposeful sampling, the researcher conducted an online search, by checking the Malaysia External Trade Development Corporation's (MATRADE) website directory (MATRADE, 2019). From the MATRADE directory, the researcher checked the organizations' websites, through convenience sampling. From the selected organizations' websites, the researcher proceeded to check their respective social media pages, which were linked to the websites.

The researcher chose this technique to identify the official social media pages for the organizations, as there are many fraudulent social media pages online. After checking the social media pages, the organization was chosen which has an active social media presence for the last six months (October 2017 to March 2018). After the initial screening, the researcher identified 129 organizations who had an active social media presence. Through email and direct phone calls, the researcher contacted 120 organizations from the list. Initially, only five organizations agreed to participate in the study, but after three months of contacting companies, seven other organizations were brought on board to participate. Thus a total of 12 organizations constituted the final sample in this process. After conducting the first three interviews, it was clear to the researcher that social CRM vendor organizations also needed to be interviewed for this research. The prior three participants clearly stated the importance of media agencies in this regard, so the researcher decided to interview the agencies as well. From an online search, the researcher found some relevant organizations and checked their websites to see whether this organization provided social media services. Based on purposeful sampling, nine relevant organizations were selected and from this, four organizations agreed to participate. So, altogether, the sample size was 16, consisting of 4 media organizations and 12 business organizations.

RESEARCH CONTEXT

The research focuses on business organizations in Malaysia. In recent years, we have seen a boom in the use of social media in business and organizational settings. Social media in business for communication purposes is used widely in the modern business world, and Malaysian business is no exception. Progressive internet innovation has brought many opportunities for the country's business community such as accumulation of consumer information and improved communication interactivity. Different forms of interaction have been made possible through social media platforms such as Facebook, Twitter, YouTube, and others. News can be sent and received around the world in seconds through these communication platforms. Furthermore these platforms can be used with minimal expense. In that capacity, social media pages are an incredible medium to distribute data to the general populace. Social media is ideal for marketing products and services, due to its wide availability.

Social media differs from traditional media in two principal ways. First, there are more individuals involved, who are both content creators and content distributors; second, communication frequently involves communication exchange, which is a social perspective of two-way communication (Chen, 2012). Marketing has always been an important activity for organizations who wish to convey information about their products and services to potential consumers. Although traditional kinds of marketing, for example, newspaper advertisements, radio, and TV are still used as mainstream marketing channels among organizations, social media has opened up many more opportunities to access potential customers/clients. In business field, rivalry is extremely intense, and it moves rapidly. A vast amount of new commodities have been created to be sold to society at large. In order to present and promote these products and services, social media is becoming increasingly important, since the expenses for printed promotional space are high.

In Malaysian context, the growth in internet usage has ballooned in recent years. According to the Malaysian Communication and Multimedia Commission (MCMC) survey (2018), the percentage of internet users in 2018 stood at 87.4%, a 10.5% increase from 76.9% in 2016. There were approximately 28.7 million internet users, an increase from 24.5 million in 2016 (MCMC, 2018). The internet has become a pivotal medium in social engagement. Text communication and visiting social networking platforms were the most common activities for internet users (96.5% and 85.6% respectively) (MCMC, 2018). WhatsApp and Facebook were the most popular communication and social networking platforms (MCMC, 2018). Participation in online banking and financial activities has also increased – more than half of internet users were using online banking (54.2%) in 2018, compared to 41.7% in 2016 (MCMC, 2018).

Social media utilization has turned out to be pervasive, and associations need to deal with this instrument to meet their key objectives. Social media has picked up a particular reputation in the current business framework, as a cheap and convenient mode of communications. Organizations are realizing it is crucial to alter their ways, to deal with CRM and grow new advertising capacities that encourage customer fulfilment. In addition to encouraging relational interchange, social media applications have empowered customers to connect with business associations, and allow them to play a functioning role in co-making their engagements (Prahalad and Ramaswamy, 2004). Currently, executives are incorporating social media applications into the existing CRM frameworks, to grow new capacities that enhance customer satisfaction and fulfilment (Trainor et al., 2014). This merger of existing CRM frameworks with social media has extended the idea of CRM, to involve more communitarian, intuitiveness, and organized means of dealing with customer relationships (Trainor et al., 2014). New terms such as 'social customer relationship management' characterize and portray this approach to creating and managing customer relationships (Greenberg, 2010a, 2010b; Lehmkuhl and Jung, 2013).

According to Garrido-Moreno et al. (2014), the concept of CRM arose in the late 1990s. As CRM has emerged with business trends, social media has been incorporated into several businesses to achieve their targeted client base to develop stronger relationships. Information gathered regarding consumer demographics and behaviour patterns shows that an organization can easily focus on clients with special promotions and develop a relationship that may profit every customer and company in the long run. CRM, together with knowledge selection and trialling, will require businesses to gather the information that is necessary to collect and analyse data in a cohesive strategy. Social customer relationship management, as a business strategy, is a technology platform to support business rules and processes, and can target and interact with customers in a better language for mutual benefits. Every business owner and customer should see value from this, in a genuine exchange of information on a social platform.

Malaysian organizations have started to use social media in this fashion. According to the Burson-Marsteller Asia Pacific (2011) report, Malaysian firms use social media for corporate communications and marketing activities. The results of the study revealed that, among the Southeast Asian organizations, Malaysian, Thai, and Filipino organizations have invested actively in social media. It was also found that South Korean, Australian, and Malaysian organizations are actively promoting their social media channels, through their corporate websites (Slover-Linett and Stoner, 2011). This shows that Malaysian organizations have started to realize the importance of social media and are taking it seriously to improve their businesses. Socialbakers' November 2018 report discusses the growth rates of a number of business organizations in Malaysia, and this month's top social media contents created by PETRONAS and Celcom Axiata. As per the report, AirAsia was the top Twitter page in numbers of consumer engagement, and Traveloka Malaysia was the fastest growing Twitter page in the numbers of fans following. Celcom Axiata was the most liked and talked about YouTube video of this month (Socialbakers, 2018).

According to Statista's 2017 survey, the number of Malaysia's internet users in 2016 was 21.93 million people. This figure is projected to grow to 23.41 million in 2022. According to Nielsen 2015 online survey, 66% of Malaysian online consumers responded to social media advertisements of online shopping portals. Malaysian revenue in the 'e-commerce' market amounted to US$894m in 2016 and revenue is expected to show an annual growth rate (CAGR 2016–2021) of 23.7% resulting in a market volume of US$2,585m in 2021 (Statista, 2017). Nearly three quarters of Malaysian respondents use social media to access promotional offerings while shopping and consumers in South-East Asia demonstrate a strong desire to use social media in forming associations with their preferred brands (Pew Research Center, 2016). According to a 2016 digital report (wearesocial, 2016) 20.6 million people were using the internet, which was 68% of the total population; 59% of the total population was active as social app users, like Facebook; and 52% of the total population use mobile social applications, such as WhatsApp. Facebook is the most popular social networking app in Malaysia, with 41% of the total population using it. WhatsApp on the other hand is the most popular mobile app, with widest usage of over 39% of the entire population (wearesocial, 2016). It is also observed that 50% of the overall social media users are engaging in e-commerce, that is buying products online (wearesocial, 2016). Several Malaysian organizations, like AirAsia, are also promoting their brands abroad using social media (Wong, 2016). AirAsia launched a Facebook campaign to raise its brand awareness in the Australian market, where the company started its initial flights and is competitive in the market. The 'give away a plane' campaign prompted Facebook users to choose up to 302 of their Facebook friends for the potential prize of a flight to Kuala Lumpur. The campaign was largely successful in attaining its objectives. As a result of the campaign, AirAsia is expecting to double the number of daily flights from Sydney and has increased its Facebook fan base by 30%. Furthermore, this single campaign generated

12,500 entries and reached about 2.2 million people on Facebook (Jung et al., 2016; Whitelock et al., 2013).

Figures such as these suggest the importance of studying the value of CRM to business contexts more widely. Previous researchers like Choudhury and Harrigan, (2014), Trainor et al. (2014) and Wang and Kim (2017) focused mainly on quantitative approaches to studying CRM, but qualitative studies from an organizational perspective are less common. So, the primary focus of the research was to identify the usage of social media among Malaysian organizations in regard to social CRM from a qualitative perspective.

MAJOR CHALLENGES IN THE FIELD

In the phase of data collection, a number of challenges were encountered and effectively overcome by the researcher. These challenges, along with the methodologies employed to deal with them, are discussed below.

Choosing the Appropriate Organization

In the Malaysian setting, it was a challenge for the researcher to find appropriate organizations with a substantial social media presence in recent years due to the lack of a database in this regard. Previous researchers in developed nations have been able to identify databases of a number of organizations as a result of their social media activity. In MATRADE's listing of organizations, however, there are a large number of organizations listed which do not always provide this data. Malaysia External Trade Development Corporation (MATRADE) is a national exchange advancement organization, under the Ministry of International Trade and Industry, and enrolment into its directory elevates Malaysian businesses to worldwide entities. The researcher used the MATRADE (2019) directory to identify organizations which could be studied in relation to their social CRM activity (Figures 19.1 and 19.2).

The organizations were randomly selected by the researcher from this database and their websites were accessed and searched. The fundamental objective of the researcher was to find the social media links from the organization's website. This was not always easy as there are many phoney pages on such social media platforms (Figure 19.3).

Pinpointing Respondents Inside the Organization

After the organization was chosen, the next challenge was to locate the suitable respondents to interview. Usually, the organizational point of contact in Malaysian establishments is the sales or customer service division, where buyers can call. However, to know more about their social media activities,

Source: MATRADE (2019).

Figure 19.1 MATRADE database

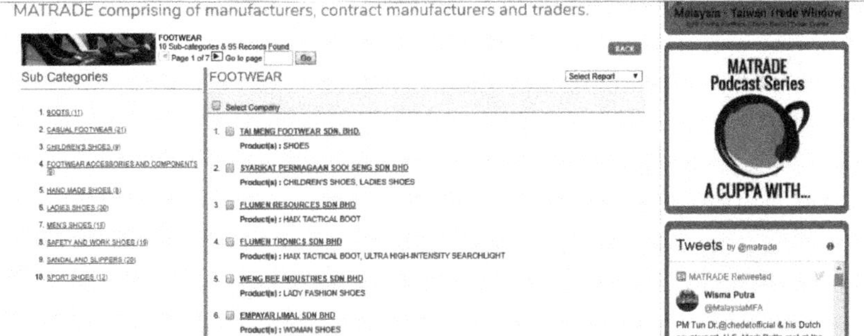

Source: MATRADE (2019).

Figure 19.2 Organization listing under each category

planning, and issues in customer relationship management, the researcher needed to interview the mid-level manager, who had access to this information. The contact details given on the website are usually of the front office, so initially the researcher went in person to the organization's workplaces. The researcher visited seven or eight organizations in the first 15 days of data collection, and still did not manage to collect the desired contact data. Two or three organizations gave email addresses to the researcher to contact. The researcher provided the organizations with the university authorization letter and consent form, which gave all the details of the research. Although the researcher was told that someone would be in contact, unfortunately no information was received from the organization as a result of this effort. The email addresses the researcher was given were also a dead end because the recipients

Here, we searched Beryl's (a famous Malaysian chocolate brand) in Facebook. We can see along with the original page, there are some other pages related with the brand came up. To get the actual social media page, the researcher need to select the page which link is provided in the organizations website.

Source: Authors.

Figure 19.3 Example of Facebook pages

never replied to any of the messages. Initially, this became a matter of great concern at the data collection stage.

Rather than going to the organizations in person, the researcher began to contact the selected organizations via telephone. This method was also not a productive one. For instance, when the researcher contacted the telecom organization, the call went to the organization's front office, from where the call was transferred to the customer care unit, where the call was later transferred to the corporate correspondence, where another email address was given. This discussion lasted 27 minutes, and the researcher needed to report the same details about the research at each of the three levels. A few organizations put the call on hold and following 20 minutes of holding the call, it would naturally cut off. Thus, using a telephone was not an appropriate technique in this situation. The email addresses provided were also in no way helpful.

Another technique employed by the researcher was the email address that was given in the 'contact us' tab on the organizational websites. This contact tab had a remark box, where one could compose a query. Some 30 organizations were contacted by using this method; seven of them responded but declined the invitation to be a part of the research. Some of the organizations responded with yet more email addresses and just one organization agreed to be interviewed.

Overcoming the Gatekeepers

As discussed in the previous segment, to get the actual respondent from the selected organizations was challenging, because of the gatekeepers. After one month of successful data collection from the first organization that agreed to be part of the study, the researcher decided to employ another technique to approach the gatekeepers. The researcher utilized Facebook messenger to contact the organizations directly. The organizational Facebook page is usually managed by the marketing department or social media division of the organization, and this meant it was easier to reach the respective department rather than through the traditional point of contact. Through this method, three more organizations agreed to be part of the interviewing procedure.

Language Barrier

While reaching out to different Malaysian organizational websites, the researcher discovered numerous Chinese and Malaysian websites. As an international research student, it was challenging for her to understand the language used on these sites. Often, those websites do not have English translated pages, and in the case of social media pages, this problem also existed. Although on Facebook there was a translation option, often it was not adequate.

The researcher also thinks that the organization did not provide sufficient and appropriate safety measures for a female researcher to conduct the study. In addition, at every point of contact, the researcher was expected to introduce herself by passport and her school's ID alongside research documents in order to access the organizations. In some cases, even with the required documents, the researcher could not access the organization, due to her being a foreign nationality. While reaching out to those organizations via LinkedIn, a few of the respondents also declined because the researcher was a foreign student. In the prior segment, it was referenced that an organization who responded through email declined to participate and this was because of the researcher's nationality. This limitation was challenging to overcome by the researcher, as were the organizations' concerns over security, which they sometimes cited as a reason not to participate in the study.

Trust Issue

Another critical challenge that was encountered by the researcher was to gain the trust of the respondents. As the researcher reached numerous mid-level managers, their worries centred on trust issues and the confidentiality of their identity. The researcher made every attempt to reassure them, as a declaration form was attached with the email invitation to all respondents, which guaranteed the confidentiality of the respondents' identity.

STRATEGIES TO OVERCOME THE CHALLENGES

The following strategies were adopted to overcome the challenges in this research.

Check Social Media Pages Before Contacting the Organizations

At this stage, the researcher examined the social media pages of these organizations to gather more data. Researchers need to discard those organizations who use a single social media platform in cases where it has not been active over the last six months before the inquiry (in this case October 2017 to March 2018). Through this screening method, 129 organizations were chosen as the sample for data collection. The researcher first needed to build her database, to choose the right organizations, to overcome the sample selection challenges.

Using Other Methods to Pinpoint the Respondents

Another crucial point of contact was through LinkedIn. LinkedIn is a social platform for experts, where any individual can contact an individual related to his/her professional interest. In recent years, LinkedIn has become a more accessible place for professionals and experts to get in touch with one another. The researcher created a professional ID in LinkedIn, and began to search for social media managers, marketing managers, and corporate communication managers of the selected organizations. LinkedIn has an option of sending a message to particular individuals that one wants to contact. The researcher contacted more than 30 individuals working in particular organizations and expert in particular field over a two-month period of data collection. Out of these, 20 people indicated enthusiasm for the study, and the researcher had back and forth correspondence with them through LinkedIn and emails to seek their participation in the interview sessions. Eight mid-level managers agreed to be interview respondents.

Another four respondents from other offices were reached by using direct telephone numbers that the researcher collected personally through meeting with them at three business conferences during the data collection period. The researcher participated in the MITEC Conference 2018, SME CEO Forum 2018, and SME Biz Convention 2018 for this reason. To be a participant in these events as a student was challenging. The researcher was appreciative for this opportunity by her supervisors, who had managed to gain her admittance to these esteemed meetings. While going to these events, the sole objective of the researcher was to become acquainted with mid-level managers of the selected organizations and get their contact details.

Taking Help from Local Students

Language was another barrier but the researcher got some assistance from her local friends, who helped her to translate and interpret messages, as Google translator was of little help in this regard.

Overcoming Trust Issue

To acquire the trust of the respondent, the researcher was consistently utilizing the university affiliated email and sent all the related research documents such as university authorization. Occasionally, the researcher's supervisors in the university also emailed some respondents to build trust in this exercise. If the respondent asked the researcher to let them see the semi-structured questions before the interview, to allay their concerns over what topics would be covered, the researcher willingly did so.

REFERENCES

Boyce, C. and Neale, P. (2006). *Conducting In-Depth Interviews: A Guide for Designing and Conducting In-Depth Interviews for Evaluation Input*. Watertown, MA: Pathfinder International.

Burson-Marsteller (2011). *Asia-Pacific Corporate Social Media Study 2011*. https://issuu.com/burson-marsteller-emea/docs/burson-marstellerasia-pacificcorporatesocialmedias.

Chen, G.-M. (2012). The impact of new media on intercultural communication in global context. *China Media Research*, 8(2), 1–10.

Chikweche, T. and Fletcher, R. (2013). Customer relationship management at the base of the pyramid: Myth or reality? *Journal of Consumer Marketing*, 30(3), 295–309.

Choudhury, M. M. and Harrigan, P. (2014). CRM to social CRM: The integration of new technologies into customer relationship management. *Journal of Strategic Marketing*, 22(2), 149–176.

Elbeltagi, I., Kempen, T. and Garcia, E. (2014). Pareto-principle application in non-IT supported CRM processes: A case study of a Dutch manufacturing SME. *Business Process Management Journal*, 20(1), 129–150.

Garrido-Moreno, A., Lockett, N. and García-Morales, V. (2014). Paving the way for CRM success: The mediating role of knowledge management and organizational commitment. *Information & Management*, 51(8), 1031–1042.

Greenberg, P. (2010a). *CRM at the Speed of Light: Social CRM Strategies, Tools, and Techniques*. New York: McGraw-Hill.

Greenberg, P. (2010b). The impact of CRM 2.0 on customer insight. *Journal of Business & Industrial Marketing*, 25(6), 410–419.

Jung, J., Shim, S. W., Jin, H. S. and Khang, H. (2016). Factors affecting attitudes and behavioural intention towards social networking advertising: A case of Facebook users in South Korea. *International Journal of Advertising*, 35(2), 248–265.

Lehmkuhl, T. and Jung, R. (2013). Towards social CRM: Scoping the concept and guiding research. *BLED 2013 Proceedings 14*. https://aisel.aisnet.org/bled2013/14.

Marshall, C. and Rossman, G. B. (2014). *Designing Qualitative Research*. Thousand Oaks, CA: Sage.

MATRADE (2019). *MATRADE Directory*. http://www.matrade.gov.my/en/malaysia-products-directory-matrade.

Mayoh, J. and Onwuegbuzie, A. J. (2015). Toward a conceptualization of mixed methods phenomenological research. *Journal of Mixed Methods Research*, 9(1), 91–107.

MCMC (2018). *Internet Users Survey 2018*. Malaysian Communications and Multimedia Commission.

Mende, M., Bolton, R. N. and Bitner, M. J. (2013). Decoding customer–firm relationships: How attachment styles help explain customers' preferences for closeness, repurchase intentions, and changes in relationship breadth. *Journal of Marketing Research*, 50(1), 125–142.

Nielsen, J. (2015). *State of the Media: The Social Media Report*. Nielsen Company. http://blog. nielsen.com/nielsenwire/social.

Parsons, A. (2013). Using social media to reach consumers: A content analysis of official Facebook pages. *Academy of Marketing Studies Journal*, 17(2).

Pew Research Center (2016). *Social Media Update 2016: Internet & Technology*. Washington, DC: Pew Research Center.

Prahalad, C. K. and Ramaswamy, V. (2004). Co-creating unique value with customers. *Strategy & Leadership*, 32(3), 4–9.

Slover-Linett, C. and Stoner, M. (2011). *Succeeding with Social Media: Lessons from the First Survey of Social Media in Advancement*. Slover-Linett Issue Paper. https://nextrends.swissnexsanfrancisco.org/wp-content/uploads/sites/5/2011/03/case_succeeding-with-social-media.pdf.

Socialbakers (2018). *Regional Social Media Report*. https://www.socialbakers.com/company/contact-us.

Statista (2017). *Global Consumer Survey*. https://www.statista.com/customercloud/global-consumer-survey.

Stelzner, M. (2012). *2012 Social Media Marketing Industry Report*. https://www.socialmediaexaminer.com/social-media-marketing-industry-report-2012/.

Trainor, K. J., Andzulis, J. M., Rapp, A. and Agnihotri, R. (2014). Social media technology usage and customer relationship performance: A capabilities-based examination of social CRM. *Journal of Business Research*, 67(6), 1201–1208.

Tuohy, D., Cooney, A., Dowling, M., Murphy, K. and Sixsmith, J. (2013). An overview of interpretive phenomenology as a research methodology. *Nurse Researcher*, 20(6), 17–20.

Wang, Z. and Kim, H. G. (2017). Can social media marketing improve customer relationship capabilities and firm performance? Dynamic capability perspective. *Journal of Interactive Marketing*, 39, 15–26.

wearesocial (2016). *Digital in 2016*. https://wearesocial.com/uk/special-reports/digital-in-2016.

Whitelock, J., Cadogan, J. W., Okazaki, S. and Taylor, C. R. (2013). Social media and international advertising: Theoretical challenges and future directions. *International Marketing Review*, 30(1), 56–71.

Wong, C. (2016). Malaysian online shopping behavior. http://www.ecommercemilo.com/2016/07/2016-malaysian-online-shopping-behaviour.html.

Index